Date Due

THIS MONOGRAPH ON "THE BASILICA OF ANDREA PALLADIO" WAS PRINTED IN VICENZA BY O.T.V. STOCCHIERO USING GARAMOND TYPE. THE PAPER USED FOR THE TEXT IS PAPERALBA FROM THE VENTURA PAPERMILL; RUSTICUS, ALSO FROM VENTURA, IS USED FOR THE SCALE DRAWINGS; AND FOR THE PLATES, LARIUS, FROM THE BURGO PAPERMILL. THE BLACK-AND-WHITE AND COLOR PLATES WERE PRINTED FROM BLOCKS BY A. MONTICELLI IN PADUA. THE DRAWINGS WERE REPRODUCED IN PADUA BY FOMERG. THE BINDING WAS DONE AT THE LE-GATORIA EDITORIALE GIOVANNI OLIVOTTO IN VICENZA.

CORPUS PALLADIANUM

VOLUME II

CENTRO INTERNAZIONALE DI STUDI DI ARCHITETTURA
« ANDREA PALLADIO »

BOARD OF ADVISORS

CORPUS PALLADIANUM

Editor of the Series: Renato Cevese

Assistant Editor: Abelardo Cappelletti

THE BASILICA

Franco Barbieri

THE BASILICA

OF ANDREA PALLADIO

CORPUS PALLADIANUM

VOLUME II

THE PENNSYLVANIA STATE UNIVERSITY PRESS

UNIVERSITY PARK & LONDON

GILDA D'AGARO, in collaboration with Maria Tarlà and Mario Tomasutti, executed the scale drawings of the Basilica, the Redentore, and the Rotonda and, with the collaboration of Pietro Pelzel, those of the Malcontenta and the Convento della Carità. Andrzej Pereswet-Sołtan, under the direction of Prof. Mario Zocconi, executed the drawings for the Villa Badoera, the Loggia Bernarda, the Palazzo Barbaran Da Porto, the Palazzo Da Porto Festa, the Villa Godi Malinverni, the Villa Pisani at Bagnolo, the Villa Pisani at Montagnana, the Villa Pojana, and the Teatro Olimpico. Prof. Mario Zocconi provided those of the Palazzo Antonini and the Villa Emo.

The preparation of the monographs of the Corpus Palladianum has been made possible with the aid of the CONSIGLIO NAZIONALE DELLE RICERCHE of Italy and of the ENTI FONDATORI of the Centro Internazionale di Studi di Architettura « Andrea Palladio » in Vicenza.

The author's sincerest thanks go to the Centro Internazionale di Studi di Architettura « Andrea Palladio » for providing the opportunity to complete this study, to Renato Cevese for his kind assistance, to Rudolf Wittkower and James Ackerman for much information and useful advice, to Giangiorgio Zorzi and Don Giovanni Mantese for their generous aid, and to Fernando Bandini, Gilda D'Agaro, Mario Tomasutti, and Andrzej Pereswet-Sołtan for their collaboration.

F. B.

To my children
Francesca and Umberto

CONTENTS

THE BASILICA OF ANDREA PALLADIO

I

THE PALAZZI DEL COMUNE IN VICENZA
FROM THE TWELFTH TO THE FIFTEENTH CENTURY

The first secure evidence[1] about the municipal buildings existing in the area occupied today by Palladio's Basilica (Fig. I, p. 15; Plates 1, 2, 3) dates back to the *Regestum Possessionum Communis Vincentiae* drawn up on January 16, 1262. To the west was the so-called *Palatium vetus*. It roughly comprised the area which is currently bounded by Piazzetta Palladio and by the great arch which leads to Piazza delle Erbe from Piazza dei Signori.[2] Contiguous to this area and near its northwest corner rose a tower, called *storta* by the sources because it inclined to one side. The plan of this tower shows dimensions which were very close to those of the Torre di Piazza or Bissara.[3] Another tower, with a base equal to that of the Torre del Tormento or del Girone, very likely rose in the angle between the present Piazzetta Palladio and Piazza dei Signori.[4]

The *Palatium vetus* was the seat of the *Camera degli Anziani* and other offices, as well as of a chapel used for the administration of justice.[5] However, the widespread supposition that the lower and basement-level rooms were set aside for prisons[6] is not tenable: " The real public prisons in Vicenza came into existence during the general reorganization that followed the 'Ezzelinian' tyranny [1260]; that is to say, they date back to the Statutes of 1264 .... Up until then the Commune used the old prisons erected by the feudal lords." [7]

The origins of the *Palatium vetus* are uncertain. Barbarano states that he saw a document in the archive of the Vicentine monastery of SS. Felice and Fortunato which is datable to 1200 and which would fix in that year the acquisition of several houses by the Commune, to be used for public meetings.[8] Magrini, more prudently, observes merely that the structure—which was a fortification as well as a civic building—must have been the first property acquired by and the municipal seat of the Commune at the time of the affirmation of its autonomy.[9] Since this event probably took place as early as the middle of the twelfth century,[10] the origins of the building would not have been far removed in time. In short, in 1262 the name *vetus* was applied to a building which might have dated back to the beginning of the Duecento, according to Barbarano's evidence, or even to the end of the previous century.[11]

The appearance of the ancient palace

is as obscure as its origins are uncertain. Successive fires, demolitions, and rebuildings seem to have involved only the roof and the top part of the building, while the underlying structure, reinforced on the inside by brick vaulting, came through relatively undamaged.[12] Nevertheless, the surviving ground-floor masonry within the Palladian arcades along the west side—which is interrupted by wide apertures for shops—and along the north and south sides (along the two stairs which today lead to the main Hall) reveals very little about the original structure. The facing of *pietre masegne* from Montecchio, executed in the middle of the fifteenth century, masks all irregularities and disguises any surviving evidence. Moreover, elements held to be remains of the ancient palace—the low, square windows at the bottom of the stairs and the arch of the door which is now walled up to about half the height of the northern one[13]—relate instead to the public prisons which were set up here in the second half of the fifteenth century and which were ready for use as early as 1474.[14] One can therefore attempt a reconstruction, albeit a hazy one, of the *Palatium vetus* only on the basis of generic references to another approximately contemporary local construction: the nearby Torri dei Loschi, which, despite their 1934 " restoration," remain in some respects a unique specimen of Vicentine building of the late twelfth century.[15]

To the west of the *Palatium vetus* was the *Palatium Communis*, rising to the height of the present Torre del Girone. According to the *Regestum* of 1262, it was closely joined to the *vetus*.[16] For the most part, it consisted of a great Hall, the seat of the Council of the Four Hundred, raised "*super archivoltis magnis*" which were built in 1222-23 during the administration of the Brescian podestà Lorenzo Strazza

Martinengo and which were the work of unidentified "*magistri de Cremona*."[17] The space occupied by the arches, subtracting the width of the portico, corresponded to the space between the five lower spans of the northern side of the present Palladian loggias (numbered from the second one by the Torre di Piazza) and the five corresponding ones of the southern side.[18] Therefore the north and south façades of the *Palatium Communis* presented the fenestrated walls of the hall, supported by five enormous arches on the ground floor.

Evidently the Commune of Vicenza acquired the palace of Gualdinello Bissari at Piazza delle Biade as far back as 1211, in order to provide a residence for the podestà,[19] and decided a decade later to accommodate the enlarged magistracy with a new building to be inserted between the *Palatium vetus* and the palace of the podestà. The *Palatium Communis* seems to have been in some way joined to this building.[20] Today the first span of the Palladian loggias on the western side corresponds exactly to what must have been the space between the two buildings. We do not actually know how this was resolved; but there was probably at that time—or at least as early as 1307—a great common stair serving the two palaces in the intermediate space.[21]

The whole space under the arches remained open to free passage, which was an acute necessity since Piazza dei Signori was much less vast than it now is. From the corner of the present Contrà del Monte to the place later occupied by the two Venetian " columns " there were modest structures suitable for shops, and it was not decided until about 1264 that these should be demolished.[22] Unfortunately, the shops were gradually moved from the piazza and crowded between the arches, to such an extent that eventually the latter came to

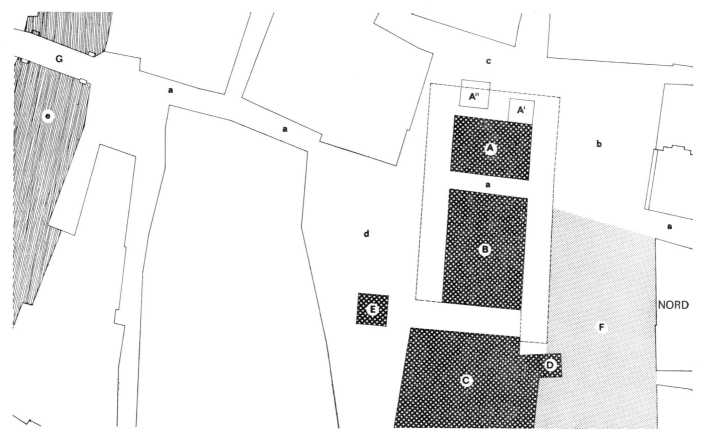

I - Vicenza: *site occupied by the oldest communal buildings.*

A - *Palatium vetus;* A' - *Turris storta;* A" - *another tower;* B - *Palatium Communis;* C - *Palazzo Bissari, formerly Palazzo del Podestà;* D - *Torre di Piazza or Bissara;* E - *Torre del Girone or del Tormento;* F - *site of the present-day Piazza dei Signori, occupied by shops;* G - *Roman bridge, today called Ponte S. Paolo, leading toward the Quartiere di Berga;* a - *course of the ancient "cardo maximus";* b - *site of the present-day Piazza dei Signori;* c - *site of the present-day Piazzetta Palladio;* d - *site of the present-day Piazza delle Erbe;* e - *the Retrone river.*

be distinguished by the popular names of the shops beneath.[23] Nonetheless, in 1262 the *Palatium Communis* must on the whole have conformed to a typical architectural solution represented by the contemporary Lombard, Paduan, and Venetian "*broletti.*" It suffices to recall the examples in Como (1214) and Milan (1228-33) or, even better, the nearby Palazzo dei Trecento in Treviso (1297) and the early Palazzo della Ragione in Padua (1218-19).[24]

Another very important urban situation was respected in the following manner: the principal street, the *cardo maximus,* which from Roman times had led down from the ancient *decumanus* (the present-day Corso) to the Ponte San Paolo and the Quartiere di Berga, was not interrupted but ran directly beneath the first arches on the western side of the *Palatium.* This is precisely the route of the present pe-

destrian passage from Piazza dei Signori to Piazza delle Erbe.[25] In fact, it is along this passage and the analogous one further toward the east that we find the remains of the thirteenth-century construction, i.e., the imposts of the arches or the upper mouldings of the large pilasters inserted in the walls at regular intervals; these were unfortunately violated or partially renovated by Bartolomeo Malacarne in his 1827 rearrangement of that section of the building.[26]

In 1236 the triumphant Frederick II, together with Ezzelino III da Romano, entered Vicenza after the resistance of the free Commune had collapsed. The city was abandoned to pillage and the public buildings were barbarously burned. It is interesting to note that in referring to this episode the chronicler used the collective expression *Palatium Civitatis* to indicate, apparently, a complex of buildings considered as a unit at that time even though only informally articulated.[27] Although the flames probably only damaged the roofs, other wooden parts, and possibly the upper part of the walls, during Ezzelino's tyranny (1236-59) the civic buildings—symbols of the lost independence—remained almost completely abandoned.[28] Only after the collapse of the tyranny was restoration undertaken, with the reconstitution of the civil magistracies between the end of 1259 and the beginning of 1260 under the Paduan podestà Aicardo di Litolfo.[29] Consequently, the *Regestum* was able in 1262 to describe the *Palatium vetus* as "*modo noviter cohopertum.*"[30]

Detailed information subsequently becomes rarer. From 1266 onward, the Commune of Vicenza lost a great deal of its vitality; it was shaken by internal battles between the Guelf and Ghibelline factions and eventually bound itself to the stronger Commune of Padua, with a guardianship pact which in actuality turned into a veritable domination.[31] It was not until 1289, during the administration of the Paduan podestà Giovanni de' Todi, that the provisional wooden stairs of the *Palatium Communis*—in use since the disaster of 1236—were finally replaced with more spacious stone ones.[32] In the following year (1290) a disastrous fire broke out in the *prope palatium* prison,[33] which was among the first public prisons established in the statutory reorganization of 1264, located (following the restoration of 1259-60) in the basement area of the *Palatium Communis*.[34] In 1291, after the damages were repaired, the learned Paduan "proto-humanist" Lovato de' Lovati (then podestà) "*fecit depingi et scribi historias de palatio.*"[35] Another fire occurred in 1293.[36] In 1307, under the Paduan podestà Vitaliano de' Lemici, the *scala magna* was open-

ed.[37] It led directly into the Hall of the Four Hundred and we have reason to believe that it was inserted between the *Palatium Communis* and the palace of the podestà.[38]

In 1312 Vicenza passed under the dominion of the Scaligeri, and life in the city became difficult, disturbed by continuous wars, famines, and plagues and by insupportable taxation and humiliating abuses of power. Meanwhile the new seignory dominated the communal Councils and, in practice, annulled any free manifestation of the popular will.[39] The political and economic situation, together with recurrent fires (in 1355, 1370, and 1374), explain the disastrous condition of Vicenza's civic buildings. Only in 1378, following an especially violent fire, was restoration begun.[40] On March 10, 1379, Avanzio da Vicenza finished the decoration of the Chapel of St. Vincent in the Town Hall. On Sunday, March 20 it was consecrated and thus was restored to the Church after having been used as a prison and otherwise profaned for almost twenty-five years.[41]

In 1387 Vicenza passed from Scaligeri domination to that of the Visconti. Conditions did not greatly improve, mainly because of the continual wars and the consequent heavy fiscal impositions.[42] The decay of the public buildings must have worsened, but we have little information regarding their vicissitudes after the end of the fourteenth century.[43]

On October 22, 1390, the Collegio dei Notai, which had its seat between the *Palatium Communis* and the Torre del Tormento, urged "*ad pulchritudinem et utilitatem*" that a change of direction be effected in the 1307 *scala magna*, in order to have it lead to a smaller adjacent room rather than to the great Hall. Since the work was of particular interest to the Collegio, it paid the expenses in advance.

The alteration was completed January 15, 1391.[44] In 1393 the great Hall of the *Palatium Communis* was reconstructed with stone vaults;[45] that is to say, the wooden trusses probably were replaced by more robust masonry arches.

On April 28, 1404, the Venetians took possession of Vicenza "by the will of all the people."[46] The supremacy of Venice, while assuring peace to the city, placed the communal magistracies in a new perspective, decidedly subordinate and provincial. On the other hand, several years were necessary for the city to balance its economy in such a way as to permit the reorganization of the countryside, which had been convulsed by the Scaligeri and Visconti wars, and to allow the founding of handicraft and industrial activity (mainly wool manufacture). For a society based almost exclusively on land ownership, these activities were needed (along with agriculture) to further the accumulation of capital necessary to any future initiative.[47] Thus we can explain the silence which during this transitional phase surrounds the civic buildings of Vicenza, even though the idea of restoring them must by then have been gaining ground.[48]

An enormous fire broke out in 1444,[49] and the structural condition of the *vetus* and *Communis* palaces became really precarious. This situation, profiting from a renewed civic prosperity, compelled a radical intervention.

NOTES TO CHAPTER I

[1] *Regestum Possessionum Communis Vincentiae*, c. 1 r.

[2] ZORZI, 1964, p. 43, n. 1.

[3] COGO, 1900, pp. 18-19. The location of the tower was identified (CABIANCA-LAMPERTICO, 1861, p. 240; BORTOLAN-LAMPERTICO, 1889, p. 312) during the excavation of the foundations for the monument to Palladio (1861); see also PERONATO, 1936.

[4] COGO, 1900, pp. 18-19: foundations of the tower appeared in 1872, in the course of the excavations.

[5] BISON, 1955, p. 42 and 1964, p. 17, thinks it was dedicated to St. Vincent: however, St. Vincent assumed the principal role among the patron saints of Vicenza only in the second half of the Trecento (MANTESE, 1958, pp. 127-129). For the location of the chapel, see Chapter III, n. 30.

[6] See *Il Palazzo della Ragione in Vicenza*, 1875, pp. 11 ff.

[7] MANTESE, 1958, p. 409, n. 95: this confirms BORTOLAN's statement, 1886, p. 19.

[8] BARBARANO, 1761, pp. 227-235. The document is no longer traceable in what remains of the archive of San Felice (now part of the Archivio di Stato in Vicenza); however Barbarano's accuracy regarding what he ascertains "*de visu*" is usually reliable.

[9] *Il Palazzo della Ragione in Vicenza*, 1875, pp. 11 ff.

[10] MANTESE, 1960, p. 43: "...by about 1115, the evolution from the *Comitato* to the *Comune* was an accomplished fact in Vicenza"; p. 45: "after 1150 the *rectores* governed the city, and in 1175 we have a record of the first podestà."

[11] Some early authors (see, for example, ARNALDI, 1767, pp. xxii ff.) date it all the way back to Theodoric; according to DA SCHIO, 1850, p. 26, there would have been an Imperial Roman palace here (for a refutation, see GIRARDI, 1924, p. 40).

[12] COGO, 1900, pp. 9 ff.

[13] COGO, 1900, pp. 9 ff.; ZORZI, 1952. The windows have an opening of circa 91 cm. per side: they now appear to be rectangular, having been partially blocked at the bottom when the two stairs were constructed (1495-96 north stairs; 1610-12 south stairs: see Chapters II and IV).

[14] BORTOLAN, 1886, pp. 20 ff.

[15] The earlier condition is documented in PERONATO, 1932, pp. 59-62; see also BARDELLA, 1933 and PERONATO, 1934. We can, it seems, pin down the dating (BARBIERI, 1959) with the information given in PAGLIERINI, *Croniche*, 1663 edition, p. 43.

[16] *Regestum Possessionum Communis Vincentiae*, c. 1 r. To indicate the complete joining of the two buildings, the text uses the precise verbal form "*coheret*".

[17] SMEREGLO, *Annales*, 1883 edition, pp. 276-277.

[18] Cf. BORTOLAN, 1886, pp. 20 ff.

[19] MANTESE, 1954, p. 270, n. 181; this confirms the statement of MAGRINI, 1845, *Annotazioni*, p. iv. Thus other traditional dates collapse, such as those of 1220 (BARBIERI-CEVESE, 1953 and 1956, p. 86) and 1226 (the latter was based on the incorrect date proposed by PAGLIERINI, *Croniche*, 1663 edition, p. 56).

[20] In this case also (see note 16 for its precedent), the *Regestum* (c. 2 r.) uses the form "*coheret*" to specify the connection of the two buildings.

[21] See notes 38 and 44.

[22] *Statuti del Comune di Vicenza*, 1886 edition, p. 134; PERONATO, 1936.

[23] BORTOLAN-LAMPERTICO, 1889, pp. 473-474; ZORZI, 1952.

[24] Cf. TOESCA, 1965, p. 720: "...one finds this Lombard type diffused throughout Northern Italy with few variants, from Novara to Genoa, and from Treviso or Padua to Bologna and Faenza." Concerning the Basilica in Padua, see CHECCHI-GAUDENZIO-GROSSATO, 1961, pp. 81-83; FLORES D'ARCAIS, 1961, p. 108; and, above all, SEMENZATO, 1963, pp. 23-30.

[25] GIRARDI, 1924, pp. 32-33. However, Girardi erroneously maintains that the *cardo* was at that time exposed in this space; instead, as we have noted, the *Palatium vetus* and *Palatium Communis* were completely joined (see note 16).

[26] COGO, 1900, pp. 9 ff.; see also Chapter V.

[27] SMEREGLO, *Annales*, 1883 edition, p. 278: " *Civitas ... fuit tota depraedata et derobata ... et ... Teotonici derobando posuerunt ignem in civitate ... et maior pars ... immo quasi tota fuit combusta* "; p. 282: " *Palatium Civitatis ... combustum fuerat.* "

[28] MANTESE, 1954, p. 270.

[29] SMEREGLO, *Annales*, 1883 edition, p. 282: " *Aicardius de Litolfo de Padua ... incipit fieri facere palatium Civitatis Vicentiae, quod combustum fuerat.* "

[30] *Regestum Possessionum Communis Vincentiae*, c. 1 r. The restorations were in large part done " *de lignamine manganorum et de lignamine carceris bericarum* " (BORTOLAN, 1886, pp. 18-19 and 1886 [II], p. 27); the term *mangani* perhaps refers (MANTESE, 1958, pp. 409-410) to stalls inserted in the arches of the ancient Roman theatre in Vicenza, the Teatro di Berga. The " *carceres bericarum,* " used for heretics by the tribunal of the Inquisition, were already located exactly at this spot and were in use in the early Trecento (MANTESE, 1954, p. 349).

[31] MANTESE, 1960, p. 52.

[32] SMEREGLO, *Annales*, 1883 edition, p. 292: PAGLIERINI, *Croniche*, 1663 edition, p. 78.

[33] SMEREGLO, *Annales*, 1883 edition, p. 293.

[34] BORTOLAN, 1886, pp. 20 ff.

[35] SMEREGLO, *Annales*, 1883 edition, p. 293. These must undoubtedly have been frescoes accompanied by titles, probably extending along the walls of the hall of the *Palatium Communis*, which was the principal building in the whole civic complex. These frescoes were almost certainly inside the building. According to COGO (1900), the traces of early paintings that were still visible at the beginning of this century on the outside wall of the palace corresponding to the stair facing toward Piazza dei Signori could have belonged to the 1291 frescoes. However, this is difficult to accept considering the asserted but undocumented age and the unexpected placement of the fragments.

In any case, the most interesting question concerns the possible author or authors of these " *historiae depictae et scriptae.* " Vicenza in the second half of the Duecento was rich in important religious buildings (S. Corona, begun c. 1261-62; S. Michele, c. 1264; S. Lorenzo, c. 1280: see CEVESE, 1965), but traces of civic buildings are lacking (BARBIERI, 1965, p. 167). Above all, nothing that is certain is left in the fields of painting and sculpture.

The Paduan Lovato de' Lovati (ca. 1230/35-1309) commissioned the frescoes. " *Filius Rolandi notarii regalis aulae notarius,* " he was a very learned scholar of ancient Latin poetry and a poet himself and was described by Petrarch as " *poetarum omnium, quos nostra vel patrum nostrorum vidit aetas, facillime princeps.* " His brilliant personality has been illuminated by BILLANOVICH (1958), who maintains that he is able to discern the sources of Lovati's humanistic culture in the codices of the ancient capitular library of Pomposa. However, Padua does not have useful indexes at present (cf. *Padova, Guida ai Monumenti e alle opere d'arte*, 1961), and neither does Pomposa, where all the surviving frescoes are of a later period. A broader investigation of the wider area to the north (especially in Emilia and the Veneto) could lead to the assembling of more data (cf. TOESCA, 1965, pp. 982-992), but one still runs the risk of arbitrary generalization.

[36] MANTESE, 1958, p. 589.

[37] FACCIOLI, 1776, p. 168, n. 21; MANTESE, 1958, pp. 590-591.

[38] In 1390 the stair was still referred to in the documents as that leading " *super sala palatii* " (ZORZI, 1937, p. 36). For the location, see note 44.

[39] MANTESE, 1960, p. 56.

[40] MANTESE, 1958, p. 590, n. 6; see also CASTELLINI, *Storia*, Bk. XIII, 1821-22 edition, p. 94; ZORZI, 1926, p. 148.

[41] CONFORTO DA COSTOZZA, *Frammenti*, 1886 edition, p. 37. MANTESE, 1958, p. 590, n. 6, suggests that the period of profanation must have been shorter, if as early as 1364 the abbot of S. Felice issued a public document in the chapel (which GEROLA, 1909, p. 33, n. 2, considers to be the same chapel as that recorded by the *Regestum* of 1262 in the *Palatium vetus*). Moreover, Conforto's term " Palazzo del Comune " does not conflict with this theory, since it must refer to the whole complex of Vicentine public building as Smereglo's analogous term " *palatium Civitatis* " did previously (see note 27).

Concerning the painter Avanzio or Avanzo, another document (see MANTESE, 1958, loc. cit.) explicitly calls him " *Avancius pictor q. ser Leonardi habitator Vincentie.* " He was certainly the same " Avancius " who in 1380 signed an *ancona*, now lost, in the Cathedral of Vicenza, second chapel to the right of the entrance (CASTELLINI, *Descrizione della città di Vicenza*, ms., I, p. 26; cf. also ARSLAN, 1956, p. 26, N. 123 a). MANTESE, 1958, p. 623, n. 134, proposes to assign to him a lost panel showing St. Anthony Abbot, dated 1383 and discovered June 3, 1812, in the antechamber of the chancellery of the Venetian podestà, when the shelves that occupied the wall were removed (ARNALDI-TORNIERI, *Memorie*, ms. copy, X, p. 916, 3 giugno 1812). This is a reasonable hypothesis, as the dates coincide and the Chapel of St. Vincent is nearby. Following MAGRINI, 1848, p. 127, who in turn had based his suggestion on BARBARANO, 1761, p. 21, several authors call this Avanzo of Vicenza " de Sammo ": but it has been noted (MANTESE, 1958, loc. cit.) that such a name would be " absolutely new to Vicenza." Additional information can be found in BORTOLAN, 1885, p. 11; GEROLA, 1909 (where the last notice concerning the artist is recorded on November 16, 1389); FASOLO, 1930, p. 64; and MAGAGNATO, 1949, p. 102. These are the only certain facts.

The discussion, however, may be extended in an effort to discover whether or not this Avanzo of Vicenza should be identified with the Avanzo who collaborated with Altichiero in Padua, in the Chapel of St. James (now S. Felice) in S. Antonio, and in the Oratorio of S. Giorgio. Supporters of this hypothesis are GEROLA, 1909; COLETTI, 1931 and 1947, pp. xliv-xlvii and lxxiii, n. 115; and ARSLAN, 1956 (loc. cit.: " without doubt "; 1959 and 1962: " highly likely "), whereas TOESCA (1951, pp. 782 ff., esp. nn. 316 and 317) and BETTINI (1944, pp. 68, 121-122, n. 5; 1960) deny it. On the other hand, the information given by SARTORI (1963), which was immediately accepted and developed by FIOCCO (1963), excludes the presence of any painter named Avanzo at S. Giorgio. PALLUCCHINI, 1964, pp. 146-147, in summarizing the problem (see also MAGAGNATO, 1958, pp. 11-12) concludes that if there was an Avanzo, he was merely one of Altichiero's collaborators and can only marginally be distinguished from Altichiero. The recent perceptive study by MELLINI (1965, pp. 87-107) reconstructs the hypothetical personality of an artist working in Padua with his probable contemporary Altichiero, with whom he maintained an autonomous and reciprocal relationship despite their shared efforts. This artist was a Jacopo Avanzi, of Bolognese origin and training but of wide culture, who had a definite Tuscan streak and was capable of emerging as the last great example of the Bolognese Trecento tradition (p. 45). Around this nucleus one can assemble a modest oeuvre which comprises, among other things, some lunettes in the Chapel of St. James, but which absolutely excludes S. Giorgio.

This Bolognese Avanzi would have already been dead by 1377. However, we should not fail to note Mellini's warning (p. 102) that " all the documents referring to [this artist] lose ... any sort of validity when confronted by the verified existence of more than one artist of the same name," and we should regard Mellini's reconstruction with these reservations in mind (cf. PETTENATI, 1965).

[42] MANTESE, 1960, p. 61.

[43] ZORZI, 1926, p. 148.

[44] *Il Palazzo della Ragione in Vicenza*, 1875, p. 17; ZORZI, 1937, p. 36; MANTESE, 1958, pp. 590-591. The concern of the Collegio dei Notai, given its particular location, seems to confirm the fact that the stair of 1307 was situated between the *Palatium Communis* and the palace of the podestà.

[45] *Il Palazzo della Ragione in Vicenza*, 1875, p. 17.

[46] MANTESE, 1960, p. 61.

[47] MANTESE, 1960, pp. 65-66; BARBIERI, 1965, p. 170.

[48] On June 2, 1436, in the lease of one of the shops arranged under the archways of the *Palatium Communis*, the case is explicitly considered " *quo Commune Vincentie fieri faceret palatium et propter ruinas seu quelibet alia impedimenta* [the tenant] *non possit comode laborare* " (MANTESE, 1964, p. 873).

[49] ARNALDI, 1767, pp. xxii ff.

II - Giovanni Bellini, *Pietà.* Venice, Gallerie dell'Accademia.
Detail of the background showing a part of the landscape and architecture of Vicenza. From left to right: the tower of the Porta del Castello, the Torre di Piazza, the Palazzo della Ragione by Domenico da Venezia, the façade of the Cathedral.

III - MARCELLO FOGOLINO, *Lower part of the Madonna delle Stelle.* Vicenza, Church of Santa Corona. Detail showing a view of Vicenza from the slopes of Monte Berico. From left to right: the campanile of the Cathedral, Palazzo della Ragione with the Formenton loggias, the Torre di Piazza, the Torre del Tormento. Below, the Retrone and Ponte Furo.

IV - MARCELLO FOGOLINO, *Predella of the altarpiece of S. Francesco Nuovo.* Vicenza, Museo Civico.
Detail showing a view of Vicenza from the slopes of Monte Berico. From left to right: the Porta and Torre del
Castello, the campanile and façade of the Cathedral, Palazzo della Ragione with the Formenton loggias, the Torre
di Piazza, the Torre del Tormento. Below, the Retrone and Ponte Furo.

V - Marcello Fogolino, *St. Sebastian.* Bassano, Museo Civico.
Detail showing Vicenza's Torre di Piazza, with Palazzo della Ragione surrounded by the Formenton loggias.

VI · MARCELLO FOGOLINO, *Destruction of the Golden Calf*. Ascoli Piceno, Palazzo Vescovile.
Detail of the background showing Vicenza's Palazzo della Ragione surrounded by loggias derived from Palladio's first project of 1546.

VII - Vicenza, *Palazzo Porto Breganze: courtyard loggia*

II

THE PALAZZO DELLA RAGIONE
IN THE FIFTEENTH CENTURY

DOMENICO DA VENEZIA'S PALACE

On March 19, 1444, the "*fedelissima Comunità di Vicenza*" decided to reconstruct the crumbling *vetus* and *Communis* palaces, and, observing that the Venetian government had already contributed to the restoration of the town hall of Padua, succeeded in obtaining a subvention of 5,000 ducats from Venice (in annual payments of 1,000 ducats) in exchange for the commitment to provide at its own expense the necessary workers and materials.[1] The doge, Francesco Foscari, announced the decision himself to the city authorities on March 20.[2]

According to some evidence, the foundations of the new building were soon laid to replace the two threatened structures,[3] and in 1445 work on the exteriors was begun.[4] This theory is usually accepted, but in actuality it seems that nothing was undertaken before 1449-50,[5] or at most that only the work of clearing the area and preparing the ground was begun. One of the greatest obstacles was constituted by the shops or " *stationes* " which had existed for more than a century and a half under the arches of the *Palatium Communis*. A delicate procedure was necessary to dispossess them, which we find recorded in documents of 1445 and 1446.[6] Between February 23 and March 2, 1450, Venice of-

fered another 3,000 ducats with the previous conditions and in annual payments of 600 ducats.[7] This was opportune, as in the course of the delays a large part of the *Palatium vetus* collapsed, on February 13, 1451.[8]

The disaster at least imparted the necessary urgency to the effort. On May 21 it was decided to employ prisoners as well on the job; actually, from March of 1450 the Doge Foscaro had allowed the people of Vicenza to convert fines into donations of money or into manual labor to help with the building.[9] Thus, by September 1457 arrangements had been made for the material for a temporary roof for the vast structure, and on the third of the month Cristoforo " de Zanichino *fornaserio* " contracted to furnish 20,000 tiles of good material, destined to last until Easter of 1458.[10] In that year the palace must have been at least partly finished, as notarial deeds were drawn up there,[11] and the new wooden roof, covered with sheets of lead, was certainly finished between 1458 and 1460.[12]

We must first consider the identity of the architect and the appearance of the *Palatium novum Communis Vicentiae*, generally called the " Palazzo della Ragione." [13] It should be noted that the *Palatium vetus* and the *Palatium Communis*, contrary to the usual opinion,[14] were not completely torn down. The lower level of the walls within the ground floor of the Palladian loggias was retained, as well as the internal dividing walls, the vaults of the rooms,[15] and the *archivolti magni* of 1222-23.[16] This explains the irregularities of the plan and the articulation of the walls of the fifteenth-century building. The surviving ground floor of the *Palatium vetus* was modified and the public prisons, formerly located below the roof, were in part transferred there.[17] Doors and windows were opened up, some of which are still visible in the north and south walls (Plate 9) along the existing stairs. The original structure, dating from the decade 1450-60, is therefore the upper one, which encloses the enormous keel-roofed Hall within broad, luminous walls, articulated at regular intervals by ogival windows and oculi (Plates 4, 5, 6, 7).

It is certain that Domenico da Venezia, present in Vicenza as *ingegnere del Comune* from 1448 to 1453, was responsible for the project.[18] Another Venetian, the *taiapria* Matteo di Giovanni, who was enrolled in the local guild of masons and laborers from 1435 and who was active at the palace as early as 1444, collaborated with him.[19] Matteo, however, would have been directly involved only in work on the dressed stone, especially in the profiles of the doors and windows and in the characteristic corner niches of the second storey, facing Piazzetta Palladio.[20] Domenico would have been the only person actually responsible for the building, which was undoubtedly the most important High Gothic structure in Vicenza—a style which, lacking an autonomous environment, had matured in the shadow of the Venetian Late Gothic.[21]

In order to reconstruct the appearance of the old palace, it is necessary to study the existing site. Passing along the upper gallery of the Palladian loggias, one can examine the Quattrocento walls on the side opposite the series of arches (Plates 6, 7) and, on entering one of the doors, one is struck by the vastness of the Hall (Plate 14). Ascending to the crowning terrace, one finds the original decoration of polychrome marble facing, as well as the part of the structure which has remained substantially intact (Plate 4).

In addition, other visual evidence is available, which is as valuable as it is inexplicably neglected or distorted. For example, in the background of the famous *Pietà* by Giovanni Bellini in the Accademia in Venice (n. 883/76), we see at the extreme left of the landscape (Fig. II, page 19), between the Torre di Piazza and the façade of the Cathedral of Vicenza, the massive bulk of Domenico da Venezia's Palazzo della Ragione, isolated and lacking the loggias which were added later.[22] Although less precisely depicted, an identical group of buildings appears in a painting from Bellini's circle, the *Madonna and Child* in the Staatsgalerie in Stuttgart (n. 1502).[23] The same group also appears, less exactly rendered but unmistakable, in a drawing by Bartolomeo Montagna now in the Louvre (Cabinet des Dessins, n. 5079), accompanied by several characteristic motifs of the Vicentine landscape.[24] Lastly, we have the recent series of scale drawings by the architect Gilda D'Agaro, who has attempted a graphic reconstruction of the western side of the building.[25]

The structure developed on an irregular, slightly trapezoidal plan[26] (Scale Drawings *j*, *k*), since it was necessary to take into account the earlier constructions. The Hall occupied the whole width of the upper storey.[27] The difficult problem of an ascending stairway was resolved by using the existing stair, which had been constructed in 1307 between the palace of the podestà and what was then the *Palatium Communis*, and which was partially modified in 1390-91.[28] Not until 1483 were these stairs replaced, and the new ones still occupied the same position.[29] The entrance to the Hall was through the still-existing door at the northeast corner (Plate 13),[30] which was located exactly opposite the door that led to the offices of the podestà; thus nothing altered the geometric clarity and simplicity of the palace's exterior.

The high walls (Scale Drawing *b*) were divided into two distinct zones: the lower zone was composed of wide rows of *pietre masegne* from Montecchio, a fortunate choice for facing the crudeness of the older masonry still preserved there; the upper zone was patterned with polychrome tessellated rhomboids in delicate yellow and rose-colored marble from Verona.

The resulting chromatic contrast was too strong. To tone it down, thick vertical ribs polygonal in section sprang from a horizontal moulding, their shafts supported on low corbels a few meters above the ground, and ran uninterrupted up the walls to the cornice. Two other horizontal mouldings traversed the lower and middle sections of the façade at the level of the floor of the Hall and at the impost of the window arches, almost as if to prevent any dispersal of the vertical accents. The already-existing irregularities must have been smoothed out at the base level. Of the old arches, only the first to the west (corresponding to the *cardo*) and, for symmetry, the third to the east were left open; the remaining ones were closed, in order to provide sufficient mass to balance visually the surviving lower wall of the *Palatium vetus* and at the same time to establish a central caesura.

Above the ogival windows, whose openings must have originally been decorated by pierced mullions,[31] the lively polychrome decoration was interrupted only by the sequence of ribs. The cornice itself, although strongly articulated by large thistle-leaf consoles, had only a slight overhang in order to avoid an unsuitable contrast of shadow. The keel-like roof (*carena*) dominated the whole mass; its ogival profile and the subtle pattern of ribbing over the whole surface made it appear as the logical conclusion to the elasticity of the vertical ribs, rather than as the passive element which unfortunately it seems to be today, despite Palladio's efforts to enliven it. Domenico had ably exploited every technical and expressive possibility of the ribs, as supports for the cornice and as buttresses to counter the outward stresses of the roof mass. Although they were introduced in this functional manner, the ribs in fact served as a dynamic formal element, animating the mass of the huge structure with their strong vertical accents.

The building's situation in the open space of the surrounding piazzas was enhanced by subtle adjustments. Its maximum width was achieved in three successive projections, from the base where it was narrowest to the cornice marking its broadest extension. At the corners (Plates 8, 10, 11 and Scale Drawing *b*), where the most weight would have been concentrated, the vertical wall ribs are carried on both sides of the corner in the upper storeys and run through progressively projecting consoles. The corners were lightened by the characteristic Venetian Gothic motif of niches with elegant fluted recesses, perhaps meant to hold sculpture (Plates 10, 11). Thus, rising without apparent strain, the great structure must have seemed to expand upward almost naturally toward the vast space of the swelling *carena*.

It is evident that in designing the *Palatium novum* Domenico da Venezia had two famous models in mind: the Doges' Palace in Venice, and the Palazzo della Ragione in Padua as it appeared after the extensive modifications of Fra' Giovanni degli Eremitani (1306-09).[32] Domenico retained the idea of the keel-shaped roof (Plates 5, 14) from the latter example, which was the more relevant prototype for the *Palatium* in every respect. His desire to minimize the Gothic structural complexity in favor of a freer treatment of surface chromaticism was typically Venetian.[33] It must have also seemed to be technically the only suitable solution for covering the immense space without the impediment of piers. However, Domenico modified the profile of the roof in respect to its Paduan prototype by reducing the ogival curve, thus disciplining its thrust into a more compact regularity.

Secondly, whereas an uninterrupted line rises from the floor to the top of the vault in Fra' Giovanni's palace,[34] eliminating any break in the continuity between walls and ceiling, in Vicenza the rectilinear walls of the Hall remain distinct from the roof. The separation is emphasized by a set-back which continues around the room, slightly above the point where the ribs rest on consoles (Plate 12). Although the ribs themselves extend a certain distance below the wooden surface onto the brick portion, almost as if to weld together the two sections by this interpenetration, the final effect is very different from that of the interior of the palace in Padua.

Fra' Giovanni's space is closed and compact, rather than spacious: one has the impression that it turns and moves following the profile of the walls.[35] The space created by Domenico da Venezia a century and a half later is more precisely formulated and more measured in cadence. While Fra' Giovanni obeyed completely and consistently the formal rules of mediaeval architecture,[36] Domenico retained only some of the more imaginative ideas. Almost as if inspired, he pursued a tendency toward an unlimited expansion restrained by the balance of a self-contained equilibrium; however, one cannot push the idea too far, nor directly associate this clarity and decorum with other " pre-Renaissance " signs in Vicentine architecture of the Quattrocento.[37]

Similarly, Domenico did not adopt the impressive model of the Venetian Doges' Palace to his needs in a servile way, but rather approached it in a critical manner, retaining his basic intuition to balance a shadowless luminosity above against a visually "heavier" counterpart, dense with shadows, below. The result obtained in Venice by running two series of arcades and loggias below—in effect, a band of strong chiaroscuro bound by grilles—was achieved in Vicenza by constructing a lower wall of the most uniform possible gray stone, interrupted as little as possible by two arches whose depth shuts out the light.

Another primary difference lies in the fact that whereas in Venice the ogival windows were opened into the continuous wall, at Vicenza they are located precisely in the transitional area between the two chromatic zones and are inserted into the rhythm of the vertical ribs. While the strength and plasticity of the frames was limited to the utmost in the Doges' Palace in order to avoid puncturing the two-dimensionality of the plane (an effect to which the original trefoils contributed),[38] in Vicenza the window splays are more articulated and are logically integrated into the architectural organism. In a second and more important variation, the superimposition of the keel-like "Paduan" roof involves a completely different dynamic, with surfaces resolved vertically through the ribbing as opposed to the horizontal "continuum" established in the Venetian prototype.

The "*Palatium novum Communis Vincentiae*" was the most conspicuous and

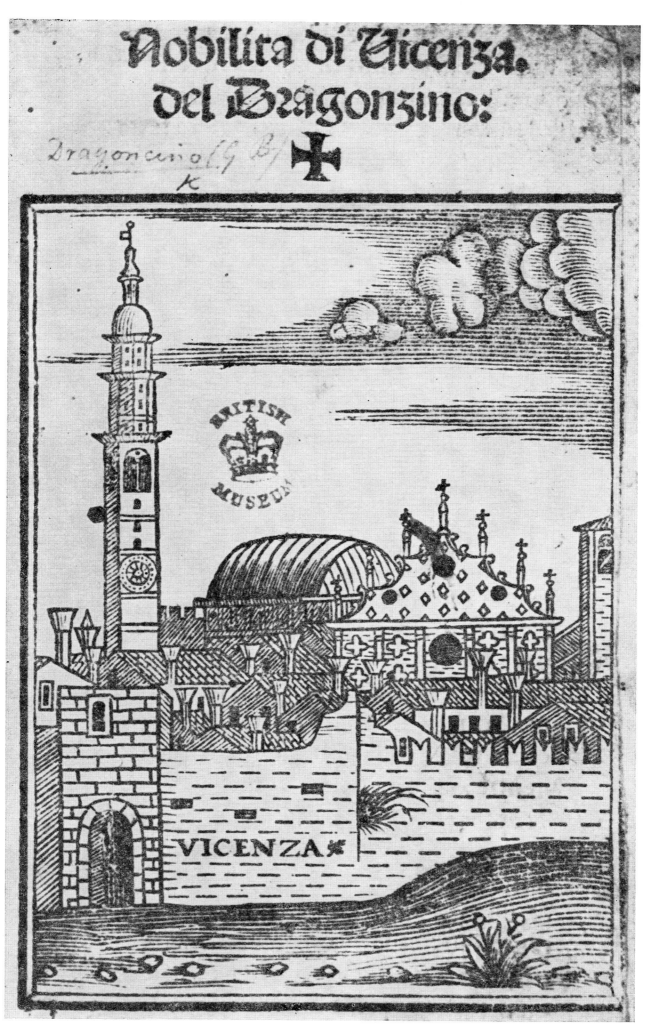

VIII - *Vicenza in the early sixteenth century.* Frontispiece of the pamphlet *Nobilità di Vicenza,*
by Dragonzino da Fano (1525)

significant architectural event in the whole inland region of the Veneto during the third quarter of the Quattrocento. The handsome, compact strength of its great mass—and the ability with which the architect used prototypes as venerable as they were challenging—placed it on a very different level from the numerous palace façades which affected a " Late Gothic " charm, fronted with balconies and pierced by apertures. These were expressions of the homage paid to Venice by her subject cities (and especially by Vicenza) in an ingenuous attempt to renew an unrenewable charm, to which the whole urban character was opposed.[39]

On the other hand, Domenico da Venezia's work shows an awareness of the diverse yet precisely defined environmental situation which already existed. It achieves a happy solution to the problem of inserting the Palazzo della Ragione into its context in the urban center of Vicenza (Scale Drawing a). Since the building was smaller and more self-contained before the subsequent addition of the loggias, it must have fit easily into the space of the surrounding piazza, at the same time having plenty of " breathing room "—especially from the moment when, in accordance with a plan which perhaps was not unfamiliar to the architect himself, the " casa della pellizzaria " at the top of Piazza dei Signori on the east side was demolished (1462). The " casa del sale " opposite the Servite Church met the same fate in 1482,[40] thus creating a continuity between the three piazzas (dei Signori, delle Biade and delle Erbe) which, joined to the smaller piazza today dedicated to Palladio, isolated the communal buildings within the heart of the city.

Since the northern side of the palace was kept almost on the axis of the opening of the present Contra' Muschieria, the western entrance of the Piazza dei Signori

remained more accessible, in addition to being scenographically more interesting. As the topographical Scale Drawing a shows, anyone who entered from that side could at that time have had an unencumbered view of the communal tower, rising several meters into the air at the corner of the podestà's palace; the tower would have been opposite them at the east and almost at the end of the foreshortening presented by the building's northern elevation. Actually, the view of the tower and the piazza was anticipated some distance away at the beginning of the Muschieria and facing the Duomo, in a different, very long perspective. The palace of the podestà must have enjoyed less visual obstruction on the western side, and from the south facing north the Piazza delle Erbe would have appeared less oppressive because the walls were set somewhat back.

THE LOGGIAS OF TOMMASO FORMENTON

Between 1481 and 1494 Domenico da Venezia's palace was encircled by the characteristic " pozzoli " (a double order of loggias). Work was initiated on June 30, 1481, when eleven columns of the lower portico facing the great square were set up.[41] Two years later the vaults of the same portico were built, and the lower columns on the western side facing the Duomo were set up; these were completed by the arches and cornices of the lower gallery. In the subsequent years of 1485 and 1486 the whole northern side facing Piazza dei Signori was finished, including the second level of loggias; in 1489 the parapets of the upper northern loggia were finished, and the Great Hall was paved with terracotta tiles.

The foundation of the eight columns of the lower southern portico facing Piazza delle Erbe dates from February 1491. The arches and cornice of that portico were constructed in August. The loggias on the western side (facing the Duomo) with the corresponding lead roof were completed in 1492. In 1493 those on the southern side facing Piazza delle Erbe were finished. Other finishing touches occupied 1494 up until November.[42]

It is possible today to reconstruct the appearance of these late Quattrocento loggias with some certainty (Scale Drawing c).[43] The lower gallery had an arcade of broad, fully-rounded arches, to each of which two small arches in the upper gallery corresponded; the latter were enclosed at the bottom by a balustrade of small columns, which in one arch were all white and in the other all red.[44] Each arch, sustained and reinforced at the impost by iron chains, was joined by cross-vaults to the wall of the palace. The arches of the upper arcade were pointed, echoing the ogival windows of the Hall (except for the two at the ends of each side, which were narrower like the corresponding arches of the lower gallery).

The series of lower arches was not, in fact, uniform. Their dimensions were determined largely by the width of the two *archivolti magni*, which were left open and which Domenico da Venezia incorporated into the ground floor of his *Palatium novum*, corresponding to the *cardo* and to the other parallel passage between Piazza dei Signori and Piazza delle Erbe (a solution dictated by the already-existing arrangement). However, the terminal arches on each side were calculated on another, smaller dimension, likewise obligatory: that of the intermediate space between the Palazzo della Ragione and the palace of the podestà, to which the first of these arches on the left on the northern side had to correspond for obvious reasons of symmetry.[45] There was, therefore, a supernumerary arch with an abnormal opening which was " set into the tower," or rather, which united the Torre di Piazza with the lower gallery of loggias on the north.[46]

Thus there were nine arches in the lower gallery on the northern side (plus the supernumerary arch, to be considered outside the unit) and eighteen arches in the upper gallery; five and ten arches were placed analogously on the western side, and eight and sixteen on the southern side. The sequence on the west was shorter, insofar as space was left at the extreme east for the "*volto va da li pozoli del pallazo de drio a la tore del Registro*": an arch which was remade in 1493-94 by Zanon Marchesini da Chiampo, over the earlier one which was pulled down in 1489 by Tommaso Formenton and Francesco da Breganze.[47] The eastern side practically coincided with the space between Palazzo della Ragione and the palace of the podestà. The fourteenth-century *scala magna*, remade in 1483 and common to both buildings, remained.[48] Perhaps during those years the ceiling of the long room and the room of about the same size above (almost at the level of the parapet) were put up; the embedded capitals from which the former was vaulted are still preserved.

Crowning the loggias was the stone cornice of the roof, covered by lead slabs and encircled with a ring of battlements rather similar to those in the Ca' d'Oro in Venice.[49] This detail, as has been pointed out,[50] is confirmed by documents[51] and by early visual evidence, in which we can see exactly how the palace was girdled by the *pozzoli*. This evidence includes the views of Vicenza executed by Marcello Fogolino in a predella now in the local Museo Civico (Fig. IV, p. 21), in the lower part of the *Madonna delle Stelle* in the Church of Santa Corona (Fig. III, p. 20),[52] and in the upper right background of a *St. Sebastian* in the museum in Bassano (n. 124; Fig. V, p. 22), although this latter painting is no longer in very good condition.[53] An additional example is the woodcut from the title page of the very rare pamphlet *Nobiltà di Vicenza* by Dragonzino da Fano (Fig. VIII, p. 29).[54]

Along the lines of more precise references, it is important to remember that the long portico in the courtyard of Palazzo Porto-Breganze (Fig. VII, p. 24) was considered as not unlike the probable structure of the loggias of the Palazzo della Ragione:[55] a valid hypothesis, even taking into account the chronological disparity.[56] A possible affinity with the surviving portions of the old cloister of S. Bartolomeo has also been mentioned,[57] but here only four embedded capitals and two columns today remain *in situ*.

One entire column (Plate 19; total height 4.2 m.) from the lower gallery on the southern side is semi-embedded in the wall of the palace of the podestà. It serves as a support for the "arch" facing the Torre del Tormento (reconstructed, as we have noted, in 1493-94 over the one destroyed in 1489) and is logically held to be analogous to the other (destroyed) columns of the lower gallery. The other column (Plate 20; total height 4.55 m.) is also on the southern side but is from the upper gallery. It is hardly visible, as it is incorporated into the first pier at the east of the second gallery of the Palladian loggias; unfortunately, the base has been damaged and the capital cut away. Two embedded capitals (Plate 17) upon which the corbels of the vaults apparently rested are now inserted into the western wall of the palace beneath the present lower gallery of Palladian loggias, at a height exactly corresponding to that of the only surviving lower column previously mentioned. The third capital, which has one volute, appears at the north-east corner at the same level as the preceding ones. The fourth is easily visible in

the lower northwest corner of the palace (Plate 8).[58]

Between the first and the second order and between the second order and the cornice are holes for the drainage of rainwater:[59] the dripstones, made in the shape of lions' heads,[60] are on a plumb line with each arch of the upper gallery.[61] The spandrels of the arches were sheathed in white and red stone, in order to harmonize with the pre-existing decorations of the palace. Of this facing, a wide band over the loggias remains; an agreement respecting them was entered into in March of 1491 with the sculptor Zanon Marchesini da Chiampo.[62] The polychromatic vivacity of the result certainly impressed the latter's contemporaries, for Lilio in 1493 described Vicenza's Palazzo della Ragione as "*una magnifica residenza fabricata veramente con singolar maestria di bianche e rosse pietre lavorate polite et recate in quadro.*"[63] The whole airy construction of the porticoes, for which stone from Chiampo and Calvene was employed, was raised several steps above the level of the surrounding piazzas,[64] not counting the much greater difference in level facing Piazza delle Erbe. Moreover, in the two year period of 1485-86, all the shops under the above-mentioned arches facing the large piazza were built.[65] They formed a typical succession of low rooms with storage areas above, and they still exist today (Plate 22)—although altered on the ground-floor level—beneath the lower northern portico of the Palladian loggias.

The complex was completed between March 1495 and April 1496 with the construction of a new stair (Plates 24, 25), placed inside the loggias on the northern side of the palace and supported on the western side. It was the work of Master Bernardino da Milano, who was assisted by Zanon Marchesini da Chiampo[66] and advised by Pietro Lombardo; the latter was paid in May 1495 for coming from Venice for this purpose.[67] On this occasion, the door to the prisons—which opened at that spot—must have been moved, and the shops which had existed there from 1485-86 must have been torn down and rebuilt (Plate 23).[68] But the most important result must have been the necessity of opening new entrances to the Great Hall, corresponding to the termination of the stairs; the two doors on the northern side of the upper loggia therefore must date back to the end of the century, as must at least one of the corresponding ones on the southern side, which permitted egress from the Hall to the loggias on the south.[69]

Partly for reasons of practical necessity,[70] the architects obviously looked to the Palazzo della Ragione in Padua for inspiration in erecting the Vicentine loggias, as they had done earlier for a model for the keel-shaped roof (a precise reference which was immediately noted by contemporary sources).[71] But this time they made a dangerous error, either through hastiness or ignorance, in assuming this model as their point of departure. The loggias which existed in the mid-Quattrocento along the northern and southern sides of the Paduan palace (the same ones which still exist today) and which the architects took as an example were not the original ones intended in Fra' Giovanni's solution, but rather those which were rebuilt after the fire of 1420. The early ones, with wooden trusses and a low roof, did not cut into the frames of the oculi which illuminate the upper part of the Hall; but in 1420 the trusses were replaced by higher cross-vaults of brick, which hid the bottoms of these frames.[72]

This expedient was excusable in Padua because of the fear of a new disaster, but it was taken as the norm by Vicenza, and thus a system of cross-vaulting was adopted for the loggias. In order to obtain enough space as well as supporting bases for the springing of the vaults, the Vicentine architects did not hesitate to break off the vertical mouldings that decorated Domenico da Venezia's palace. Even worse, in connecting the new vaults to the existing walls, the polychrome marble " skin " surrounding the structure from the windows up was broken, revealing the raw brick beneath.[73] It was then necessary to construct some small brick piers (Plate 21)—today concealed in the thickness of the Palladian vaulting in the upper gallery—in order to support the incrustation above, which had been left in place and which evidently threatened to slide down. The error was obviously repeated right to the end: the upper loggias covered the under-sections of the oculi, exactly like those in Padua.[74]

These technical defects are largely symptoms of a more serious and fundamental uncertainty. But apart from structural considerations, it is certainly true that the loggias fully answered the requirements of a site destined for a public market and, at the level of the upper galleries, demonstrated themselves to be consistent with the interior architecture.[75] In the process of joining the lower portico to the Romanesque module of the *archivolti magni* and the upper portico to Domenico da Venezia's Late Gothic rhythms, it is not difficult to perceive how motifs born of quite diverse practical and expressive necessities would have been reconciled with far more ease than coherence. As a result, the surrounding space was encroached upon, altering the calculated balance achieved through the smaller size of the previous structure.

If one seeks formal justification, it could be said that the loggias were meant to attack the solemn monumentality of Domenico's palace and to dilute or dissolve it in the search for an uninterrupted continuity of surrounding space. Proof of this would be, among other things, the insistence on joining the lower arcades of the northern façade to the Torre di Piazza, or the arch slung between the southern *pozzoli* to the nearby Torre del Girone. Moreover, the polychromatic effect of the loggias, with their undeniable though incoherent vivacity, actually takes up motifs from the second half of the Quattrocento. This recalls the caprices of that " *urbs picta* " in which façades were enlivened by frescoes, and in which wide Gothic or vaguely-Renaissance filigrees and rows of porticoes—not dissimilar in context to those of the piazza's loggias—ornamented courtyards and flanked streets.[76]

We are dealing here with a much smaller Vicenza—a fact too often forgotten in the face of its subsequent development—before high-rise buildings interrupted the low horizontal continuum of its streets and piazzas, which must have appeared so uniform in effect that the mass of the *Palatium novum* would have seemed jarringly isolated. Thus, only after the additions of the porticoes could one imagine that the city attempted to realize in this building effects analogous to those of the ancient palace in Padua.[77] Unfortunately, insofar as we can reconstruct it, the attempt does not seem to have achieved a formal dignity—to such an extent that one wonders whether those involved really knew what they were doing. The beautifully-measured precision of Domenico da Venezia's palace was altered and disturbed by the juxtaposition of a "foreign" element, the product of another land: a land that claimed Lorenzo da Bologna and Angelo da Verona, that saw the activity of Bartolomeo Montagna, Giovanni Buonconsiglio, and " lo Speranza," and that prepared the way for the Verla and for Fogolino.[78]

The unhappy solution involved the most commonplace structural require-ments, as the collapse of the loggias in 1496 demonstrated. The result of the work was therefore unsuccessful in meeting its presuppositions; but it bequeathed to those who needed to attack the same problems the lesson of its deficiencies, if anyone knew how to grasp them. Andrea Palladio confronted the problem some seventy years later, starting from the same premises but avoiding the errors, even within the new and different limitations imposed on him by the cultural situation he represented. We can sense the measure of the discrepancy between the two solutions, despite their functional similarity, in the knowledge and deliberation with which he confronted the task; and except for some understandable Late Romantic sentimentality,[79] one feels little regret for the lost Quattrocento loggias.

Tommaso Formenton of Vicenza supervised the long and sometimes exhausting work of erecting the loggias. He came from a local family of *marangoni* or carpenters, and by 1467, after the death of Matteo di Giovanni, he became *ingegnere* of the Commune of Vicenza.[80] According to some, he was merely the faithful executor of another's project, an opinion which has been strongly disputed.[81] In actual fact, reliable documents and the logical conclusions drawn from them prove that Tommaso had charge of a drawing or model of the loggia complex,[82] and that he coordinated under his direction the work of a troop of sculptors, masons, and carpenters.[83] The subsequent summoning of Formenton to Brescia in 1489 to work on the communal loggia there confirms the fact that he had acquired a certain renown for his work in Vicenza. He had charge of work on the loggias up until 1491, the next-to-last year of his life; another master, Zanon Marchesini da Chiampi, appears in a document of December 12 of that year as " *magister fabrice pallatii*," evidently for the purpose of lightening the load of supervision for Formenton, who was already past sixty.[84] On January 16, 1493, we find Master Giovanni Fuger da Rivolta as *ingegnere* of the Commune.[85]

Even aside from the documents, the attribution to Formenton is convincing. His image as a builder and practical engineer—

his transfer to Brescia having ended with nothing accomplished[86]—fits in well with the nature of the Vicentine loggias. They were added, as we have seen, to a building already complete in itself, without much troubling over either formal coherence, morphological correctness, or structural necessities.

NOTES TO CHAPTER II

[1] SELVATICO, 1859, pp. 9-10 (transcription from the Archivio di Stato in Venice, *Deliberazioni del Senato*, Vol. 1 *Terra*, c. 122).

[2] Archivio di Torre della Città di Vicenza, *Codice membranaceo vecchio*, c. 99 (transcribed by ARNALDI, 1767, p. cxvii).

[3] *Cronica ad memoriam*, 1884 edition, pp. 17-18.

[4] *Cronicha che comenza dall'anno 1400*, 1889 edition, p. 4.

[5] ZORZI, 1926, pp. 149-151.

[6] ZORZI, 1926, p. 150.

[7] SELVATICO, 1859, p. 10 (transcription from the Archivio di Stato in Venice, *Deliberazioni del Senato*, Vol. 2 *Terra*, c. 133); Archivio di Torre della Città di Vicenza, *Codice membranaceo vecchio*, c. 116 (transcribed by ARNALDI, 1767, pp. cxvii-cxviii).

[8] *Cronica ad memoriam*, 1884 edition, p. 21: "*1451. Adì 13 di Febraro giorno di S. Fosca sonando le 14 hore cascò una gran parte del Palazzo vecchio del Comune di Vicenza.*" Similarly in *Cronicha che comenza dall'anno 1400*, 1881 edition, p. 5.

[9] ARNALDI, 1767, pp. xxix and cxviii, Doc. C.; ZORZI, 1926, p. 151.

[10] ZORZI, 1926, pp. 151-152.

[11] ZORZI, 1926, p. 152. MANTESE, 1964, p. 878, considers the main reconstruction of the palace to have been almost completed by about 1450; he cites a document of April 30, 1450, written " *in comuni palatio novo* " (n. 18). But the wording is ambiguous, since " *palatio novo* " could mean the *Palatium Communis* of 1222-23, in contrast to the older *vetus*; moreover, Foscari's dogal of March 2, 1450 (noted also by Mantese) warned that " *comunitas inceperit fabricari facere... palatium... et de ea fabrica restet magna pars fieri* " at that time.

[12] ZORZI, 1926, pp. 152-153: a deed of March 21, 1460, stipulated explicitly " *in comuni palatio novo cohoperto plumbeo.*"

[13] Called " della Ragione " because " *ibi redditur jus,*" as the documents often state. Concerning the public function of the *Palatium* and the magistracies that had offices there, see FORMENTON, 1870, pp. 11 ff., for their listing and structure; for an exhaustive examination from the juridical and political viewpoints, see VENTURA, 1964, pp. 121-125.

[14] Cf. *Il Palazzo della Ragione in Vicenza*, 1875, pp. 11 ff.

[15] COGO, 1900, pp. 9 ff.

[16] ZORZI, 1952.

[17] BORTOLAN, 1886, pp. 20 ff.

[18] ZORZI, 1926, pp. 147-153. Concerning the problem of the proposed chronology of Domenico, see BARBIERI, 1965, pp. 170, 172-173, and esp. p. 178.

[19] Concerning Matteo, see ZORZI, 1926, pp. 58, 147; also 1952 and 1964, p. 43, n. 2.

[20] ZORZI, 1964, p. 43, n. 2.

[21] Cf. BARBIERI, 1965, pp. 169-170.

[22] From 1481 to 1494 (see below). The painting by Bellini is usually dated ca. 1502 (PALLUCCHINI, 1949, pp. 188-189; MOSCHINI-MARCONI, 1955, pp. 75-76), but because the detail shows the Palazzo della Ragione still minus its loggias, it is difficult to think that a view of Vicenza around 1500 is represented (ARSLAN, 1956, p. 23, N. 121 d). The painter could have easily used earlier sketches, which could have dated back to 1483 when he was commissioned to paint a Resurrection of Christ for the Duomo in Vicenza (HEINEMANN, 1962, I, pp. xix, 54) and perhaps worked in the city. At that date the work on the loggias had just begun; it involved the lower gallery, which is the part that would not have appeared in Bellini's painting, as the lower part of the palace is hidden by other buildings. Moreover, it has already been pointed out that the landscape at the right in the same panel shows a view of Cividale looking from the banks of the Natisone, which indicates the situation of the area around 1480 (MUTINELLI, 1958). PEE (1939, pp. 12-13) noted this evidence, but he erroneously associated it with the palace encircled by its future loggias (see also n. 53).

[23] HEINEMANN, 1962, I, pp. 8-9; II, fig. 203.

[24] Concerning the drawing (ca. 1485), see PUPPI, 1962, p. 150, fig. 36; for the first notice associated with the palace in Vicenza, see BARBIERI, 1956 (II), pp. 19-20.

[25] Commissioned and owned by the Centro Internazionale di Studi di Architettura Andrea Palladio in Vicenza; executed in 1961-62 by Maria Tarlà and Mario Tomasutti.

[26] Measurements of the angles: NE. 87°7', S. 88°5', N. 92°2', SE. 91°6'.

[27] Long sides: 53.32 meters (north); 53.44 (south). Short sides: 21.6 (east); 20.72 (west). Area: 1128 square meters, with a maximum height of 25.5 meters to the crown of the roof.

[28] See Chapter I, n. 44.

[29] ZORZI, 1926, pp. 36-37, Doc. p. 181: on May 8, 1483, Biagio da Santorso undertook to remove a stone vault already constructed near the door of the podestà's palace and replace it with " *unum remenatum,*" in order to make " *scallam palacii que fiet prope turrim.*"

[30] The interior and exterior mouldings clearly indicate that it was done in the last decades of the Quattrocento. The lunette above the inside architrave, which is clearly reminiscent of Padua

and Donatello (cf. the arched tympanum with crossets on the main altar of the Basilica in Padua), can be compared to the *ancona* on the altar of the small church of the Castello Colleone at Thiene and to that of the *Pietà* on the Pojana altar in S. Lorenzo (see ZORZI, 1959, pp. 347-350; figs. 203-206).

[31] As seems evident from Bellini's *Pietà* in the Accademia noted earlier. The profile of the mullioned windows of the palace can be compared to those existing today on the façade of the Cathedral; the latter was constructed in 1467 by Domenico da Venezia's collaborator, Matteo di Giovanni, in Domenico's manner and following his project (see ZORZI, 1926, pp. 153-154; 1952). According to ZORZI, 1964, p. 51, the hall of Domenico da Venezia's palace would have been illuminated by two large doors on each of the long sides and by two windows on the shorter (western) side, as well as by six oculi in each of the long sides in the upper section. The other ten windows and the six lower oculi on each long side as well as the other two windows and the lower oculi on the west side would have been opened later, in 1543. But it should be noted that the document of April 16, 1543, presented as proof (*Provisionium*, VI, cc. 633-634: not IV as accidentally transposed by ZORZI, 1937, p. 23) should be read as indicating that Giovanni Martino di Andrea and Ambrogio di Domenico, both masons from Lake Lugano, undertook at that time to put in the twenty windows on the long sides and the fourteen oculi " *existentes in palatio, ... illis modo et forma quibus est fenestra ... inter officium prestitum et appellationum in capite palatii.* " This was a simple work of adjustment, the exact extent of which is not clearly apparent; but in any case it was not of great importance, considering the modest compensation: six troni for each window and three troni, ten marchetti for an oculus.

It would have been unthinkable on Domenico da Venezia's part to illuminate a hall of that size and height (see n. 27) with only six windows of which only two were on the long sides, and it would have been impossible for anyone to open at least twenty-two new windows in the body of the old masonry a century after its erection. On the other hand, the oculi were a different matter. Domenico's palace must have had only the six lower oculi on the long sides and the two lower ones on the west side and not the upper ones which today are visible but blocked up. We can deduce this from paintings and engravings and by the fact that actually only those eight are open to illuminate the Hall. The six upper ones on the long sides and the two upper ones on the west side must have been opened later (after 1549), when the Palladian loggias partially obstructed the original lower ones. They were subsequently closed again at an unknown date (probably shortly thereafter), when it was noticed that they compromised the building's structural stability. In fact, the above-mentioned document of 1543 speaks of only fourteen oculi to be worked on, not twenty-eight; and in 1547 the palace still had only the six original oculi on the long sides, as shown in Fogolino's fresco of that date in the Bishop's Palace in Ascoli Piceno. See Chapter IV and Fig. VI, p. 23.

[32] FLORES-D'ARCAIS, 1961; SEMENZATO, 1963, pp. 31-39.

[33] Cf. SEMENZATO, 1963, pp. 37-38.

[34] FLORES-D'ARCAIS, 1961, p. 111.

[35] Ibid.

[36] SEMENZATO, 1963, p. 33.

[37] MURARO, 1959.

[38] ARSLAN, 1965, p. 58.

[39] Cf. BARBIERI, 1965. For a different judgment concerning Domenico da Venezia's building, see PANE, 1961, p. 143, who speaks of " Late Gothic preciosity " and a " dangerously formalistic interpretation, " undoubtedly with excessive severity.

[40] BARETARO, *Chronica ab anno 1444*, 1890 edition, pp. 9, 12; also *Cronica ad memoriam*, 1884 edition, pp. 25, 34; *Cronicha che comenza dall'anno 1400*, 1889 edition, pp. 6, 8; CASTELLINI, *Storia*, Bk. XV, 1821-22 edition, pp. 220, 238-239. Among the modern writers, see MANTESE, 1958, p. 388.

[41] *Cronica ad memoriam*, 1884 edition, p. 33: "*1481. Adì 30 giugno in Vicenza furon drizate in piedi 11 colone di soto delli pozzoli del Palazzo per far li detti pozzoli di preda.*"

[42] The precise sequence of events as derived from the *Cro-*

nica ad memoriam, 1884 edition, p. 36, is as follows: "*1483. ... furon fatti li primi volti di quadrello de pozzoli del palazzo verso la piazza grande e furon drizzate in piedi cinque colone dalla testa del detto palazzo verso il Domo, e furon fatti tutti gli archivolti con tutte le cornici alla detta testa* "; p. 38: " *1485 e 1486. Fu fatto il pozzolo di sopra ... verso la piazza grande, cioè furon poste in piedi tutte le colone di sopra et fatti tutti li volti ... di quadrelo e tutti furon coperti di piombo* "; p. 42: " *1489. Fu fatto il pezzo di pozzoli ... verso la piazza grande con le colonelle di preda rossa et bianca; fu salisà la sala grande ... con quadrelli di terra cota* "; p. 43: " *1491. Dal mese di Febraro ... furon drizate in piedi 8 colone ... verso la piazza delli frutti ... e del detto anno per tutto agosto fu compido di far* [the lower portico on that side] *... 1492. Furono forniti li pozzoli di sopra e li volti* "; p. 44: " *di quarelo e coperti di piombo dalla testa ... verso la Chiesa del Domo* "; p. 45: " *1493. ... furo, fatti tutti i pozzoli di sopra e li volti di quadrello e coperti di piombo ... verso la piazza delli frutti ... e furon fatti ancora quelli della testa ... verso la chiesa del Domo, e fu compido di far tutto del mese di Novembre.* "

[43] Cf. *Il Palazzo della Ragione in Vicenza*, 1875, pp. 44 ff. and esp. pl. III (drawn by G. Bettio), figs. ii and iii (a useful and reliable graphic reconstruction); COGO, 1900, pp. 19-20; ZORZI, 1926, p. 166, n. 1; 1964, pp. 43-44.

[44] ZORZI, 1926, p. 166, n. 1.

[45] In the lower gallery of this space between the two palaces where the " Borsa Merci " is now, the span of the entrance arches at the two sides would exactly correspond to the respective arches of the Quattrocento loggias; cf. *Il Palazzo della Ragione in Vicenza*, 1875, pp. 48-49.

[46] DALLA POZZA, 1943, pp. 132-133. This is why the *Cronica ad memoriam* states (see n. 41) that on June 30, 1481, eleven lower columns were set up on the north side: one was evidently the one which was placed against the tower in order to support the connecting arch.

[47] The work was completed in 1495-96 by a facing in white and red stones and the erection of a " *camera nova* " over the arch (Arco degli Zavatteri), with Bernardino da Milano and Zanon collaborating. Concerning the whole question, see ZORZI, 1926, pp. 112-113, 193-196, 196-197, n. 1; for Zanon and Bernardino, see n. 66 below.

[48] See n. 29.

[49] ZORZI, 1926, p. 166, n. 1.

[50] COGO, 1900, pp. 19-20: " ... this [hypothesis] occurred to me when I found several pieces of Gothic crenelation hidden above the vaults of the eastern loggia (which is now closed), near the balustraded attic of the Basilica overlooking the Pescheria. These were undoubtedly removed when the Gothic loggias were replaced by the ' classical ' ones, and they must have been stored above the vaults, which were conveniently near-by." Today the surviving pieces are at the Museo Civico in Vicenza (Plate 15). They are clearly Venetian in type and are analogous to those on the façade of Palazzo Porto-Breganze; there, however, they are blocked by the Settecento attic (BARBIERI, 1965, p. 180, n. 24).

[51] Several payments are proof that the upper loggias terminated in crenelations, according to ZORZI, 1926, p. 166, n. 1. The payments were for breaking the latter up and clearing them away after the collapse of the loggias in 1496 (see also Chapter III).

[52] BARBIERI, 1962, pp. 125-129; ARSLAN, 1956, pp. 64-65, N. 355. The two paintings, datable between ca. 1515 and 1520, in fact postdate the collapse of 1496. However, during those years the loggias—notwithstanding the gravity of the disaster—were a long way from being dismantled (Chapter III), especially along the southern side, which is the one represented in the two views.

[53] PUPPI, 1966, pp. 20, 58; pl. 3. The reference to St. Sebastian was previously made by PEE, 1939, pp. 12-13, who, however, connects it to the Bellini *Pietà* in the Accademia in Venice (which, as we have seen, instead reflects an earlier aspect of the building). PUPPI, 1966, (II), p. 19, proposes in a general way the idea that a pair of paintings by Bartolomeo Montagna also indicate the appearance of the loggias of the Vicentine palace. As Puppi himself has kindly clarified for me, we are con-

cerned here with a very brief glimpse at the left of the Papafava *St. Peter* and a much more ample view at the right of the *St. Jerome* in Ottawa (PUPPI, 1962, figs. 68, 91). The reference seems too vague, however, as the painter represents two series of porticoes quite different in cadence and articulation from the porticoes in Vicenza.

[54] DRAGONZINO DA FANO, 1525. See n. 52, which is also valid for the date of this evidence, although the sides of the palace represented here are in part different. I wish to thank Dr. Ferdinando Bandini, who kindly furnished me this information.

[55] CEVESE, 1953 and 1956, p. 110.

[56] Palazzo Porto-Breganze would date back to about the fifth decade of the Quattrocento (BARBIERI, 1965, pp. 172-173).

[57] ARSLAN, 1956, p. 7, N. 39.

[58] There is a disparity of about 18 cm. in respect to the floor of the loggias between the level of the embedded capitals and the height of the column. The disparity is due to the inclination of the floor toward the outside for the drainage of rainwater. Some authors consider (*Il Palazzo della Ragione in Vicenza*, 1875, p. 52; COGO, 1900, p. 21) that these three embedded capitals are remnants of Giorgio Spaventa's modifications of 1498-1500, which is a completely untenable suggestion (see Chapter III, n. 21).

According to tradition, after the collapse of 1496, and especially after the early decades of the Cinquecento, the material from the progressive demolition of the loggias had been gradually reused for other local buildings, and traces of it reportedly have been found. Thus ZORZI, 1937, p. 14, n. 1, states that: " the stairs that ascend from the Corso... to the minor portal of the Church of S. Corona were flanked by two orders of small columns that were given to the Holy Fathers of the Church by the Vicentine community, taken from among the columns that made up part of the upper order of the loggias of Palazzo della Ragione. ... Many other scattered capitals of the same style can be seen in the streets and on the porticoes of the city." The capitals and shafts of the columns in the cloister of S. dei Servi have the same provenance according to ZORZI (loc. cit.), and ARSLAN agrees (1956, p. 157, N. 1081), although with some reservations. CEVESE, 1953 (II) and 1956 (II) considers it " probable " that the portico columns of Casa Zilio (Contrà S. Lucia, civ. N. 46) are of the same origin and suggests a relationship with those in the cloister of S. Maria dei Servi, and also with several in the east porticoes of Piazza Biade. In my opinion (BARBIERI, 1953 and 1956, p. 340), the two large overturned Quattrocento capitals now in the southern portico of the cloister of S. Pietro may have come from the destroyed loggias of the Palazzo della Ragione.

From a documentary point of view, we know only that one column of the palace was assigned to Pier Antonio Civena and was evaluated on May 9, 1526, before its delivery, by Giovanni da Pedemuro (ZORZI, 1937, p. 80). Some columns were given to the Church of S. Maria degli Angeli, and a column, a base, and a capital " *volto in canton* " were given to Alvise Capra (ZORZI, 1937, n. 14, n. 1), all of which have completely disappeared. Regarding the capitals and shafts in the cloister of the Servite church, stylistically we would be concerned only with those on the northern side, and a simple comparison of measurements with the portions of the surviving loggias still *in situ* is sufficient to exclude them. The same is true for the Quattrocento columns and capitals of Piazza Biade and of Casa Zilio. Only the comparison with the two capitals in the cloister of S. Pietro (Plates 16, 18) remains convincing: the measurements correspond in such a way that one is convinced that the larger one comes from the lower order and the smaller one from the upper order of the loggias. The difference in structure does not seem a reason to reject the hypothesis, considering the frequency with which capitals of the most varied types alternated in the same building. A portico capital on the western side of Piazza delle Erbe possibly suggests a provenance from the Palazzo della Ragione. I would like to thank the architect Andrzej Pereswet-Sołtan, who provided the necessary technical data for this note.

[59] ZORZI, 1926, p. 166, n. 1.

[60] See n. 59. According to Zorzi, it is not rare still to come across these dripstones in some private houses in Vicenza; however, more precise information is required.

[61] *Il Palazzo della Ragione in Vicenza*, 1875, pp. 44 ff.

[62] ZORZI, 1926, pp. 192-193, n. 2: Zanon undertook " *a far condurre a Vicenza tute e singole priede bianche e rose anderà e bisognerà e intrarà de la cornice di volto di sotto fino al compimento di merli de sopra,*" i. e., up to the crenelations which crowned the loggias. ZORZI, 1926, p. 166, n. 1, suggests that on that occasion the facing of the top part of the interior of the Gothic building (above the loggias) was also executed. On the other hand, such facing already existed in Domenico da Venezia's palace and was the evident model for the subsequent work. Concerning Zanon, see n. 66 below.

[63] LILIO, *Breve descrittione del mondo*, 1551 edition, pp. 132-133.

[64] Cf. *Il Palazzo della Ragione in Vicenza*, 1875, pp. 44 ff., and DRAGONZINO DA FANO, 1525: " *A la pubblica piazza pervenuto... / vidi il palazzo, il qual magno reputo, / di piombo il copre una cuba formosa / le sue colonne con superbo aiuto / alzan dintorno una loggia pomposa.*"

[65] *Cronica ad memoriam*, 1884 edition, p. 38.

[66] *Cronica ad memoriam*, 1884 edition, p. 49; for the contract agreed to by the two sculptors on March 13, 1495, see ZORZI, 1926, pp. 196-197, n. 1. Concerning Bernardino and Zanon, see ZORZI, 1926, pp. 103-121, 189-200 and 1959, p. 358. For a survey of their activity in Vicenza, see *Guida di Vicenza*, 1953 and 1956, and ARSLAN, 1956. It suffices here to emphasize the very close analogy (already mentioned by ZORZI, 1926, p. 115, n. 5) between this stairway of the palace and the one in the presbytery of S. Corona, also by Bernardino (ca. 1502).

[67] ZORZI, 1937, pp. 35-37.

[68] The whole was executed by Bello da Rivolta in 1496; for the payments, see ZORZI, 1926, pp. 186-187 and n. 4.

[69] Judging from the moulding, this was probably a question of the one furthest east; the other, near the top of the Seicento stair, must be the one dating from the second half of the Settecento (see Chapter V). In any event, inside the Hall we can see the flattened arches which were inserted in the masonry of the two long sides above the doors in order to reinforce the structure during the work on the doors themselves. The span is wider than that of the earlier windows, and the ogival curve and the profile of the mouldings are also different.

[70] Considering the clear, secure structural premises set out by Domenico da Venezia, it does not really seem that the loggias were required " in order to cover up the confused execution of the various parts of the building " (ZORZI, 1964, p. 43).

[71] SANUTO, *Itinerario*, 1847 edition, p. 108: " *el palazo di Ragion* [in Vicenza] *si fabricava, et è a modo quello di Padoa.*" Among modern writers, FLORES-D'ARCAIS, 1961, pp. 108, 112; SEMENZATO, 1963, p. 32.

[72] PROSDOCIMI, 1961.

[73] The violation is particularly evident along the cornice of the ogival windows. In fact, now that the marble covering has been removed, the projection of the cornice onto the wall in back becomes excessive and overly brusque because the thickness of the moulding, originally meant to be covered by the marble slabs, is visible.

[74] See n. 72. We do not know if this is why an oculus of the palace was also destroyed at some later point in the demolition of the loggias. Today it is missing from the lower row on the southern side and was probably replaced by the opening for a sundial which the *Deputati* of the city presented on November 25, 1530, to the canons of S. Giorgio in Alga, officiants of the Church of S. Rocco (ARSLAN, 1956, p. 149, N. 1012). The proposal of Arslan and of CEVESE, 1953 (III) and 1956 (III), p. 280, to identify this " *oculus lapideus palatii nuper colapsi* " with the one actually inserted in the façade of S. Rocco seems logical; nevertheless, there is a remarkable difference in their profiles.

[75] ZORZI, 1964, p. 44.

[76] Cf. BARBIERI, 1965, esp. n. 15; CEVESE, 1964.

[77] SEMENZATO, 1963, p. 42.

[78] Cf. LORENZONI, 1963; PUPPI, 1959-60, 1962, 1963, 1964-65, 1966, 1967.

[79] Cf. SASSELLA, 1884, pp. 15 ff.: The old palace would

have been " of superb beauty and a glorious monument for Vicenza... if [it] had been restored in the early ogival manner." See also HOWELEY, 1887.

80 Concerning Formenton (born ca. 1428 in Vicenza; enrolled in the guild of masonry-workers from April 25, 1480, on; died in 1492), see MAGRINI, 1872. ZORZI provides fundamental information (1926, pp. 155-179); for revisions and clarifications, see ARSLAN (1956), the *Guida di Vicenza* (1953 and 1956), and MANTESE (1964, p. 877, n. 13).

81 Cf. MAGRINI, 1872; *Il Palazzo della Regione in Vicenza,* 1875, pp. 25-33; and esp. FORMENTON (1863; 1867, p. 374; 1872).

82 ZORZI, 1926, pp. 163-169; also 1964, p. 90.

83 Enumerated with punctilious exactitude by ZORZI, 1926.

84 ZORZI, 1926, p. 198; concerning the restrictive meaning of the expression " *magister,*" which does not negate the attribution to Tommaso of the loggia's design, see also ZORZI, op. cit., p. 201, n. 2.

85 ZORZI, 1926, pp. 183-186.

86 As earlier guessed by MAGRINI, 1872, this was confirmed after some early hesitation (1926) by ZORZI, 1964, p. 90. Concerning the narrow limits of Formenton's artistic personality, see also FIOCCO, 1961, pp. 169-170.

III

FROM THE COLLAPSE OF THE LOGGIAS
TO THE APPROVAL OF PALLADIO'S PROJECT

FROM 1496 TO 1542

On Wednesday April 20, 1496, scarcely a year and a half after the conclusion of the work, "*cascò tra le 19 e 20 hore una gran parte delli pozzoli... cioè tutto il canton verso le pescarie con tutte le colonne et volti di sotto e di sopra con tutta la coperta di piombo.*"[1] The same source reports the principal cause of the disaster, which concerned the southwest corner of the loggias: "*fu tutto per difeto delle catene di fero che eran tropo sotili, che si rupero, e per difeto delle colone di soto che erano tropo sotili, et in particolar quella ch'era sopra il cantone.*"[2] The recent excavation by modern scholars confirms the diagnosis.[3]

The disaster had been anticipated on other occasions, though it was fortunately avoided. We have, in fact, information about repeated precautions taken in earlier years: in 1491 Giovanni da Rivolta had even reconstructed an arch of the palace itself "*verso le pescarie,*" demolished as early as 1489 by Tommaso Formenton because it threatened to collapse.[4] We know positively that on March 19, 1495, when Bernardino da Milano and Zanon Marchesini da Chiampo entered into a contract for the construction of the new northern stairway, they committed themselves at the same time to prepare by April of 1496 "*quatro collone de la grosseza de quelle*

sono ali cantoni de i portigi cum capitelli e basse de sua pria e mettere in opera a tute sue spese."[5] But fate would have it that the collapse of April 20th preceded the execution of this plan to replace the corner supports.

However, it was quickly arranged to clear the debris and to shore up the most endangered arches,[6] at the same time searching for suitable remedies. Antonio Rizzo, then working in the Doges' Palace, was summoned from Venice; only three weeks after his arrival a model with his first suggestions was exhibited, with payment to a Master Domenico " *marangon* " on May 11, 1496,[7] accompanied by a brief report.[8] Rizzo, having ascertained that the loggias were made rather poorly, proposed pulling them down; when reconstructed, the lower arches would have smaller openings in order to obtain a rhythm identical to that of the upper portico—an overall effect which was perhaps not far from what the same architect achieved in the loggias on the eastern side of the courtyard of the Doges' Palace.[9] But as the expense would have surpassed the citizens' resources, they fell back on more simple expedients: the city surveyor suggested a simple reinforcement of the structure, exchanging the columns for piers, especially at the corners where they would strengthen the foundations.[10]

This time the remedy, examined by one

IX - Sebastiano Serlio, *Design for a palace*. From *Regole generali di Architettura*, IV, 1537

" Alexius *peritus architectus* "[11] and by many other competent citizens, seemed too casual. Consequently, on July 3, 1496, the Council of the Hundred decided to start new consultations.[12] But they ended up by turning again to Rizzo: on July 7 Alvise Pace was charged with seeking him out directly in Venice,[13] and on July 15 his new, definitive proposals were discussed and approved.[14] Albeit unwillingly, the Council accepted the idea of demolishing the Formenton loggias and remaking them with an equal number of arches in the two orders and with the lower columns polygonal in section "*dato modello seu designo per dictum Architectum.*"[15] Meanwhile, they beseeched the Venetian government to allow Rizzo to remain in Vicenza, and on August 4 the destruction of the *pozzoli* was begun, starting on the western side " *verso el domo* ":[16] the material salvaged was carefully saved, so that once the lower arcades were remade one could put the columns and balustrades of the upper order back into service. Two years later, on the 8th of March, Zanon Marchesini da Chiampo committed himself to prepare the stones needed to proceed with construction of the new loggias.[17]

In the meantime (1498), Rizzo had been accused of embezzlement and had fled to Ancona. Giorgio Spaventa, who succeeded him in the office of chief architect of the Venetian Republic, advised several modifications which were approved on March 22, 1498.[18] The columns were to be replaced with square-based piers only at the corners; the lower portico should retain its rhythm, thus avoiding the proposed doubling of the arcades and their anticipated demolition; moreover, it would suffice to replace thirteen columns " *sopra la piaza e per testa del Palazo*," to secure the columns well to each other and to the inside wall, to replace the stones slabs of the upper portico's pavement with compressed ter-

racotta (to stop more effectively the infiltration of water), and to repair the roofs.[19] The saving permitted by these proposals was welcome: in 1499 the stonemasons prepared the mouldings,[20] and by August of 1500 the lower arcades of the western side were already restored up to the cornice which marked their separation from the upper gallery, in accordance with Spaventa's ideas.[21]

But turbulent times intervened. In 1502 Julius II and the anti-Venetian coalition proclaimed a " holy war " against Venice. The Venetian defeats at Agnadello and Mirabello (1509) followed, and in the alternating phases of the struggle Vicenza was occupied on the part of the troops of the Hapsburg Emperor Maxmillian. Only after 1520, with control changing many times, was the city able to regain a relative calm; fortunately it remained apart from the worst of the events provoked by the reciprocal conflicts and alliances between Venice, Clement VII, Charles V, and Francis I.[22]

Obviously during such crises the anticipated reconstruction of the loggias remained suspended, and the great structure of the palace was practically abandoned. Only the necessary maintenance was kept up: in 1509-10 Bartolomeo d'Arsiero and Lodovico da Viadana worked on the roof; on September 7, 1512, a wooden beam of the framework supporting the loggias threatened to collapse; in 1518 Domenico Pagan constructed a wall for the new north stair.[23]

Only on March 1, 1525, when it was ascertained that the upper loggia facing Piazza dei Signori was manifestly in danger of falling, were two distinguished citizens, Ludovico Capra and Francesco Gualdo, charged to consult with experts and architects " *ne tanta machina ruat.* "[24] On the 15th they were authorized to spend twenty ducats " *pro conducendis dictis protis et architectis,* "[25] and on May 9, 1525, Francesco Gualdo was reimbursed the four gold scudi which he had paid to an expert whom he had summoned especially from Venice.[26] In all likelihood this was Antonio Scarpagnino,[27] at that time overseer for the Venetian Republic and already known in Vicenza for other important works executed some years earlier.[28] However, the fact remains that his intervention must have been largely in the nature of preservation and was destined to provoke the resignations of Gualdo and Ludovico Capra in protest.[29]

Perhaps as a consequence of that action, in March of 1527 a propping-up of the endangered loggias (especially along the northern side) was begun. Payments toward that purpose are registered in 1527, 1528, 1529, and in May of 1532.[30] On February 12, 1528, Bartolomeo Brugnoli da Lugano undertook the construction of three shops under the lower southern loggias at the head of the arch facing the Torre del Girone.[31] In May of 1532 Scarpagnino returned to Vicenza; on the 29th, after a talk with the *Deputati* of the city, he took on a contract for the task of repairing as well as possible the precarious condition of the roof, and especially of the enormous *carena*.[32] Two subsequent notes of January 31 and July 29, 1534, clearly refer to the melting of the necessary lead.[33]

On April 12, 1535, the sculptor Francesco di Battista Matteazzi was entrusted to supply all the stone to erect another three shops under the loggias, facing south " *inter columnas palatii.* "[34] Everything notwithstanding, a document of September 28, 1535, lamented that the loggias were collapsing " *cum maximo hominum apotecarumque... damno,* " not to mention the dishonor to the city; therefore, three illustrious citizens were appointed and proceeded with the repairs " *medio peritorum.* "[35] On November 25 of the following year all the income from the rent of the communal lands of Campo Marzo was set aside for the restoration, and the arrival of Jacopo Sansovino as consultant was announced as near at hand: " *quem quotidie expectamus.* "[36] An optimistic expression, as the great architect did not arrive until 1538.

During those years the old Formenton loggias along the northern and southern sides remained standing, propped up and in sorry condition. Those along the western side, rebuilt in 1500 according to the last Rizzo project modified by Spaventa, were hardly completed in the lower gallery. In order to resolve a situation which had become stagnant since Sansovino had failed to arrive, it seemed opportune to persevere with the Rizzo-Spaventa idea, with the firm intention of completing it. On July 30, 1537, 150 ducats a year were added to the 249 ducats already in deposit until the work was completely finished;[37] evidently the palace in Vicenza was to be the " Palace of Unsuccessful Intentions. " Finally, in the early part of January, 1538, Sansovino arrived in Vicenza.[38] On January 29, 1538, Giovanni Trento was reimbursed the ten scudi he gave to the architect to pay for his transfer " *causa videndi reparationem palatii fiendam.* "[39] But, after all the waiting, it seems that Sansovino limited himself to mere advice—both here and on the occasion of his last visit to Vicenza, which fell between March and April of the same year (1538) when he came to work on the problem of the apse of the Cathedral.[40]

The whole of 1538 passed with nothing accomplished, and thus on February 15, 1539, two scudi were again paid for a consultation requested with the architect Sebastiano Serlio.[41] We must rely on the letter of the act of payment[42] that the money was compensation " *pro faciendo unum designum seu modellum* "; but the total silence which descended afterward concerning Serlio's possible " *invenzione* " aroused the insinuation that the Bolognese had made neither a design nor a model, but had contented himself with pocketing the two scudi—which perhaps was excessively cynical.[43] Little, however, could have been concluded by Michele Sanmicheli, who came to Vicenza in November 1541 and in January 1542 and remained in the city with his family and two horses a good twelve days in all. He stayed in Pedemuro Sanbiagio with Giovanni da Porlezza, who was reimbursed on January 31, 1542, for the expenses sustained.[44]

It was enough to make one lose patience. But the administrators of the city, besides being unlucky, were also—to their eternal credit—sufficiently tenacious, as proved by the deliberation of November 30, 1542, which was unanimously approved by the Council of the Hundred.[45] Here, after sorrowfully confirming how the rebuilding of the loggia had been initiated over forty years ago and was still " *numquam perfectum*," they confirmed their determination to place a time limitation on completing the building. Deploring the loss of the " *scripturae in hac materia* " (the destruction of the Rizzo and Spaventa drawings in the fire of 1508),[46] they emphasized however that " *extat tamen opus* ": one section was complete (the surviving Formenton loggias), one incomplete " *bellis supervenientibus* " (the west side, the reconstruction of which had stopped in 1500 on the lower gallery, due to the political events). Therefore they could make a decision concerning the main body of the building; or better, " *ad tolendum omnem dificultatem contradicere intendentium*." As word of the fame of Giulio Romano—" *architecti non vulgaris immo celebris et nominati*," who was then in Mantua—had reached the Council, it was decided to turn to him. The merit of the artist chosen and the fame of his recent works in Mantua—which was enhanced by that of his works spread throughout the Veneto, echoes of the distant and glorious sixteenth-century Roman *Maniera*—seemed finally to guarantee a sure and satisfactory solution to the problem. But subsequent events turned out very differently.

From 1542 to 1549: Giulio Romano and Palladio

Valeriano Valle went directly to Mantua to summon Giulio Romano in December 1542,[47] perhaps making the trip with Andrea Palladio.[48] Giulio came at once to Vicenza, remaining there fifteen days. On January 3, 1543, he was paid fifty ducats for his trip and " *videndi pallatium et faciendi modellum causa fabricandi dictum pallatium*." [49] This model was accompanied by drawings for several variants, by notes of expenses, by three plans to clarify the urban arrangements of the surrounding area, and by a full report " *circa fabricam podiolorum*." [50] It was, however, a case of " *parturiunt montes*."

On close examination, Giulio formulated very sensible proposals, in part dictated by a Solomon-like ability to compromise: his judgment, as has been wittily noted,[51] was "quite similar to that of a modern but not very intelligent government inspector." It seemed to him " *che non si debba patire de ruinare il pallazo cum speranza de refarne uno più bello, massimamente per essere l'ediffitio... molto magnanimo et honorevole*." Rather, he advised " *che se seguisse la fabrica al modo che è cominciata verso il domo cum le colone più grosse*": that is to say, he urged the continuation of Rizzo's plan as modified by Spaventa, which was begun in 1500 on the western side and halted at the lower gallery. Thus the columns and capitals which were already made but which had become useless after the suspension of the work would be put to use. Giulio carried his homage to the Spaventa project to the extent of advising, as Spaventa had, the use of iron chains to bind the arches and columns together. And, "*volendo l'opera più bella et più richa e senza guastar niente,*" one could double the cadence of the columns of the lower gallery at a later date. So that the trouble of costly foundations could be avoided, each column added in the middle would rest on a sturdy underground arch thrown between the bases of the existing columns.

In strengthening the Formenton columns on the ground floor and standardizing their sections according to the larger column envisaged by Spaventa for the corner piers, Giulio showed in an accompanying sketch how they could "*vestire*" the aforesaid columns and "*farli li pillastri dintorno.*" In the end, he reconfirmed the initial concept: "*perché mi pare cossa de importanza, non consentirei mai... de ruinar la fabrica per haverne a fare novo modo, perché è impossibile acordarse cum l'ornamento quale è atorno al palazo in forma terzacuta et todescha.*" And if at all costs they wanted "*far altro novo dissegno, ... bisogneria disornare et spogliar* [the building] *de pietre e ferramenti, il che cavati che siano strazeria tutta la fabrica et discatenerà il tutto ne mai con quella fermezza di prima si riporranno in opera.*"

In conclusion, with the number of arches in the two rows of loggias equalized, the edifice would have actually assumed—despite the importance of the plan's advocate—the same physiognomy as that of the Rizzo project.[52] Giulio Romano seemed rather concerned about examining a new arrangement for the stairs; he especially wanted to remove Bernardino da Milano's late Quattrocento stair, "*perché rompe l'ordine et guasta lo portico di sotto et lo pogio di sopra,*" and the older one as well

(the one rebuilt by Biagio da Santorso in 1483 and located between the Palazzo della Ragione and the palace of the podestà), and to move both of them "*ne li cantoni verso il Domo.*" Then "*saranno più comode et espeditte e non impedirano li poggioli e dariano più fermezza alla fabrica.*"[53]

For a more suitable division of the shops and the pedestrian passageways under the Hall, he offered three variant solutions. The first, "*quale a me piace di più et a ogni architecto pensa debba piacere,*" advocated unencumbered porticoes on the ground floor with the intermediate aisles equal in size. The second plan modified the existing situation only slightly, improving the position of Bernardino's stair. The third plan "*saria de più utilità et cum maggior numero di botteghe et cum le vie espeditte cum altro modo di scalle*"; it contemplated in addition a different placement of the prisons, which were at that time located on the ground-floor level of the palace facing west.

Finally, the architect formulated an interesting proposal, which unfortunately is like the others in being difficult to reconstruct in detail due to the loss of the drawings and plans which accompanied the report. Desiring that "*li successori ornare et dar fine alla fabrica del pallazo,*" it was agreed to lower the level of Piazza dei Signori while raising the level of Piazza delle Erbe, in such a way that "*d'intorno tutte le piaze siano a un pari*" and so that within the vast, uniform area the great building would be isolated. The immense piazza resulting "*se doveria circundare di portici ad uso dun claustro o almen quanto si potrà.*"

Here Giulio produced one of the most interesting urban plans of the Cinquecento, corresponding to Sangallo's contemporary projects for the Piazza in Loreto.[54] Giulio did not indicate however, whether he envisaged the Rizzo-Spaventa type of portico with one or two orders, or something more "modern." Nevertheless, it is enough to take account of the Palazzo della Ragione's situation within its urban context, to realize that the project—besides being enormously difficult to execute—cut heedlessly into an organism whose body had been determined by centuries of vicissitudes. Moreover, Giulio's broad and detailed discourse seems to reveal two contrasting requirements. On the one hand, while denouncing prudence at least, if not respect for the existing Late Gothic loggias, he seems to feel the hesitations and critical apprehensions peculiar to the new enigma of Mannerism, of which he was such a distinguished exponent.[55] On the other hand, while admiring the regular, closed piazza with its circuit of porticoes, he adhered to the more genuine, abstract Renaissance idea of the "*piazza salone*":[56] the result was his own peculiar combination of "classical jargon and mediaevalist compromises."[57]

The fact remains that Vicenza's Council of the Hundred had started out boldly supporting the "foreigner" but subsequently became, if not almost hostile, much more cautious. On January 25, 1543, when the reports prepared by the architect were put under discussion, they decided to follow one of the solutions offered by him, to be settled at a later date; but, it was always emphasized "*firma manente parte anni 1498 cui non intelligatur modo aliquo per presentem partem derogatum.*"[58] Since in the Council's session of March 22, 1498, Spaventa's modifications of Rizzo's project for restoring the loggias had been approved, the freedom of choice was effectively diminished. In addition, the decision was certainly not very enthusiastic, showing barely sixty votes in favor against forty votes opposed. It was a question of a concerted manoeuvre among the various groups to turn down what was not satisfactory to them, while avoiding the troublesomeness of a rejection. They therefore concluded by voting "no" under the specious aspect of approval. In fact, when as far back as July 15, 1496, Rizzo's project had been accepted,[59] it was decided not to undertake another project if such a one did not obtain at least three-fourths of the votes. The condition was never rescinded, and it was not verified in this particular emergency.[60]

The documents are silent for the rest of 1543 and for the two-year period of 1544-45,[61] until March 5, 1546, when—the curious situation having by that time dragged on for half a century—the *Deputati ad utilia* submitted to the Council of the Hundred "*ex omnibus quae extant designis... designum novissime presentatum per magistrum Joannem et Andream Palladium vicetinos.*"[62] According to this project, "*forma conspicuum*" and not very expensive to execute, the work on the palace could finally be concluded. However the *Deputati* themselves proposed that in order to permit a more thoughtful decision based on direct observation, one of the arches envisaged in the chosen design should be constructed in a wooden model, which would be displayed exactly "*subtus unum ex arcubus palatii.*" Thirty gold ducats were designated for this purpose, which included the honorarium for the two architects.

The Council of the Hundred approved this with eighty-four votes in favor and nineteen opposed. The delicate carpentry-work was immediately subsidized on March 6th and was paid in full on January 31, 1547.[63] This actually concerned the lower gallery;[64] while the costs, which had risen to 102 ducats as compared to the 30 ducats envisaged, signified that it was not merely a question of a finished arch, almost life-size, but that the model had to be modified over and over again.[65]

The discussions were not finished, however, but were further complicated by the deaths of two of the *Provveditori alla fabbrica* and the resignation of the third[66] and by other causes, in particular by controversies raised "*circa electionem designi.*"[67] In order to shorten the delays, on September 6, 1548, the Council of the Hundred appointed two new wardens—Gabriele Capra and Girolamo Chiericati—with eighty-six votes in favor and eight opposed; to these Giovanni Alvise Valmarana was added on September 24th.[68] The three were charged with reviewing and reporting to the Council the terms of the fifty-year-old question, the origins of which few could recall, and with submitting at the same time not less than three "*designa sive modella*" for a definitive choice. One of these had to be the "*designum sive modellum vetus,*" that is to say, the 1496 Rizzo project with the Spaventa modifications of 1498. In order to simplify the procedure, it was decided that the winning project need obtain only one-half plus one of the votes on the first ballot.

For some months the question seems to have been set aside. We know only that on October 27, 1548, the *Deputati ad utilia* hired Andrea Palladio to make "*quatuor dessigna palatii,*" upon payment of fifty pound-weight of small coins.[69] More silence follows until April 11, 1549, when they arrived at the conclusive debate. The *Provveditori*, in accordance with the mandate they had received in September of the preceding year, submitted three designs in competition: 1) of necessity, the "*modellum vetus*" which had been begun on the western façade of the palace; 2) by their choice, Giulio Romano's project (proposed again after the rejection, in substance if not in fact, of January 1543); 3) a "*modellum ligneum Andreae Palladii architecti vincentini,*"[70] evidently constructed from the designs made the previous October (1548).[71] First to speak was Alvise Valmarana (described as "*luculentissime*" by the town clerk, who displayed his most aulic style for the occasion); he supported "*apertis argumentis et rationibus architecturae.*" Girolamo Chiericati ("*elegantissime*") followed, holding the audience "*cum maxima omnium attentione.*" In the voting, the Palladian project triumphed with ninety-nine votes in favor and only seventeen opposed. One is continually reminded of the impassioned, albeit rhetorical, statement that by its sanction the Council of the Hundred actually determined the destiny of Andrea Palladio, and with it the splendor of Vicenza.[72]

NOTES TO CHAPTER III

[1] The "*Pescarie*" were and are the two city quarters to the southwest of the Palazzo della Ragione: from the Piazza delle Erbe to the Ponte S. Paolo (*Pescarie Nuove*) and from the Piazzetta Palladio, through Contrà Giacomo Orefice and Contrà Garibaldi, to the apse of the Cathedral (*Pescarie Vecchie*); cf. GIAROLLI, 1955, pp. 338-339.

[2] *Cronica ad memoriam*, 1884 edition, p. 48.

[3] Cf. PANE, 1961, p. 143.

[4] Cf. ZORZI, 1937, p. 24 and 1926, pp. 110, 112, 196-197.

[5] ZORZI, 1926, pp. 196-197, n. 1.

[6] Bernardino da Milano directed the work of clearing; he was reimbursed on September 17, 1496, together with Zanon Marchesini da Chiampo for the expense of hiring the "*caro mato*" used for that purpose (ZORZI, 1926, pp. 113-114 and 198, n. 4). Other shoring and demolition operations involved Gasparo da Malo, Giovanni Fuger da Rivolta, and the brothers Andrea and Pietro Bonvicini da Valsolda; among other things, they spent from August 4 to August 13 taking away the crenelations over

the loggias (ZORZI, 1926, pp. 100-101 and n. 5; p. 166, n. 1; p. 186. Cf. also ZORZI, 1959, p. 358).

[7] ZORZI, 1937, p. 25 and n. 3.

[8] As ZORZI correctly deduces (1937, p. 25; also for the chronology) from an examination of the subsequent report by Rizzo on July 15.

[9] Cf. BASSI, 1962, pp. 46 and 51-52, fig. 37: the intervention of Rizzo in work on the Ducal Palace began in 1483 and ended in 1498.

[11] Who may perhaps be identified with the Bergamese architect Alessio Aleardi, who at that time was employed by the government of the Venetian Republic (ZORZI, 1964, p. 44). See also ZORZI, 1959, p. 358; 1961 (IV), pp. 501-503.

[12] See ZORZI, 1937, pp. 26 and 128-129 for the full text of the resolution.

[10] Archivio di Torre della Città di Vicenza, *Libro Albo Vecchio*, c. 187 (transcribed by ZORZI, 1937, pp. 127-128).

[13] ZORZI, 1937, p. 13 and n. 2.

[14] Archivio di Torre della Città di Vicenza, *Libro Albo Vecchio*, c. 189 (transcribed by ZORZI, 1937, pp. 129-130).

[15] Unfortunately—whether it was a model or a drawing—this was lost, probably in the fire that broke out on September 9, 1508, in the Torre del Girone or del Tormento, where the Communal Archives were stored (ZORZI, 1937, p. 30).

[16] ZORZI, 1937, pp. 27-28; see also *Cronica ad memoriam*, 1884 edition, p. 48: " *la comunità di Vicenza fece getar giù tuti li pozoli dela testa del... Palazzo perché volevano cascare e per occasion di fare due pilastroni di preda quadri sopra li cantoni e per rimeter tutte le colone di sotto più grosse.*" This is a clear allusion to the Rizzo project. It is also clearly indicated that the crenelations on the loggias were removed on this occasion.

[17] ZORZI, 1926, p. 198 and 1937, pp. 28-29.

[18] ZORZI, 1937, pp. 7, 13-14, 33-34.

[19] Archivio di Torre della Città di Vicenza, *Libro Albo Vecchio*, c. 192 (transcribed by ZORZI, 1937, pp. 131-132).

[20] ZORZI, 1937, pp. 29-30.

[21] *Cronica ad memoriam*, 1884 edition, pp. 52-53: " *1500 ... furon drizzate tutte le colonne alla testa del Palazzo di Vicenza che era rovinato verso le Garzerie per far li pozzoli al detto palazzo e fu fatto sino alle cornici dove andavano le colonelle di pozi d'Agosto.*" According to ZORZI (see n. 18), the March 22, 1498 deliberation with which the Spaventa project was approved produced no sequel, and the execution of the Rizzo project continued (cf. also PANE, 1961, p. 144 and n. 4). It is difficult to see the reason for this, considering that the Spaventa proposal " *omnibus de ... consilio placuit exceptis vigintinovem in contrarium extantibus.*" When later documents refer to the Rizzo project, they always do so by way of the Spaventa modifications; see the deliberation of January 25, 1543 (n. 58), in which it is explicitly stated, " *firma manente parte anni 1498 cui non intelligatur modo aliquo per presentem partem derogatum.*" However, we must remember that the hypothesis that the embedded capitals with Ionic volutes still existing on the western side and at the northeast corner of the palace constitute proof of Spaventa's modifications (*Il Palazzo della Ragione in Vicenza*, 1875, p. 52; COGO, 1900, p. 21) is without foundation. In fact, Spaventa never alluded in his report to the possibility of changing the embedded capitals, as he evidently used those which supported the vaults of the Formenton loggias, to which the surviving capitals clearly belong (see Chapter II, n. 58).

[22] MANTESE, 1960, pp. 65, 71.

[23] *Il Palazzo della Ragione in Vicenza*, 1875, p. 23; BORTOLAN, 1886 (III), p. 8; *Appunti di Storia Vicentina*, 1910, p. 45; ZORZI, 1937, pp. 7, 14. According to MANTESE, 1964, p. 881, it seems that the work entrusted to the carpenters Bartolomeo d'Arsiero and Lodovico da Viadana was then postponed, but later the contract was renewed with the same individuals (on December 10, 1520).

[24] ZORZI, 1937, pp. 7-8.

[25] ZORZI, 1937, p. 8.

[26] ZORZI, 1937, p. 38, nn. 3-4.

[27] ZORZI, 1937, pp. 37-40.

[28] On August 13, 1521, he and Giovanni da Pedemuro were paid 289 ducats for having put in the floor of the old Loggia del Capitaniato (the predecessor of the present Palladian structure), using white and red stone.

[29] ZORZI, 1937, pp. 8, 38-39.

[30] ZORZI, 1937, pp. 8-9, 39. During these years (MANTESE, 1964, p. 884) they also had work undertaken in the Chapel of St. Vincent. This was the old chapel still existing in the *Palatium vetus* (see Chapter I), which the documents describe as " *in comuni palatio, prope carceres* " (MANTESE, ibid., p. 874), i. e., in the lower part of the *Palatium vetus* which was later incorporated into the western section of Domenico da Venezia's palace.

[31] Today these shops, for which Brugnoli received an advance of two gold scudi two days later (ZORZI, 1937, p. 14), no longer exist. For other peripheral work in the palace during those years, see MANTESE, 1964, pp. 81-84.

[32] Archivio di Torre della Città di Vicenza, *Libro Provisioni IV*, c. 389 (transcribed by ZORZI, 1937, p. 133); see also ZORZI, 1937, pp. 9, 22, 39-40. As early as 1529 Battista, the carpenter for Bernardino Facio (called " Rossetto "), had received the commission to maintain the lead covering of the roof in good condition (MANTESE, 1964, p. 883, and n. 36). But as soon as Battista received the 3000 lbs. of metal acquired for this purpose (through the city's resolution of March 19, 1529), he sold them!

[33] However, not until March 26, 1544, was Scarpagnino paid for a final inspection of the roof; in his absence a certain Bernardino Cappelletto, called " cohopertor palatii," supervised the work (ZORZI, 1937, p. 40, n. 3).

[34] ZORZI, 1937, pp. 99-100, n. 2. Today these shops have disappeared.

[35] ZORZI, 1937, p. 10.

[36] Archivio di Torre della Città di Vicenza, *Libro Provisioni V*, c. 383 (transcribed by ZORZI, 1937, p. 141); also ZORZI, 1937, pp. 10, 14-15.

[37] ZORZI, 1937, p. 15.

[38] ZORZI, 1937, pp. 48-50.

[39] Archivio di Torre della Città di Vicenza, *Libro Provisioni V*, c. 710 (transcribed by ZORZI, 1937, p. 142).

[40] ZORZI, 1958, p. 281. The traditional regret for having lost all evidence regarding Sansovino's ideas (cf. *Guida di Vicenza*, 1953 and 1956, p. 88) is more suggestive than well-founded.

[41] ZORZI, 1937, pp. 15, 50-51.

[42] Archivio di Torre della Città di Vicenza, *Libro Provisioni V*, c. 930 (transcribed by ZORZI, 1937, pp. 142-143).

[43] ZORZI, 1937, p. 50; 1960, p. 10. According to FRANCO (1937, pp. 61, 63), a precise design by Serlio for the loggias in Vicenza actually existed; subsequently, DALLA POZZA (1943, p. 104, fig. 26) noted that the design (fig. iii) by SERLIO (1537, c. 33v.-34r.) reveals a theme analogous to that later developed by Palladio in his loggias. It has been pointed out (BARBIERI-CEVESE, 1953 and 1956, p. 88) that this perhaps allows us to gain some idea of the solution offered by the Bolognese architect. Cf. FORSSMAN, 1965, p. 40, n. 2, who considers Serlio's design for " *logge sopra logge* " in the fourth book (1537) of his treatise (a repetition or variant of his design for the Basilica in Vicenza) to be very practical. Concerning this question, see also WILINSKI, 1965, pp. 119-120. Moreover, PANE (1961, p. 144) properly notes that the presence of Serlio in Vicenza can be considered much more important and effective for the local artistic culture than the single event of the restoration of Palazzo della Ragione, or his probable plans in regard to it. For Serlio's stay in Vicenza, see DALLA POZZA, 1943, pp. 65-87 and BARBIERI, 1952, pp. 28-33; PANE, 1961, p. 46, n. 7, is in substantial agreement.

[44] Archivio di Torre della Città di Vicenza, *Libro Provisioni VI*, c. 316 and 377 (transcribed by ZORZI, 1937, pp. 143-144); see also the clarification by ZORZI, 1937, pp. 17, 52; 1960, p. 90; 1964 (II), pp. 105-106. Sanmicheli's intervention followed two important deliberations of July 5 and September 6, 1541 (ZORZI, 1937, pp. 15-16), in which for the first time the possibility of

examining new " *mudella vel dessigna* " for the palace in addition to the old Rizzo-Spaventa compromise was expressly mentioned. The payment to the architect for one of his trips from Verona " *causa faciendi mudella pro palatii fabrica* " was decided on November 15, 1541. However, we no longer have a record concerning these " *mudella* "; either they were not made, or they were immediately rejected. The possible Sanmicheli project for the Vicentine loggias has never been identified, although a brief indication by FIOCCO, 1960, p. 6, suggests a different result from Dalla Pozza's. WILLICH (1935) speaks generally of numerous models by Sanmicheli for the palace in Vicenza; and LANGES-KIOLD (1938, p. 23) advances the hypothesis that the drawings by the master, which were later lost but which existed during his lifetime, were used by his nephew and follower Domenico Curtoni for building the " Gran Guardia Vecchia " (1610) in Piazza Bra in Verona. This hypothesis has occasionally been repeated (cf. JACINI, 1958, p. 44).

In this case as well as in that of Serlio, the opportunity for direct contact between Sanmicheli and the Vicentine artistic circles through the agency of the Pedemuro studio—as early as 1530 the vehicle for transmitting Sanmicheli's style (cf. PUPPI, 1958; BARBIERI, 1960)—was much more important.

[45] Archivio di Torre della Città di Vicenza, *Libro Parti* I, c. 141 (transcribed by ZORZI, 1937, p. 144).

[46] Concerning this disaster, see n. 15.

[47] ZORZI, 1937, pp. 53, 55. Valle was reimbursed with ten gold ducats on December 9, 1542: Archivio di Torre della Città di Vicenza, *Libro Provisioni* VI, c. 559 (transcribed by ZORZI, 1937, p. 144).

[48] ZORZI, 1954, p. 121, n. 35; however, ZORZI, 1958 (II), pp. 16, 137, himself places Palladio's Mantuan trip in the years 1540-47, without returning to the 1542 hypothesis; this appears quite reasonable to me.

[49] Archivio di Torre della Città di Vicenza, *Libro Provisioni* VI, c. 569 (transcribed by ZORZI, 1937, p. 145).

[50] Archivio di Torre della Città di Vicenza, *Libro Parti* I, c. 145 (transcribed by ZORZI, 1937, pp. 145-146); cf. also ZORZI, 1937, p. 53; 1960, p. 90; 1964, pp. 44-45. Unfortunately, the drawings, plans, and notes are all lost.

[51] PANE, 1963, p. 60.

[52] ZORZI, 1937, p. 54. However, in a subsequent deliberation of January 25, 1543 (see n. 58), the Council of the Hundred explicitly admitted that Giulio Romano's proposal " *preterquam in circumstantiis et additamentis* " had been found " *conformis opinionibus aliorum... architectorum de quibus in... parte 1498* ": i. e., Rizzo and Spaventa.

[53] This must therefore have been a question of exterior stairs to the loggias; two drawings show the plan and " *il modo de dirizarle.* " Giulio Romano's words confirm that the old stairway of 1483 had not been demolished in 1496, when the one by Bernardino da Milano was being erected (cf. ZORZI, 1937, p. 36).

[54] LOTZ, 1966, pp. 123-124.

[55] NICCO FASOLA, 1960; TAFURI, 1966, pp. 48-54.

[56] Cf. LOTZ, 1961, pp. 85-88.

[57] TAFURI, 1966, p. 52.

[58] Archivio di Torre della Città di Vicenza, *Libro Parti* I, c. 149 (transcribed by ZORZI, 1937, p. 147).

[59] See n. 14.

[60] Cf. ZORZI, 1937, p. 55.

[61] ZORZI, 1937, pp. 11, 17. The document, which is assumed to be dated October 27, 1545 (*Il Palazzo della Ragione in Vicenza*, 1875, p. 11) is recorded for that year by DALLA POZZA, 1943, p. 95; however, with a different interpretation it should actually be dated October 27, 1548 (see ZORZI, 1950). Concerning the document of April 16, 1543, relative to the windows of the Hall, see Chapter II, n. 31.

[62] Archivio di Torre della Città di Vicenza, *Libro Parti* I, c. 274 (transcribed by ZORZI, 1950, Appendix, I). This undoubtedly concerns Palladio and Giovanni di Giacomo da Porlezza (see Chapter IV, n. 85). The latter, along with Girolamo Pittoni da Lumignano, was responsible for the famous Via Pedemuro studio which took in the adolescent Andrea di Pietro (at least from 1524 to 1537-38); see ZORZI, 1949 and 1958 (II), pp. 1-4. Mention should be made of both the misunderstanding by ARNALDI (1767, pp. xlii-xliii)—who identified that Giovanni with Giandomenico Scamozzi, at the time (1546) barely twenty years old—and the curious argument about it with Temanza which followed (BARBIERI, 1952, pp. 42-43); cf. also MAGRINI's hypothesis (1855, pp. 58-62) that Palladio's full name had been Giovanni Andrea. The double name, which would have come about through a copyist's error could have been read as " *per magistrum Joannem Andream Palladium vicetinum.* " MAGRINI (1845, pp. 158-159, *Annotazioni*, p. liv, n. 73) and other of his collaborators (*Il Palazzo della Ragione in Vicenza*, 1875, pp. 61 ff.) produced some rather substantial justification in support; moreover, Palladio's contemporary DONI (1555, p. 155) calls Palladio " Giovanni Andrea." BARICHELLA, 1880, p. 14, shares Magrini's opinion, but LAMPERTICO (1880, pp. 5, 13-14, 18) and subsequently (with greater authority) ZORZI (1922, pp. 3-4, n. 2) both demonstrated the inconsistency of Magrini's captious interpretation.

[63] Archivio di Torre della Città di Vicenza, *Libro Provisioni* VIII, c. 441 (transcribed by ZORZI, 1950, Appendix II); *Libro Saldi segnato* 1625, c. 127 (transcribed by DALLA POZZA, 1943, pp. 205-206).

[64] In fact, the model was to be displayed under one of the arches on the Piazza dei Signori level so that everybody could easily examine it.

[65] DALLA POZZA, 1943, p. 114.

[66] ZORZI, 1964, p. 46.

[67] See document referred to in n. 68.

[68] Archivio di Torre della Città di Vicenza, *Libro Parti* I, c. 366 (transcribed by ZORZI, 1950, Appendix, III); see also ZORZI, 1964, p. 46.

[69] Archivio di Torre della Città di Vicenza, *Libro Provisioni* VII, c. 914 (transcribed by ZORZI, 1950, Appendix IV). Concerning the problems connected with the interpretation of this and the following document (n. 70), see Chapter IV.

[70] Archivio di Torre della Città di Vicenza, *Libro Parti* I, c. 384 (transcribed by ZORZI, 1950, Appendix, V). Actually, since the existence of precise designs by Sansovino, Sanmicheli, and Serlio himself was questionable (as we have seen), the possibilities confronting the *Provveditori* were few indeed.

[71] It was executed by Martino Dezin, son-in-law of Giovanni da Pedemuro, and paid for the following May 27, 1549, with seven gold scudi (ZORZI, 1964, p. 47, n. 36; p. 323).

[72] *Il Palazzo della Ragione in Vicenza*, 1875, p. 44.

IV

THE PALLADIAN LOGGIAS

THE PREMISES

When in February of 1546 Palladio worked out his first project for the loggias of Vicenza's Palazzo della Ragione—which was later presented jointly with Giovanni da Pedemuro[1]—he was in the middle of his second and longest sojourn in Rome, which had begun in September 1545.[2] His stay in Vicenza was therefore brief. As soon as he had obtained preliminary approval on March 6, 1546, he went back to Rome, where he remained until the end of July, 1547.[3]

In Rome, Palladio painstakingly deepened his archaeological knowledge, which was broadened through excursions into surrounding areas and in Lazio. He met famous colleagues and *letterati*, including Michelangelo, at gatherings in the hospitable house of Giangiorgio Trissino in Campo Marzio.[4] In addition, he carried out a modest but interesting activity in the construction of two altar canopies for the Church and hospital of Santo Spirito in Sassia: they were almost certainly commissioned to him after September 1546 on the death of Antonio da Sangallo, who first undertook the vast complex.[5] The canopy for the hospital, which is the one that survives,[6] serves to conclude Palladio's first independent phase of activity as an architect; it was begun just before 1540 and follows his youthful experiments in

the circle of the Via Pedemuro workshop. These early attempts and phases have now been clarified with considerable precision, in all their vicissitudes.

Research on the architect's early work is sufficiently advanced to deny to Palladio's projects for the loggias any trace of the improvised character of "first works." We have one secure early date, that of Villa Godi, dated to 1540; subsequently, the loggia projects represent a remarkable comeback after at least a five-year period of inexplicable silence, interrupted only by participation in the work for the decorations for Cardinal Ridolfi (1543).[7]

Several works can in fact be credited to Palladio's "novitiate," which dates from the time between 1523 and 1524 when the adolescent Andrea di Pietro fled from Padua to Vicenza and worked in the studio of Giovanni and Girolamo da Pedemuro, until 1537-38 when he began a more independent life. Among these works, in which the pupil's collaboration becomes testimony to a special sensibility,[8] are: the portal of Santa Maria dei Servi (1531); the Godi chapel and sepulchral monument in the since-destroyed Church of S. Michele (1532-33); the Dall'Acqua altar in the Cathedral (1534-35); and the approximately contemporary Da Schio tomb in the Cathedral. In 1536-37 Master Giovanni and his studio were working at the Villa Godi in Lonedo. It is likely that the near-

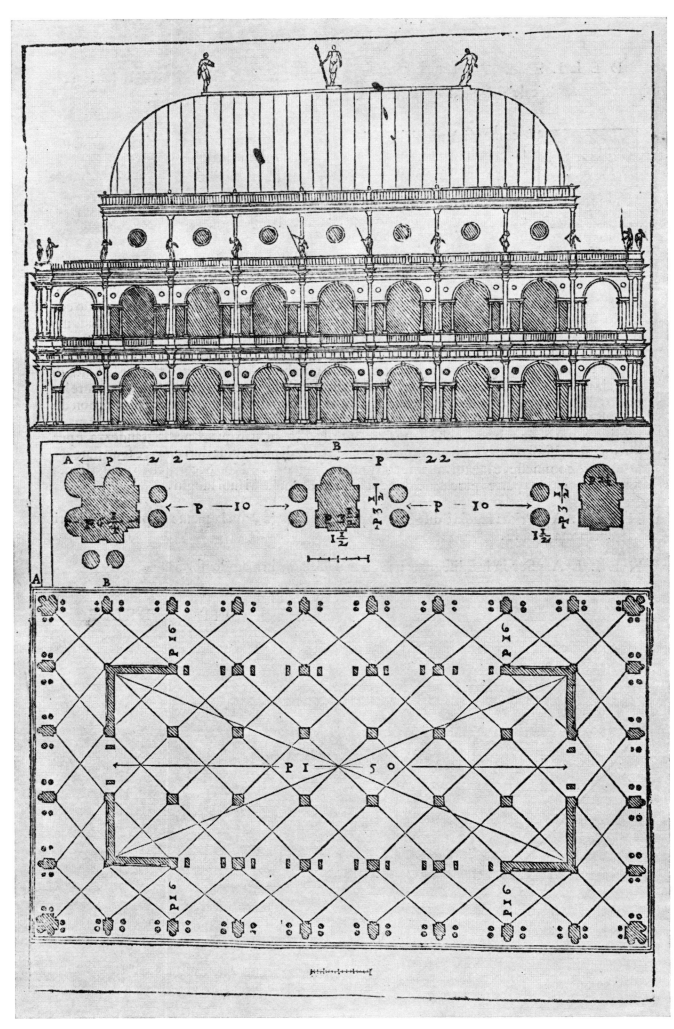

X - ANDREA PALLADIO, *Elevation and plan of the " Basilica " in Vicenza.*
From *I Quattro Libri dell'Architettura*, 1570, III, xx

by Villa Piovene was begun a little later; here Andrea appears for the last time in the position of a subordinate. He must have become aware of a capacity which he was not allowed to develop without heavy restrictions.[9]

The decisive meeting with Giangiorgio Trissino took place between 1537 and 1538, and Andrea's modest patronymic was changed to the aulic "Palladio": thus he initiated his completely personal activity. In 1540 Palazzo Civena was begun.[10] The designs for the Palazzetto Da Monte and the Villa Marcello in Bertesina fall within the same years (1540-41).[11] In 1541-42 —if not somewhat earlier—we have the plans for the Villa Pisani in Bagnolo[12] and around 1541-44, the design for the Villa Valmarana in Vigardolo[13]: so much for the secure dates. The controversial little Villa Cerato at Montecchio Precalcino, considered to date around 1540-45,[14] and the Villa Muzani alla Pisa near Malo (c. 1545)[15] may be added to the list. Moreover, the conception of Palazzo Thiene is said with sufficient reliability to fluctuate between 1542 and 1545,[16] and that of the Palazzo Iseppo Porto must have been definite immediately after the architect's return from Rome, or after 1547.[17] To complete the picture one might mention some minor works, such as the Orgian Monument (1541-42) at Monte Berico[18] and the festive decorations (1543) for Cardinal Ridolfi.[19] Projects datable between the end of the fourth decade and the first five years of the fifth decade are recorded in a number of drawings in the collection of the Royal Institute of British Architects in London.[20]

From this complex of works, attempts, and simple "*invenzioni*," the "curriculum" covered by the artist from the age of twenty-three to about forty emerges clearly, covering his transformation from a stonecutter to the profitable and prestigious profession of architect. At the outset, in the stagnation of building activity in Vicenza following the League of Cambrai (1509),[21] the few fresh illuminations available to the young architect came from the frequent contacts between the Pedemuro studio to which he was attached and the studio of Michele Sanmicheli, whose teaching was for many years afterward fundamental for him.[22] Actually, we know of no securely datable building of importance executed in the city and countryside between 1525 and 1540 which was conceived and matured outside Giovanni da Pedemuro's sphere of influence. The only exception is the Villa Cricolo, which allowed Giangiorgio Trissino—who was renovating it according to his design in 1537—to introduce a new, albeit modest, factor into the stagnant situation. This work derived from a source which was both Raphaelesque and Roman, and which therefore was extraneous to local affairs.[23]

Shortly afterward (between 1537 and 1540), the first two books by Sebastiano Serlio, who had been living in Venice since 1528 began to circulate in the Veneto;[24] in addition, the author himself was in Vicenza in 1539.[25] Palladio did not seem to have been as much interested in the theoretical possibilities of Serlio's individual thoughts—these were destined to bear fruit later in another area, with Giandomenico and Vincenzo Scamozzi[26]—as in the repertory of architectural forms and ideas which were disseminated through his books. These forms and ideas became the most authoritative ones of the period,[27] as well as the most tested. Their source was the influential circles of Roman "classicism"; they were derived ultimately from Bramante but were filtered through the freer and more contemporary interpretations of Raphael and, above all, of Peruzzi, culminating in the "mannerism" of Giulio Romano. Thus they were divested of many of the literary and ar-

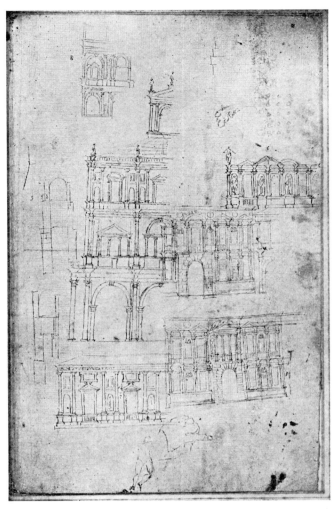

XI - ANDREA PALLADIO, *Sketches for loggias and palace façades*. London, R.I.B.A., X, 15

chaeological hindrances present in the work of their precursor, Bramante.[28] And yet, as has been observed,[29] these ideas were retardataire, part of a culture at least a generation older than that of the thirty-year-old Andrea. This is an important factor in understanding the architect's fortune in the backward atmosphere of provincial Vicenza.

Concurrently, around 1537-38 Palladio began travelling: he took small trips in the Veneto to Verona, Padua, and Venice, as well as longer ones to more distant points, such as Mantua and Pula.[30] As a consequence, the architect came directly in contact with other *ambienti* and other personalities, from Sansovino to Falconetto (who was closely associated with Cornaro) and from Scarpagnino to Giulio Ro-

mano; some of these were sooner or later approached personally by Vicenza regarding the problem of the loggias.[31]

The trips to Rome in 1541 and 1545-47 were a much more decisive factor. Through them Palladio could finally know at first hand forms he had met and admired through reading Serlio and Vitruvius (the latter was a habit to which he had been introduced by Trissino). He discovered, with a fresh view, both ancient and "modern" Roman architecture.[32]

An essential fact regarding Palladio's trips to Rome was, above all, the enthusiasm with which we see him embrace during the fifth decade of the century the "modern" idiom in the development from Bramante to Giulio Romano, up to the first hints of Michelangelo's late maturity. Michelangelo was near a decisive turning point; he had been disturbed for more than twenty years by an internal dialectic that had begun as early as Bramante's death and that was later accentuated during the anguished years between the 1527 Sack of Rome and the 1529 Siege of Florence, when the very civilization of the Renaissance threatened to collapse along with its greatest centers.[33] His architecture was then of such a nature as to demand from those who confronted it a selective capacity, an ability to discriminate among figures and currents. We can read in this respect a simple recapitulation in Palladio's treatise of 1570, which amounts to a confused dossier of artists all understood with very little subtlety as continuations of Bramante. Only Michelangelo and Serlio are seen as concerned with "*metter in luce la buona e bella Architettura.*"[34] As a Renaissance symbol we find two illustrations of the Tempietto of San Pietro in Montorio, once again as an "archaic" example of classicist purism.[35]

This attitude on the part of the young provincial architect is understandable, if we recall that he was raised on the books of Serlio and Vitruvius under the tutelage of Giangiorgio Trissino.[36] The latter was a systematic Humanist, a "melancholy pedant" who was able to determine the formation and destiny of his pupil to such an extent—and who was so resolved to make him his own creation—that he changed his name to the pompous one of "Palladio." The change of name occurred about 1540,[37] almost as if it were a viaticum for the Roman journeys. The artist's whole youth was spent in an environment like that of Vicenza, which, after having waited until the fourth decade of the century to welcome the first Sanmichelesque "classicists,"[38] had then lazily cherished them for a decade. Only after 1540, with the intensification of external contacts, could this environment dedicate itself wholly to the new culture.

It is thus clear that the impassioned ardor of the neophyte and the determination of the self-taught artisan-turned-architect would have prevented Palladio from participating in the "crisis of distrust of classicism" which was present as early as the fourth decade in the most advanced Roman circles. This crisis became even more pronounced after 1540 and was soon destined to be aggravated by the terrible presence of Michelangelo and to erupt in the anguished and subtle dilemmas of full mannerism.[39] We must deny any possible influence of Palladio on this development[40] and insist on the substantial isolation and the diversity of the ambience in which he matured. In this way his integrity and strict precision, which were the sole capacities for vivifying a world of worn-out forms, may be justified.[41] We can thus comprehend how the formal point of departure derived from mannerist sources would have had a completely new significance, involving a seriousness and moral strength that sug-

gest a commitment different from and greater than that offered by the mannerists.[42]

Through his vaguely anachronistic integrity and his obsolete moral rigor, Palladio rediscovered the antique in the mid-Cinquecento as no one else did, directly and systematically.[43] He drew from that experience the main foundation for his building activity. In this respect, the confidence the artist expressed in the value of the models he proposed is unlimited. We have no hint of an "historical" interpretation of architecture—capable, if not of comprehending, at least of accepting a vocabulary different in provenance from the much-admired "classical" repertory. Palladio thus rejects the broadened perspective introduced by antithesis within the problematical nature of mannerism, in which "the expressionistic elements... that had characterized 'Gothic art' for centuries no longer appeared abnormal...."[44] Nor does one note in his approach any anticipation of Scamozzi's critical attitude, which was shortly to prove capable of putting any source—even the most authoritative—to the scrutiny of rational choice.[45]

In this sense, the over-simplification of Palladio's thought at times proves completely disconcerting. He does not introduce any substantially novel concepts in his treatise of 1570, in comparison with Vitruvius and Alberti, the two most frequently cited authors. The true novelty and fascination of the *Quattro Libri* lies in the essential and unpretentious tone with which the author adheres to the concrete reality of experience.[46]

First as an apprentice and subsequently throughout his life, Palladio loved to work on the site; thus, as has been acutely observed,[47] he was bound not just to Vitruvius, but to all the great Greek treatise writers, from Theodorus of Samos to Polycleitus and Hermogenes. A unified tradi-

XII - ANDREA PALLADIO, *Portico of the Theatre of Pompey: elevation.* London, R.I.B.A., XI, 2r

XIII - ANDREA PALLADIO, *Portico of the Theatre of Pompey: interior.* London, R.I.B.A., XI, 2v

tion from the Byzantine craftsmen through the Venetian workshops and guilds links him with the ancients. In his approach to antiquity, Palladio followed his own instinctive and personal manner. While respecting the essential nature of Roman architecture, he transforms it through his interpretations. His graphic reconstructions, from his drawings of the 1540's to the edition of Vitruvius and the *Quattro Libri*, offer a series of opportunities to sample and define the nature of his creative spatial vision. In his choice of themes, we find that most of Palladio's exercises concern Late Imperial buildings, with such a clear persistence of preferences that the coincidence of availability must be excluded[48] and we must presuppose a particular taste on his part.

In order to explain this we must turn back to the artist's Venetian origins: "Venetian"[49] in the sense of the continuation of the Late Antique and Byzantine traditions in Venice, which was a distant but direct and uninterrupted link with the classical tradition. From this originates Palladio's profound accord with antiquity, which was so great as to enable him to revive certain effects peculiar to antique art.[50] On the one hand, if one emphasizes Palladio's tendency to render perceptible the play of pictorial effects inherent in architectonic structures, a certain analogy results with late Roman works. On the other hand, one may more aptly point out his clear predilection for solutions providing a united and articulated continuity of forms fixed in space.[51] Through that pre-

a) Palladian loggias: overall view of the northern and western sides

dilection, the artist moves from the Venetian and Byzantine interpretation of the Late-Antique "continuum" toward a re-proposal of the suggestive aspects of the great Roman forensic and thermal complexes.

Both theses, within their limits, are convincing and are useful in avoiding the danger of a purist, "neo-classical," or coldly archaeological interpretation of Palladio's art. But, on the other hand, they give rise to misunderstandings if, through over-simplification, they are taken as absolute definitions of a style which in actual fact is much more complex. One need only recall how in the wake of the illuminating contributions of the early research[52] a whole "pictorial" pseudo-criticism of Venetian architecture arose, which dealt in allusive, non-characterizing generalizations; one finds repeated as if by rote the idea that Venetian architecture is color, as if such an affirmation signified something over and beyond the critical process of reconstructing an individual artistic expression.[53]

The typical Venetian architecture which had been elaborated in Venice itself and of which Palladio could see notable examples in the environs of Vicenza (from the Quattrocento patrician residences to Domenico da Venezia's palace) was a unique and coherent example of "chromatic" vision, articulated in rhythmical sequences of surfaces. Here the "continuum" was realized in conformity with Byzantine sources through a succession of extended façades spread out like tapestries.[54] In contrast, Palladio's earliest and simplest ideas—as well as those which between 1540 and 1546 constituted the necessary basis for the more complex statement of the Vicentine loggias—clearly tend to be articulated in depth. Consequently each element is taken up in its three-dimensional value and in the accentuated relief of its precise volumetric definition, and wide spatial scan-

sions are organized around well-thought-out central nuclei.

In this sense, the artist's approach toward the "antique" helped him to acquire a certain syntax essential to the development of his style. Determining effects were obtained by a more varied and conjoined flow of spaces, as is demonstrated in the early projects where the square or rectangular central rooms of the normal Venetian floor-plan are replaced by livelier spaces, with cross-vaults and tunnel vaults which are clearly derived from the ancient baths. These spaces were capable of being—with very different results—both coordinating and propelling elements of a circular spatial dynamic.[55]

Analogously, this articulation of the structure "in depth" proceeding from the inside outward animates and transforms the framework of the exterior shell. Starting from what might be called a traditional acceptance of the building-box defined within the two-dimensionality of the wall, and varying it with the almost dreary proportions of the Villas Godi and Piovene (which, however, were conditioned and restricted by outside factors[56]), Palladio moved toward the more marked projections of several unexecuted studies[57] and subsequently passed to even more active and daring ideas: to "three-dimensional" façades, in which the columns played against the walls behind articulate and gauge the depth of the façade itself.[58] The first complete achievement of these ideas on a large scale was the palace created in 1550 for Girolamo Chiericati, with its façade of superimposed loggias.[59]

However, Palladio's interest in the "poetics" of the open form goes back some years to his early efforts between the fourth and fifth decades;[60] it explains certain aspects of the solution he provided in 1546-49 for the problem of the loggias in Vicenza. Precisely this instinctive need to project the structure in three dimensions as a free spatial entity—freeing it plastically from the tyranny of the floor-plan understood as a boundary—appears to be characteristic of Palladio's working method.[61] The originality of his rediscovery of the antique derives from this, as does the possibility of his foreshadowing future developments toward the Baroque of Bernini, at least on the level of spacious scenographic effects.[62]

It is necessary to emphasize the fact that only Palladio's fervent and total adherence to an uncompromising classicism could permit him, in the middle of the Cinquecento, to conceive a facing for the Palazzo della Ragione which was destined to become a triumphant assertion of this classicism. Faced with the pre-existing Quattrocento building, all of the other architects consulted had been much more prudent. Either they had mainly advised the restoration of the old loggias, or they had shied away from the question.[63] In his 1542 report, Giulio Romano expressed great perplexity concerning the method of harmonizing the new Cinquecentesque forms with the work of Domenico da Venezia; this demonstrates the hesitant state of mind, no longer capable of systematic rejections, with which the more highly developed and open-minded Mannerist currents regarded the "Gothic" phenomenon. The latter, formerly considered an abnormality, had become at least comprehensible—if not actually acceptable—in certain aspects.

Giulio Romano's position, with its hesitancy and compromises, perplexed the leaders of a city such as Vicenza; to them, the classicist example (partly because of Trissino's influence and partly due to Vicenza's provincialism and its distance from the great centers of culture) seemed the ultimate in ideal beauty. Giulio's argument was judged poor and mean, and was cast aside and substantially rejected.

At the same time, it was certainly during these discussions with the various architects who were consulted between the fourth and fifth decades that Palladio, who was not at all lacking in worldly wisdom,[64] clearly realized the demands of the ambience within which he chanced to live. He abandoned his initial timidities, such as the rhythmic distribution of flat pilaster strips over broad surfaces and the play of simple, balanced masses. The Palazzo Civena and Palazzo da Monte were followed during the two year period of 1540-42 by the more stately and imperial Villa Pisani and Palazzo Thiene, which were undoubtedly more agreeable to his patrons. The projects of these years,[65] although sometimes only unrealized exercises, would have been unthinkable outside of a precise relationship with a definite social " humus," whose needs the architect had to satisfy and whose tastes he had to meet. It does not seem essential to ask whether these projects responded to precise commissions; they were a demonstration of the artist's ability, which he prepared to offer to those whom he considered to be his future patrons.

In this light, one can understand how and why in March 1546 Palladio's project for the loggias was approved by a large majority; it was a completely unexpected success, overtaking *ab externo* the sequence of events. It has been said that for Palladio " to slip in uninvited " and gain acceptance for his own project after some of the most important authorities of the time had had their say was a difficult accomplishment.[66] Indeed, no one would have dared to present uninvited any sort of proposal to an assembly like Vicenza's Council of the Hundred—which had never proclaimed a public competition, but had from time to time chosen on its own initiative the architect considered to be most suitable. However (according to the March 5, 1546 document[67]), the Palladian project, dispatched with a truly inexplicable audacity, unexpectedly arrived between February and March of 1546 to confront the *Deputati ad utilia*. Only then, after all the time that the affair had dragged on, did the providential bolt of lightning dissolve all doubts.

During the years immediately following 1540, the ex-stonecutter Andrea di Pietro had (through the agency of Trissino) been binding his fortunes ever more closely to the aristocracy of the city. A few families of landed aristocracy, disturbed by nostalgia for the old regime as opposed to the new mercantile nobility of Venice, dominated that small provincial world;[68] throughout its dominions, the rich and powerful metropolis reduced the provincial representatives to the humble rank of subordinate administrators.[69] Thus the nobility of the city placed the defense of its own privileges at the center of its duties; membership in a Republic it did not respect impeded the sentiment for the public good, and individual interests transcended the higher interests of the state.[70]

In such a situation, those who shunned the attraction of the landed estates—or because of hereditary questions did not have the right to enter into them—concentrated on the art of war. Vicenza, rich in towers and castles, was regarded with suspicion by the Venetian Republic more than any other Venetian province because of a certain spirit of independence; a heroic and self-sufficient atmosphere, quite unusual in the other inland territories, flourished there.[71] Pietro da Porto and Antonio Caldogno were in the service of Charles V, and Leonardo Valmarana was in the service of Austria. Orazio Angarano was a captain in the papal forces, Giulio and Cesare Piovene served in France, and Ottavio Thiene was a captain under Henry II of France. All these were bitter and powerful enemies of Venice.[72]

Even superficial historical research fully confirms the anti-Venetian bias in Vicentine ruling circles:[73] a bias composed of cynicism[74] and deriving from class privilege, social power, and family honor.[75] The standard-bearer of that world was Trissino, who was able after more than two and a half centuries to admire Dante's great, reactionary, northern-oriented dream of the Holy Roman Empire—a dream which was already dead in Dante's time. Trissino was thus enclosed in his political beliefs without popular consent, which isolated him spiritually and rendered him the immature aristocrat, even in literature.[76] He was so persistent as to ask for and obtain the privilege, vainly sought by others, to participate at the crowning of Charles V as Emperor in Bologna in 1530 by holding the train of the pontifical mantle. The sovereign rewarded his constancy by naming him Count Palatine.[77]

It was natural, therefore, that within the Venetian domain the cultural structures of the inland cities—even the largest, such as Padua, Verona, and Vicenza—displayed with respect to Venice a recognizable urge to preserve their own forms and traditions;[78] and it became inevitable that Vicenza, lacking Padua's university (which next to Venice was the main focal point of Venetian culture[79]) as well as Verona's contacts with Lombardy and Mantua, was the stronghold of this traditionalism. The fate of the interpretation of Aristotle's *Poetics*, framed within the limits of Venetian Aristotelianism and in resolute opposition to Florentine Platonism, is an example. For the Venetian Andrea Navagero, and especially for the Veronese Girolamo Fracastoro (who introduces Andrea as interlocutor in his dialogue *Naugerius sive de poetica*), Aristotle's work goes back to the nucleus of the Platonic *eros* and is redeemed by this contact from the danger of becoming a manual of operative tech-

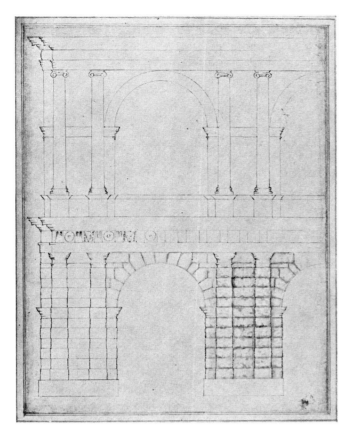

XIV - ANDREA PALLADIO, *Design for the loggias of the Palazzo della Ragione.* London, R.I.B.A., XIII, 9

nique. Trissino, on the other hand, considered it in the normative sense as a complex of ideal rules; the Aristotelian definition of tragedy was regarded as an incontrovertible canon,[80] from whence derives Trissino's *Sophonisba.*

In this closed atmosphere—and in the climate of bitter political decadence that deprived it of any authentic faculty of command, permitting only a certain financial fluidity directed toward land investments[81] —the local nobility developed an understandable yearning for escape; but there was no escape for the repressed desire for power, except to build palaces and villas of a splendid immensity, which were often impossible to realize.[82]

From the moment that, having left the Pedemuro studio to become Trissino's pupil, Andrea di Pietro renounced his name to call himself "Palladio,"[83] he became— together with his patron but in another field—the best qualified representative of

a widespread ideal of thought and life. Certainly his supporters, convinced of the cause's value and by that time aware of the artist's ability, would have wanted him to have the official recognition that would have accompanied the commission for the Palazzo Communale. However nothing could be done until 1543, since up until that year the local conservatives were consulting more officially-approved figures, from Serlio to Giulio Romano. The virtual elimination of the latter in January of 1543— obviating the necessity of awaiting his death[84]—marks a turning point in favor of Palladio's supporters. It also indicates that by that year the idea of creating an open manifesto of triumphant classicism in the heart of the city in the form of the new loggias had gained ground against Giulio's doubts and hesitations. The tempo increased: when Palladio departed with Trissino for Rome in the autumn of 1545, he carried with him a precise charge to acquaint himself with examples of Roman art; and we know that as early as the following February of 1546 the compliant artist was already on his way back with a first project for the loggias.

From then on it was up to others, shrewder and more qualified in managing public opinion, to discover the way to get the project accepted: first by proposing it to a Council which had not in actual fact ever requested it. Then came the "*fictio*" of defining as " *novissime presentatum* " a project which must have been hatching for years in certain circles, and the necessity of getting the signature of the old master Giovanni da Pedemuro. The latter was certainly completely extraneous to the design as such; but his name, since he had worked so much about the palace, would have been a guarantee of continuity, especially for the older councilors.[85] The not-exactly-overwhelming result initially achieved (the approval in principle of March 5, 1546, which, however, was subject to a more considered examination of a wooden model of one arch) was due to the resistance of the conservatives.[86] This explains the half-peremptory, half-triumphant tone with which the *Deputati ad utilia* attempted to force the situation before the Council of the Hundred. The *Deputati* had already studied the choice " *elegerunt anima,* " pointing out the design which they thought should be followed: " *iuxta quod palatium ipsum fabricari debeat.*"

However, the waiting period lasted three full years and only ended in success on April 11, 1549.[87] The intervening time was necessary for the Palladian faction to overcome the lingering uncertainties and the thinly-disguised opposition of those who loved the symbol of the old arcaded Quattrocento city—with its Late Gothic elegance represented by the collapsing Formenton loggias—and dreaded losing it under the impact of new ideas. Meanwhile, Palladio had reached Rome shortly after the decision of March 1546 and did not return before the end of July 1547. Not until then was he able to see the wooden model of his first design, which had been completed in January of that year during his absence.[88] The project, delivered in 1546, now belonged to others and became the banner of a faction which by the September 6, 1548 decision of the council[89] was to win another success.

The difficulties which sprang up after the approval of March 5, 1546, were made sufficiently plain by the delay of over two years and could not be ignored. They were apparently of two kinds: on the one hand, they concerned the Palladian design itself and the model deriving from it, which on careful examination did not appear to be completely convincing; on the other hand, " *circa electionem designi,*" they certainly involved the precipitous way in which the project, signed by Palladio and by Master Giovanni, had suddenly and unexpectedly been presented. Even to many of those who had approved it, the precedure perhaps seemed too brusque in retrospect and above all too unilateral.

Under the threat of a new delay, Palladio's supporters again took the initiative and on September 6, 1548, reproposed the question, which had dragged on through so many tedious and tenacious delays; this time they accepted the possibility of a confrontation, but limited to a field of only three competitors. The Palladian faction thus ably and subtly manoeuvered in such a way as to obtain two undeniable advantages at the outset.[90]

Three convinced supporters of the architect were elected wardens in charge of reporting on the questions: Gabriele Capra, who had charge of the Ridolfi celebrations of 1543; Girolamo Chiericati, who two years later requested a plan from Palladio for his new palace in Piazza dell'Isola; and Alvise Valmarana, who from 1543 onward had been on cordial terms with the architect.[91] Moreover, to make an eventual victory easier, the majority of at least two-thirds which had been decreed by the deliberation of July 15, 1496,[92] was declared no longer necessary, and only a simple majority was required. A little more than a month later on October 27, Girolamo Chiericati (who was also a *Deputato ad utilia*) overcame the "*fictio*" of using Giovanni da Pedemuro as a figurehead and with his colleagues charged Girolamo Barbarano to pay Palladio alone for four new designs for the loggias, modifications of the initial project.[93]

However, the artist's silence continued, even on April 11, 1549, when the conclusive meeting took place. There were authoritative figures upholding his faction —Girolamo Chiericati and Alvise Valmarana argued for it—but Palladio himself never appeared either in person or by means of a written report to defend his own cause, as all the other architects consulted before him had done. Yet he must have known that the stakes were high, and that this first important official commission for the city would be very useful for his future career. His silence therefore confirms the degree to which his work on the loggias had been done on commission, in compliance with the wishes of patrons who dreamed of reviving a whole world and had seen in Palladio the instrument with which to realize this. Palladio as an artist had been slow in maturing (at that time he was forty years old), but since 1546 he had been complete master of all his powers of form and composition.

However, even if Palladio had had to wait until this moment for his great opportunity, classicism in Vicenza had won its battle on all fronts with Giangiorgio Trissino as tutelary. Trissino died in 1550, but a few years afterward (in 1555) the Accademia Olimpica was founded, and his ideas —which until then had been based on the enthusiasm of innovators—received both official sanction and the doctrinal force deriving from a systematic re-examination. During the same period Palladio enjoyed his most productive time, creating some of his noblest works. In fact, one never again finds the artist engaged during such a short period on such a complex of works for such a vast program. One might even conclude that a similar situation has not fallen to the lot of any other architect;[95] but few other architects have been so closely bound in chronology to the internal as well as to the external events of a social milieu.

The milieu was certainly not unambiguous. Beneath an apparent uniformity, Vicenza was full of ferment of various kinds, even including infiltrations of Lutheran heresy.[96] But it was the ruling class of landed aristocracy, with its notable economic resources, that offered the most fa-vorable climate for the expansion of Palladio's genius.[97] From the third and fourth decades and even before, with the damages suffered in the campaigns for the League of Cambrai indemnified, this element was certainly the most prosperous one. It is, in fact, necessary to go to 1576-80, to the first conscious tests of Scamozzi's critical attitude (Palazzo Trissino near the Duomo and the " Rocca " at Lonigo) or to the Mannerism of artists such as Alessandro Maganza or the Albanese, in order to understand that mutable climate. Especially significant was its pursuit of severer habits of life and thought, an approach which was not unrelated to the stimulating ferment of the Counter Reformation.

The fact remains that through a chronological coincidence, through general habits of living and working, and through a considerable debt of gratitude, Palladio was the hero of that triumphant yet immature moment of Vicentine classicism. As a result of this particular situation, the initial victory of his designs and their definitive sanction in 1549 initiated Palladio's destiny as an artist, and he was more or less aware of it. The success of the loggias and the consequent rush of commissions that followed it attest to the approval of the " Establishment " in Vicenza, which rewarded the architect's compliance when confronted with the impositions of official rhetoric. This compliance was so great as to cause Palladio to enroll in 1555, " *homo novus,*" in the society of nobles of the Accademia Olimpica. The architect bowed to the fashion of harnessing his children —the grandchildren of a poor Paduan miller—with the pompous " classical " names of Silla, Leonida, Orazio, Marcantonio, and Zenobia.

On the other hand, if Palladio did not wish to or could not due to prudence and economic necessity extract himself from the prevalent megalomania, it was still necessary for him to preserve his artistic freedom and principles. This must have been an arduous undertaking in that situation and certainly was not realized without inner torment, even though any torment was well hidden behind the appearance of a serene and even happy adjustment on the architect's part.[98]

It is now the critics' task to reconstitute the course the architect followed in order to arrive at the splendid success of his accomplished work, regardless of his obligations to tenacious and provincial classicist conventions. In fact, Palladio's situation was that of a worker who entered his studies by way of service and in whom the " building fever " grew slowly, in the shops and through fleeting contacts with the educated. He grew into manhood and advanced in his profession by tolerating the eccentricities of the nobles and by being always willing to grant the requests of indebted patrons,[99] and perhaps inner conflicts belied his apparently undisturbed adjustment.[100] It is not easy to understand how such an artist issued from so ill-administered a baptism, in which two eminent pedants, Trissino and Vitruvius, were the godfathers.[101]

One need only remember that from the same climate of classical revival in Cinquecento Vicenza came Trissino's unhappy *Sophonisba* and above all his *Italia liberata dai Goti*, his long poem in the Greek and Roman manner which was " famous for never being read." [102] It cost Trissino twenty years of wasted effort and was published between 1547 and 1548,[103] exactly when the first model for the Palladian loggias was being displayed in the main piazza. It was, in fact, Palladio who on his return from Rome in July 1547 carried back a section of the paternal poem to Ciro Trissino, the son of the learned humanist.[104] Perhaps in an understandable error of perspective, the coincidence of events would have seemed at the time almost a happy one. These events were separated, however, by the subtle and immense gulf which runs between the sterile labor of " junk writing " and the delight of poetry.

THE GENESIS OF THE LOGGIAS

An early sketch for the loggias of the Palazzo della Ragione can probably be identified in a sheet in London (R.I.B.A. X, 15; sketch at the top left), which contains other sketches of façades and details of plans.[105] The drawing (Fig. XI, p. 52) was once considered to pre-date the architect's first trip to Rome (1541),[106] as it appeared to reflect only Venetian influences and to exhibit the virtuosity of the late Lombard production. It is now thought to be related to Palladio's projects for the municipal loggia in Brescia (1549-50).[107]

Moreover, after the stimulating contacts with Roman buildings from the autumn of 1545, the master was obliged to revise on the basis of the new texts all the possible precedents relative to the question. As has been observed,[108] Palladio wanted (or rather was compelled) to resolve his problem in accordance with a classical vocabulary. The Roman pier with half-column seemed to be the only scheme which could guarantee the structural stability necessary to avoid a second disaster for the loggias like that of 1496. One of the examples of this type easily available to the architect was the famous portico of the Theatre of Pompey in Rome, which Palladio would have known through Sebastiano Serlio's engraving.[109] Palladio himself furnished three drawings of this (R.I.B.A. XI, 2: recto and verso): the plan, the elevation, and the inside of the portico (Figs. XII, XIII, p. 54).[110]

To estimate how valuable the suggestion from antiquity must have been for the architect in the development of his design,

XV - ANDREA PALLADIO, *Design for the loggias of the Palazzo della Ragione.* London, R.I.B.A., XVII, 22

it is enough to note the obvious correspondence in cadence of the arches and piers and, even more, the way in which the solution of the corners is indicated. Two paired vertical elements meet at the pilaster; the external one concludes the rhythm, turns, and begins the sequence at the side. Although the plan shows clearly that the element at the vertex is square in section, the analogy nevertheless remains evident through the articulation Palladio later applied to the three free corners of the loggias.

This antique motif had been re-elaborated by architects in the early Cinquecento from Bramante to Sangallo and Sansovino, in the simple aspect of a pier with engaged column and in the more complex aspect of a corner pier with columns and a pilaster at the vertex. Examples are Bramante's project for the Palazzo di Giustizia in Rome (the courtyard); the courtyard of Palazzo Farnese (ground floor); and the Libreria Vecchia di S. Marco and the Villa Garzoni by Sansovino.[111] Especially interest-

ing in this regard is the weight-bearing corner structure of the Church of San Biagio in Montepulciano, begun in 1519 by Antonio da Sangallo the Elder and almost certainly known to Palladio through stops there on his way to Rome. Here the correspondence to the later solution in Vicenza is completely apparent, especially in regard to the prominence of the frieze and the projection of the cornice.

However, the Vicentine loggias proposed infinitely more complex problems than those of Pompey's portico or of any other possible source. The height of the two storeys of porticoes, taken individually or together, was by that time definitively fixed. Even if the levels of the fallen loggias need not have been respected, the windows of the Hall with their fixed height were complete obstacles, as well as the oculi above; the lower row of oculi (the original row by Domenico da Venezia) had to be above the roof-line of the loggias if they were not to be blocked. Moreover, the number of arcades was fixed by the proportions of the inner walls and their sequence. On each side the arcade had to end with a smaller unit; it was necessary here to comply with the dimensions of the first arch on the left on the north side, which was a narrower arch corresponding to the pre-existing passage between the podestà's palace and the Quattrocento Palazzo della Ragione.[112]

As if that were not enough, the division of the Late Gothic wall of the second storey causes a pier, polygonal in section, to project between each window. The cross-vaults of the upper loggias rested on these. As the new Cinquecento version demanded (in logical conformity with the classical arrangement) that the same proportion of arcades be maintained above and below, there would have been one arch in the upper loggia for every two pre-existing arches. Consequently the supports for the vaults would have had to rest on the above-mentioned internal pilasters, with only every other one actually being put to use.

Thus, both vertically and horizontally, the dimensions within which Palladio could move were fixed in advance with almost no margin[113]—including that of the depth of the porticoes, which was set by the span of the end arches of the loggias. In addition to all these restrictions, the width and cadence of the upper windows was not uniform; and since this was the key measure for the whole articulation it would have caused a considerable deformity in the proportion of the piers, making the measurements of the interaxes different. At first sight, this difficulty seemed to preclude any satisfactory solution.

If in this situation Palladio had insisted on the alternative of arches and simple piers, even though inspired by better-articulated and more diverse models, he could have had little confidence in his solution. Another of the architect's drawings (R.I.B.A. XIII, 9; Fig. XIV, p. 58), per-

haps the earliest surviving one which directly and effectively concerns Vicenza's loggias, demonstrates this.[114] There are reminiscences in it[115]—in addition to the usual examples of the Theatre of Marcellus and the Colosseum—of the Basilica Aemilia in the Roman Forum, which Palladio later honored with a citation in his *Quattro Libri*.[116] The second order is a clear derivation from the three upper arches in Falconetto's Cornaro Odeon;[117] the first order shows in two distinct passages (one unshaded and the other lightly shaded) a marked predilection for the vigorous effects of rusticated surfaces. Recollections of the ancient Porta Maggiore mediated through Giulio Romano[118] create a framework of a decidedly Sanmichelesque flavor, in the "mitered" stones of the arch, the distribution of the stones of the columns, the profile of the mouldings, and above all in the taste for rugged stony surfaces.[119]

Unquestionably, we are fluctuating between reminiscences of the Porta Nuova (1533-40) in Verona, especially in the outer façade, and recollections of the "keep" in the fort of S. Andrea al Lido (begun 1543). The latter constitutes a close resemblance in its lower section to the inner façade of Porta Palio, except that it is heavier in the excessive width of the vaults and in the high plinth running around the base of the piers and is badly resolved in the brusque solution of the corners. If Porta Palio dates (as seems likely) after March 1546,[120] we would have here a clear anticipation of it in a minor key. This and other motives confirm the hypothesis that the drawing,[121] which is Sanmichelesque in the contrast of surfaces between the two storeys, actually represents the project presented "*novissime*" by Palladio and Giovanni da Pedemuro to the *Deputati* in March 1546 and approved on the 5th of that month.

The slightly scholastic adherence to the

methods of Sanmicheli might be explained by recalling the document countersigned not only by Palladio but also by Master Giovanni, for whom Sanmicheli still constituted the most modern point at which one could safely aim.[122] This is not a question of suggesting that Giovanni (who was a necessary figurehead in signing the project, as we have noted) might actually have shared in the design, which was beyond any of his capabilities, but rather of admitting that only in the ambit of the Pedemuro studio could the climate necessary for producing such a drawing have been found. The studio was the center of Sanmicheli's influence in Vicenza, and Palladio remained at home there even after his emancipation of 1537-38. Moreover, autograph works by Sanmicheli must have been available there, since they sometimes served as the basis of the remarkable achievements of that studio.[123]

But the most effective confutation comes from another source. The "*designum novissime presentatum*," from which the model exhibited to the public under the arcade of the Palazzo della Ragione had been taken, must have been something very new—especially to artists and men of culture, to judge from the controversy it aroused. The tone of the Council's decision of March 5, 1546, with its approval in principle by a large majority, actually indicated the expectation that the design would be executed; this belief prevailed at least until late in 1547, when difficulties appeared upon careful examination of the model.

This same early Palladian project appears in its entirety in a fresco by Marcello Fogolino, in the Palazzo Vescovile in Ascoli Piceno. There, in the twelfth panel of a cycle of *Scenes from the Life of Moses* (Fig. VI, p. 23), at the bottom of the scene showing the destruction of the Golden Calf, is a view of Vicenza which seems to be united in a fantastic marriage with an idealized version of the Castello in Trent.[124] Vicenza's Palazzo della Ragione stands out clearly between the Torre di Piazza and the Torre del Tormento. However, it is not shown in the view which would seem most logical, still surrounded at least in part by the surviving Formenton loggias, but rather by a double order of arcades between wide piers. A simple comparison with the drawing examined earlier (R.I.B.A. XIII, 9; Fig. XIV, p. 58) is sufficient to convince one of the derivation of this architectonic motif;[125] it is accurate and precise and is certainly not a fantasy of the painter, who signed and dated the frescoes in 1547[126]—exactly at the time when the problem of the "*designum novissime presentatum*" was of immediate interest and possibly close to execution. Fogolino's evidence is especially valuable because it adds something not visible in the drawing: i. e., the systematization of the upper part of the palace above the loggia galleries, regularizing the six existing oculi on the long sides between vertical pilasters. This is a "classicizing" version of Domenico da Venezia's Late Gothic forms, and it unquestionably did not originate in the painter's mind but was derived from a precise source which served him as a guide.

However, the frank eclecticism of the Palladian project, which joined onto a Sanmichelesque basis the most diverse contributions from archaeology to Falconetto to Giulio Romano, does not solve the crux of the problem. The discrepancy in the interaxes could have been resolved in a less displeasing manner by leaving the spans of the arches uniform and varying only the width of the robust piers; but the latter, multiplied in the long sequence, assumed a visually oppressive weight. Moreover, with the intrusion of flat surfaces, the inside course of the loggias would have seemed closed and badly adapted to the purpose of the open ambulatory for which it had been destined by location and function. Moreover, at least one window out of three of the Great Hall was blocked by the impending back wall. All these inconveniences are anticipated by Fogolino with absolute clarity. Nor can we see, given a similar arrangement, how it could really have helped to insert niches in the piers between the half-columns,[127] an expedient which was intended to modulate the tense compactness of the storeys but which was incapable of breaking the oppressive design.

It is useful to note how in the initial drawing, especially in the framing of the upper gallery, the point of departure is *in nuce* already present and capable of being elaborated later. If the project was unadaptable in practicality as a result of the excessive width of the mass of the piers, it must have been precisely on this vertical structure that Palladio concentrated.[128] After the criticism and the arguments which followed the 1547 model he projected certain necessary modifications, which are now unfortunately lost but which can be reconstructed rather accurately.[129]

For the whole width of the piers, the projecting impost moulding of the arches forms a continuous band located at a height of about three-quarters the height of the pier. This horizontal band is balanced by two vertical elements (namely the shafts of the attached half-columns). However, it is only occasionally interrupted by them, although we are conscious of their continuous recurrence. Rather than intersecting, these elements are juxtaposed almost on distinct planes and at the same time complement the unity of the pier from the furthest-projecting half-column to the one most set back into the wall:

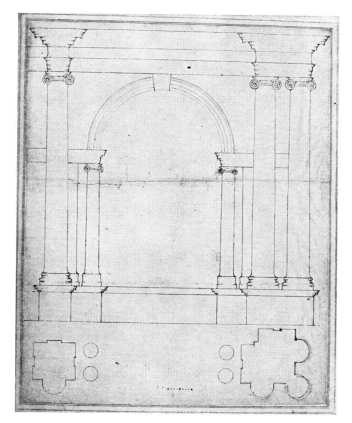

XVI - ANDREA PALLADIO, *Design for the loggias of the Palazzo della Ragione.* London, R.I.B.A., XIII, 8

an effect destined for subsequent development in Palladio's work. The order of the columns underlines the ascending rhythm, or rather marks its scansion in the continuity of the loggias; the set-back surface guarantees the organic unity of the support. The impost moulding fixes the arches' continuous concatenation. Each subsequent modification had to take these fundamentals into account.

It must have very quickly become apparent that an abundance of half-columns placed rather far apart, instead of accentuating the vertical progression, would slacken it, just as the uniform course of the friezes and the cornices above becomes monotonous in its enormous length. Because of this, the version which was finally carried out (Plates 44, 45) retained only one half-column, which was shifted to the center of the pier; there, isolated, it assumes a confident boldness and a springing elasticity. Similarly, Palladio broke the continuity of the entablature, making it project in correspondence with the shafts. The whole structure is thus filled with movement and better utilizes the precise rhythm of the ascending members, which are strongly emphasized from the base up to the balustrade statues.

The result is much more decisive, since at the sides of each half-column the wall is opened in accents of rectangular and round voids, in order to concentrate the dynamic tension at the center. This tension is enhanced by a chiaroscuro contrast formed by the illuminated central element and the dense shadows of the deep apertures at the sides. The new articulation no longer treats the pier as an inert mass meant to guarantee structural stability *ad abundantiam*, but rather as an element capable of developing dynamically, giving us a key to the original significance of Palladio's intention.

The moulding of the arch imposts, distinctly demarcated by the dark void beneath, unites the arches in a more compact development with its skillfully-freed profile. But above all the course of the loggias is no longer a uniform sequence of alternating solids and voids, of light and shadow continually flowing along a plane surface, as proposed in the initial project. By concentrating on the piers, the architect clearly made a choice between the members: the arches are understood as connected pauses, while the accents fall decisively on the strongly-realized piers. Thus the active structural members coincide with the visual accents in true structural honesty. Since the piers are solid three-dimensional masses articulated in depth, the arches—and the entire loggia as well—acquire depth and three-dimensionality. From this the dynamic character unfolds, based on the pursuit of vertical rhythms and united by the flow of the sequence of arches. This is revealed especially

in the foreshortened view (Plates 27, 28, 30), in which piers and half-columns seem to spring from the plane of the set-back arches and the problem of an interpretative selection among the various elements becomes apparent. Another fact which the artist obviously took into consideration in thus energetically enlivening his rhythms was that a complete frontal view, even of the shortest side, is virtually impossible due to the narrowness of the space in front compared to the extension of the façades.

The presupposition of the aulic and imperial Roman spirit remains valid in its suggestiveness, which is as generic as it is strong; the majestic and expressive structure is truly capable of evoking history in the epic sense.[130] But, justifiable enthusiasm aside, a more careful reading of the whole context causes one to reflect on the way the fundamental characteristics of ancient Roman architecture emphasize " the anti-classical dimension of the continuum " [131] and consequently the development of immense spatial stretches, whereas in the Vicentine loggias Palladio's capacity for dramatization introduces a fundamentally different principle by dynamically accentuating the pier projections. The sustained tension of the vertical rhythm alters any possible uniformity and establishes a concise dialectic with the uninterrupted succession of arches bound by the recurring impost mouldings. This does not negate Palladio's overriding interest in the unified continuity of forms;[132] however, a new aspect of his vision is apparent in the loggias.[133]

Regarding again the solution of the angle piers (Plates 26, 28, 30), there are some obvious precedents that we have summarily noted; careful research might gather additional prototypes, from archaeology or from other Cinquecento sources.[134] The piers are very robust—the collapse of 1496 had actually involved one of them—and introduce the insertion of a column at the angle in place of the standard square-sectioned pilaster. This expedient was a practical necessity (see Scale Drawings *j* and *k*) because the masses of the angle piers, following the obligatory course of the loggias, could never have a straight right angle at the corners, but must always present a section varying from ninety degrees, being less at the northeast and southwest vertices and greater at the northwest one.[135]

In fact, it is at the northwest corner, which is the one most visible, that the deviation from the norm is greatest. This corner (Plate 30) was one of the places where work was begun,[136] and the necessity arose to mask the anomaly by using a round-sectioned shaft—a solution which was afterward extended to the other two corresponding positions at the northeast and southwest. In this way a homogeneous, fluid development between the sides of the building was established. The whole corner structure acquires an exceptional prominence through the repetition of the attached half-columns, by which the progression of rhythms in each elevation is defined.[137]

It is hardly necessary to emphasize that here the final idea was developed only by patient work in transforming the structure of the piers. In the first project, they were reduced to a banal juxtaposition of orthogonal walls at the corners, but today they are bundles of self-contained energy. The piers are so suggestive that some scholars have resorted to an "historical" explanation of them, almost insinuating that Palladio was reflecting Romanesque and Gothic examples.[138] This is certainly too abbreviated as an hypothesis, but it is nevertheless useful as a further confirmation of the artist's very personal style.

Later the architect was able to free himself from the forms imposed by his own theoretical presuppositions in order to adhere to the concrete demands of the construction; in fact, Palladio's independence had already been noted by nineteenth-century critics, at least during that century's more open-minded periods: "The design which we see... realized is extraordinary in its grandiosity and in its beauty; it is harmonized marvelously with the external projection of the Hall and with the enormous vaulted roof. It harmonizes because of a certain organic nature which recalls the Middle Ages."[139]

Palladio, as we know, abhorred Gothic architecture; but in this specific case, he permeated himself to such a degree with the structural requirements of the building in joining his loggias to Domenico da Venezia's palace that he almost approached a reminiscence of polystyle piers. The nineteenth-century critic continues: "Everything... contributes to impressing on the building a character which is not purely and strictly classical"; he concludes with this astonishing judgment: "Confronted by this building, anyone who did not know that it was by Palladio would not think at first that it was his." If, in fact, we think of Palladio as a creator of pure and abstract forms and if, following the standards of his patrons, we see him as pursuing the illusion of an ideal classicism, then the design of the loggias—calculated within the limits of a very precisely-defined situation—does not fit into the picture. In fact, it does not seem to belong to Palladio at all.

The visual separation of the loggias from the palace, almost as if they were an independent concept and only pertained to antiquity by coincidence, does not grasp the real generative process of Palladio's work any more than it can explain it. The error seems to go back to the architect himself, who in his old age permitted the publication of two illustrations of

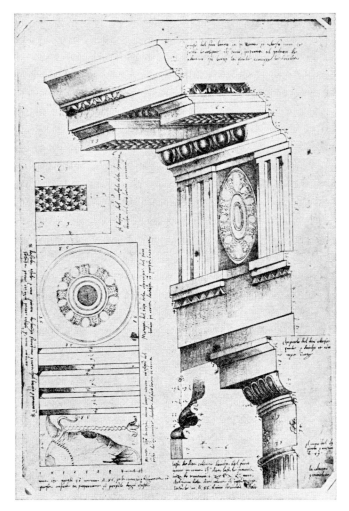

XVII - GIOVANNI MARIA FALCONETTO, *Cornice of the Basilica Aemilia* (inscriptions and measurements by ANDREA PALLADIO). Vicenza, Museo Civico, D 32

the Basilica in his *Quattro Libri* of 1570 (Fig. X, p. 50, and Fig. XXIV, p. 94).[140] The first one especially, which shows the great edifice free on all sides in space, is well within the bounds of a fantastic re-elaboration. If the actual building disappeared, Palladio's idea as transmitted by these graphically rather modest drawings would appear as little more than an exercise. Even worse, one would deduce from them the foolish wish to alter or ignore the existing facts in order to create a grandiose effect in illusory freedom. Although we must admire the splendid graphic balance of the treatise, we are aware of what value is to be placed on the major part of the engravings in it, in respect to the genesis of Palladio's de-

signs.[141] Yet it is precisely because of these inauspicious plates that too often in the course of the centuries the loggias have been considered a free variant or a modulation of a free and abstract theme, and they have been condemned to whatever extent this variation or modulation did not respond to some pre-established canon.

Thus the "purists" have been scandalized. Scamozzi attacked the excessive heaviness of the lower order;[142] later, "rationalists" noted that the supposed uniform and harmonious succession of the arches within the rhythm of the piers was not at all the perfect syllogism that the premises would have required, but a ductile organism capable of absorbing and concealing variations and profound disparities. Consequently, one must admire the ability with which the architect was able to deal with such a difficult situation, drawing up an elevation and graphically reconstructing the building in order to preserve it in its "ideal" form.[143]

Later, some critics called the "licenses" outrageous. They objected to the use of a Doric frieze with triglyphs (which in their origins were beam-ends) to mask the cross-vaulting behind,[144] as well as to the plinths of the Doric columns (whose projection extends the upper step of the portico),[145] the excessive projection of the Doric cornice in comparison with the Ionic,[146] and the way in which the columns of the smaller orders act as imposts for the arches, without the bases required by the manuals but rather with the shafts resting on short, round, slightly-projecting plinths.[147] Even recently, it has been said that "the real Palladio is not in that noble but impersonal range of arches... with the squat columns, which were still far from the magnificent, graceful, velvety shafts of his maturity";[148] and it has been emphasized that "the upper corner arch abutments... through reducing the module for the [Serlian aperture] exclude the use of oculi for the corner bay."[149]

Actually, this was certainly not the case where the architect could allow himself to depict the "perfect" form outside of the factual circumstances: considering the previous historical vicissitudes of the building, those circumstances had determined all the errors or uncertainties that might be found in the abstract in the Palladian loggias. For example, by simply "inventing" for the loggias' location and specific function the particular type of base used for the columns of the smaller orders, Palladio produced rectangular openings in the lower gallery sufficiently wide for a comfortable pedestrian passageway (Plates 44, 48). This was a necessity if the loggias were to be (as the earlier ones were and as the site required) a comfortable meeting place for citizens and merchants.

These practical requirements were resolved with perfect formal coherence. The "abnormal" bases for the columns of the smaller order are aligned with the "regular" bases of the larger columns and with the projection created by the bottom of the central core of the piers; in this way, the logical fusion of this core with the smaller coupled columns which flank it and which are an integral part of its structure is confirmed. But short-sighted theoreticians, truly annoyed at this point,[150] have been known to interpret the protruding edges of the central sections of the piers as small pilasters of the minor order, buried in the columns of the giant order. On close examination, it is exactly the apparent detachment of these edges—almost as though they were extraneous to the central core of the pier and were related to the small paired columns of the minor order, rather than vice versa—which serves to relate the small columns to the internal core. This ambivalent feature has provoked the suggestion that the loggias are only a grandiose sequence of Serlian apertures.

The same might be said of another of Palladio's designs (R.I.B.A. XVII, 22), in which each interaxis on the second storey contains this same typical motif (Fig. XV, p. 62). The motif, which is certainly related to the Vicentine loggias,[151] can hardly be considered an improvement over the first design and in any case it must have been very quickly abandoned. Although it ingeniously recapitulated some important moments of the architect's earlier development (such as the rusticated arcades of the lower portico of Villa Pisani at Bagnolo, or the Serlian aperture planned for the upper portico of Villa Valmarana at Vigardolo),[152] it nevertheless produced some undesired effects. Since the continuity of the line at the imposts of the arches was broken, each Serlian aperture, isolated in itself, tended to become the central element of the wall and assumed in the spatial organization an importance equivalent to that of the piers—which, for their part, were excessively wide and projected too slightly. In addition, there was an unfortunate discordance between the two porticoes, since the lower one was composed of large rusticated arches, and the calligraphic simplicity of the friezes of the two orders was carried to the extent of completely sacrificing the Doric frieze. Actually, the Serlian aperture was turned into a text-book exercise, and the compositional interest moved away from the vital nexus of the piers and slipped unprofitably into the intermediary zones. It is a little difficult to think of this architectural idea as preparatory to a definitive solution.[153]

If this direction had been pursued it would have been impossible for the loggias to have assumed their characteristic three-dimensional development, unfolding their framework in depth as they do. The discovery of this new "dimension" came only when the first enormous pier, opened up at the sides and compressed at the center, was completely revealed in its transformation from an inert surface to a disciplined framework of forces within a perspective scheme. Only in such a context could the pairing in depth of the small columns (an integral part of the framework) be unfolded.[154] These arch-supporting columns had perhaps been initially conceived as simple small pilasters with flat surfaces, as were the rectangular apertures in the masses of the large piers. The transition from the flat surfaces of the piers to the turned shafts of the columns must have been suggested to the artist by the necessity to comply better with the effect of the central projecting half-column, as well as by the need to modulate the sides of the piers in a continuous development—freely isolating them in space and rendering them totally accessible in all their organic development.[155]

Palladio emphasized this development with extreme care in the smallest structural details. On the outside, the width of the pier was precisely fixed; in the upper order (Plates 45, 46) it presented a unified and compact podium set beneath the sides of the base of the central half-column and beneath the small side columns. This podium was intended to project perceptibly onto the balustrade closing off the arch. The balustrade, on the other hand, is set back and railed, so that its jutting edge emphasizes without equivocation the boundary of a structure in which the arch and the balustrade are perceived as substantially distinct.

Passing along the porticoes inside the galleries, one feels the distending pauses of the arches within the marked rhythm of the columns (Figs. 35, 40, 41, 42). It is impossible to reunite (especially in a complete perspective view) the *disiecta*

membra of the Serlian apertures, so imposing is the effect of the enormous tripartite piers. Upon careful examination, another unexpected and fascinating aspect of Palladio's solution emerges: in consequence of this animated articulation, the pier is not just enveloped but permeated by light: a warm, live atmosphere which becomes an integral part of its full plastic bulk. It was precisely the artist's understanding of the structure's three-dimensionality and his emphasis on it that enabled him to attain such coherent pictorial effects and suggestive chromatic variations, anticipating one of the most important aspects of his work to emerge later in the façade of Palazzo Chiericati (1550-51).

The ultimate effect of the loggias is the realization within an apparent uniformity of an internal development which is extremely interesting and varied, not only because of the encounter between Domenico da Venezia's elegant Gothic details and the new forms—which was perhaps the source of some uncertainties and perplexities[156]—but above all because of the complex play of fifths articulated on the outside wall in ternary cadence. The scheme of the "open" piers is ambivalent yet overwhelmingly effective; whereas on the three piazzas they energetically hammer out the rhythm of the sequence, from the inside they mould the otherwise monotonous continuity of the galleries—"an effect that is greatly enhanced when the loggias are viewed from an angle revealing the full light that pours through them."[157]

Serlio's frequently-proposed design for a palace "*copioso di lumi*" (Fig. IX, p. 40),[158] was intended to resolve a fundamentally different problem. His problem was to subdivide a series of approximately square surfaces in the second order (the areas bounded by the Ionic pilasters, the Doric frieze, and the upper cornice), which occur above the lower row of arches where

b) Palladian loggias: detail of the western side

XVIII - Andrea Palladio, *House of Raphael in Rome.* London, R.I.B.A., XIV, 11

one sees a curiously extravagant door with a tympanum inserted in the back wall. Serlio's manual does not, in fact, emphasize the pre-eminent function of the pier, much less the plasticity of its framework. On the contrary, he aimed at realizing a balanced alternation of solids and voids, of dark zones and brilliant whites. Serlio thought of the theme as one which could be inserted into the two-dimensional polychrome façades stretching along the Venetian canals. Thus the famous Serlian aperture, the focal point of the whole composition, was in effect simply a modernization, classical and mannerist at the same time, of the Venetian Gothic aperture.[159]

By 1537, Sansovino, still in Venice, had conceived his Library, which was another precedent for the Vicentine loggias.[160] Palladio, in the train of several noblemen, was in Venice toward the end of September of 1548—just at the time when, after the Council's decision of September 6th, he had begun to re-examine his first project of 1546.[161] After the collapse in 1545 of the vault of the Library's Hall, reconstruction of it had been begun. A beamed roof had been chosen, and the building was therefore certainly in a state that would have allowed it to be completely examined.[162]

It is undeniable that certain formal analogies exist between Palladio's work and that of Sansovino, and that these are explainable in the light of Palladio's admiration for his contemporary.[163] But these are merely surface analogies and in the last analysis are deceptive, because they indicate only a nominal and extrinsic resemblance.[164] Palladio's loggias and the

Venetian Library only superficially appear to be analogous sequences of arches alternating with piers, although the piers of the Library show the same formula of engaged half-columns, similarly derived from and influenced by the Roman-Bramantesque ambience.[165] The Serlian archway on paired columns illustrates the depth of the division that separates the work of the Tuscan architect, so careful in its articulation of surfaces, from Palladio's vigorous constructive power and the solemn and clear monumentality of his work.[166]

Fundamentally, if the vocabulary of the Vicentine loggias recalls the language of Sansovino, the syntax and the grammar are exquisitely Palladian.[167] Whereas the Library remains the principal comparison and was the ideal model for the loggias to have imitated,[168] it was employed, if at all, to enable Palladio to overcome certain immature residues of the styles of Sanmicheli and Giulio Romano. As a result, he abandoned the ambiguity represented in the first project by the contrast of the rustication of the lower gallery with the smooth surface of the upper gallery, reducing the whole to smooth stone (as has been correctly noted).[169]

Because of Palladio's astuteness as an experienced builder, the technical accident that had happened to his colleague three years earlier served him as a stimulus toward more discerning calculation of the weight-bearing elements. Sansovino, constructing *ex novo* after the pre-existing building had been demolished, was not bound by an internal framework but had instead to adapt himself to the typical " continuum " of Venetian buildings. Although we may assume that a formal analogy between the Library and the Vicentine loggias exists, it would be arbitrary as well as useless to try to isolate points of accentuated tension in the articulation of the Library; these, on the other hand,

have great dramatic prominence in the Basilica. The uniform development in cornices and friezes fixes the perpetual flow of rhythms in Sansovino's Library, imposing a concatenated " modular " reading of the very long façade between the distinct caesuras of the sharp, jutting edges of the corners.

It is impossible to overemphasize the fact that Palladio was making a " restoration " in renovating the loggias surrounding an already-existing Late Gothic nucleus,[170] and the architect's assumption of Cinquecentesque and classicizing forms constituted a remarkable obstacle in this regard. It is also necessary to emphasize a fact that is unfortunately overlooked when the loggias are considered apart from the context for which they were created: the palace inside them had not only been conceived by Domenico da Venezia according to a different vocabulary, but had been conceived without loggias. It was an organism sufficient and complete in itself, and the old Formenton porticoes must have always seemed just an addition to it, incapable of melding with the great central body.

In fact, the Formenton loggias were joined on in a rather banal fashion, which neglected even the basic structural requirements;[171] the gigantic *carena* augmented the insecurity of the construction by the pressure it exerted on the outside walls, and the palace very quickly shrugged off its superfluous harness. That superfluous quality would have remained in the new Palladian version, despite its beauty as an abstract " *invenzione*," if the architect had not been able to justify the loggias on the functional and visual plane and to make them appear as an apparent necessity. This was a task of almost absurd difficulty, in the face of which the example of Sansovino's Library would have been perfectly useless.

The conception of the new loggias seemed to ignore past events and to insist on perpetuating an error, which arouses the suspicion that perhaps Palladio's clique of protectors and patrons—who were infatuated with classicist rhetoric and whom he could not refuse—proposed it, and he was obliged to follow it. However, it was then up to the architect to validate his "*invenzione*," both in relation to the pre-existing building and—even more difficult—to the urban situation.

What saved the architect from perpetrating a similar crisis within such a restrictive situation (and from producing a brilliant and suggestive but equally irrelevant exercise) was only the intelligent humility with which he approached the original Quattrocento building. He quickly singled out the structural essentials of the palace, as well as the possible constructional difficulties. Tall pilasters accent Domenico da Venezia's broad walls; in strict coherence, a distinct vertical cadence is emphasized in the Palladian loggias. In the upper portico, the "Late Gothic" pilasters corresponding to the Palladian interaxes remain free and preserve their full value in the articulation of the surfaces (Plate 41). On the upper level they coincide with the spans of the Cinquecento arches beneath, and their axes coincide with the masks of the keystones (Plates 3, 29). Thus they emphasize the points of greatest tension of the voids beneath and seem to reassert on a projecting plane the rhythm of the articulation. This small detail points up the uselessness of the illustration in the *Quattro Libri* (Fig. X, p. 50),[172] where the middle pilaster is eliminated at the attic level and the oculi are lined up in a facile, obvious symmetry.

Moreover, in Palladio's loggias the moulding of the imposts of the arches stretches out horizontally and continues through the various turnings of the

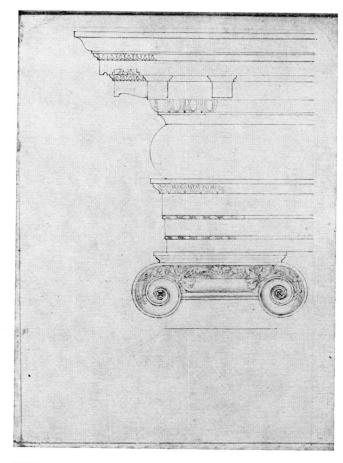

XIX - ANDREA PALLADIO, *Ionic capital and entablature.* London, R.I.B.A., X, 6

structure, recalling the analogous fascia of the Quattrocento wall—which is also just at the impost of the pointed arches of the windows and doors. The separation of the storeys between the new Palladian screen and the Quattrocento wall set back behind but emerging above the roof of the loggias was masked by the statues placed above the central element of each pier. In this way the ascending line of the great half-columns seems to continue upward and, in the normal perspective view from the piazzas, gives the illusion of reaching through the figures above to the cornice on which the *carena* rests (Plates 26, 27). Consequently, although it is naturally anchored to the internal core of the building, this line almost seems to discharge its elastic tension onto the Palladian piers ready to contain it: an effect inversely proven by the rather unfortunate aspect

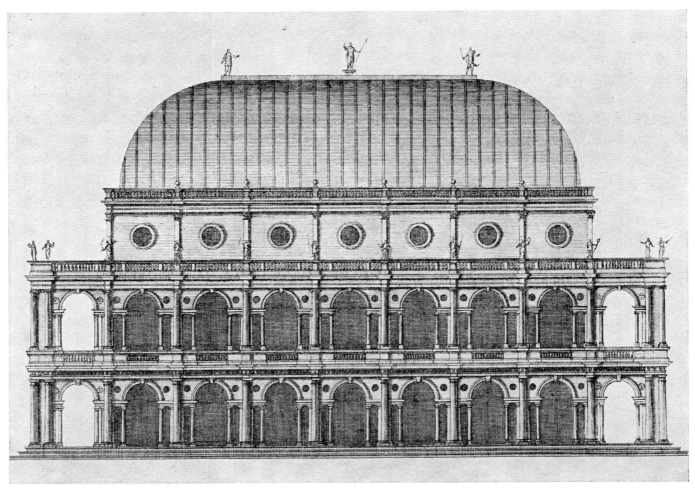

XX - FRANCESCO MUTTONI, *Palladio's " Basilica ": elevation.* From *Architettura di Andrea Palladio vicentino,*
V, 1744, pl. xix

of the southern side facing Piazza delle Erbe (Plate 34), where some of the statues are missing.

Inside the loggias, the genius with which the architect attempted effectively to unite totally diverse structures is always impressive. Those who had expected long corridors with barrel vaults along the lines of the Sansovino Library saw instead an articulated succession of cross-vaults constructed of bricks set on edge and left exposed (Plates, 35, 36, 39, 41). Moreover, the sumptuous external facing of sharply-edged stones is limited on the inside to the profiles of the arches and to the core of the piers and their smaller lateral columns (Plates 35, 40, 42). The boldness of the joining is plainly evident, especially in the upper porticoes (Plate 41), which are free of shops. On one side the Palladian arcades meld with Domenico da Venezia's wall, repeating above it and at equal intervals short sections of Cinquecentesque moulding which served as imposts for the new cross-vaults. On the other side (Plates 39, 40) the cross-vaults—by the very character of their visible brickwork and by their form, the web profile of which accentuates the elasticity of the linear distance—extend to the Cinquecento structure the characteristic Late Gothic aspect of the palace. It has been aptly observed that in order to make possible " the graft of a new formal vocabulary onto an old one, it was necessary that an element of the former be transferred to the latter." [173] In addition, there are conscious parallels in the choice of materials. Domenico da Venezia's building was completely finished in stone, and that is how the visible upper part of it appears;

thus Palladio's shell for it was executed in stone from Piovene. This is exceptional in the architect's oeuvre, as he usually worked in brick, stucco, or plaster.[174]

The close succession of the cross-vaults within the loggias has an important effect in the overall context, and this is technically confirmed by the way in which Palladio articulated and animated the piers, starting from the heaviness of the initial design. Each cross-vault clearly marks the middle axis of the pier (Plates 35, 38, 42), which it emphasizes without equivocal lateral zones of less resistance where the mass might be lightened with impunity. In the same way, it indicates the intermediary arch as a blank pause between elements under tension. Consequently, the cross-vaults (Plate 36, 40) also suggest the immediate idea of a system of forces springing from an inner core and balanced on the outside by the heavy piers, thus accentuating the sensation which we feel in looking at the building from the piazzas (Plates 26, 27). The enormous, swelling *carena* almost seems to dilate, while the buttressed surround of loggias suggests a centrifugal thrust to provide the necessary equilibrium.

Since the dangerous tendency to push the walls outward was an unfortunate defect of the old palace,[175] we must admire in this new light the architect's subtlety in drawing from an actual structural deficiency—which could have been differently obviated—another valid reason to justify the active presence of the loggias so that they surround Domenico da Venezia's building with a series of apparently necessary reinforcements. The suggestive force of the distinctly calculated links renders them logical—or, at least, opportune—fulfillments of the initial idea, which the original architect had never in fact envisaged.

The apt observation can be made that "the very purpose of art, even where architecture is concerned, [is] to give life to invention."[176] However, when put to the test as in this specific case, the compromise that makes the invention acceptable lies in this demonstrable fact: the centrifugal pressure exercised by the walls and discharged through the cross-vaults eventually returns to the pier, the fundamental and determinative motif in the articulation of the loggias.

The grouping of the loggias around the Quattrocento nucleus in such a close and purposeful connection determines a very different urban situation from that of Sansovino's Library. Sansovino's concept was that of a *piazza salone* with uniform continuous walls, opened at the bottom in very long porticoes. Thus he supports the typical assumption of the High Renaissance, in which the piazza is no longer conceived along a perimeter outlined by independent buildings but becomes an area bounded by unified façades, i.e., a unified space.[177] In Vicenza, since the problem involved utilizing a building isolated on three sides (Scale Drawing *a*, Plates 1, 2, 3), every presupposition for a similar realization was lacking; only Giulio Romano unrealistically desired one. Whereas Sansovino encased a " vacuum " within his arcades, for Palladio there was no other choice but (starting from the center) to organize and dominate the surrounding spaces. Only in that way could the Cinquecento loggias, which were actually even more obtrusive than those by Formenton, be inserted into an urban texture which had been developed and organized without them—a texture for whose specific dimensions Domenico da Venezia's building had been uniquely calibrated.[178]

Today we almost succeed in forgetting this fact, and we gloss over certain absurdities: for example, at the southwest corner the pier is repressed by the closeness of the surrounding buildings, and the cornice almost touches the adjacent wall

(Plate 31). Such "errors" are masked by the forceful suggestiveness of Palladio's structure, with the hammering rhythm of its piers and the dynamic continuity of its arches, which acts like a tension-conducting wire.[179] The surrounding space is invaded by the loggias and at the same time is peremptorily encroached upon.[180] Whereas the Quattrocento Palazzo della Ragione had to appear in all its lucid structural beauty when viewed from the open area of the piazza, the Cinquecento loggias compress the surrounding voids, subjecting them and finally reuniting them around their central point.[181] In re-employing within the calculated elaboration of the loggias the beautiful Late Gothic *carena*, Palladio seems to have discovered a centripetal function that the latter did not possess formerly, or at least did not possess so decidedly.

In the face of the complexity and astounding originality of the results, all explanations of Palladio's "*invenzione*" pass from the realm of the generic to that of the concrete. The search for exact antecedents becomes extremely problematic. From the vast Mannerist repertory, certain of Giulio Romano's motifs must be cited, such as the Serlian archways on combined columns of the garden façade of Palazzo del Tè;[182] indeed, the idea has recently been suggested that the concept of the Vicentine loggias originated entirely from designs by Giulio Romano.[183] But this leads to the suggestion that if Giulio had discovered the decisive formula, he should also have been able to apply it when he was officially invited in 1542 to do so.

To say the least, it is astounding to think that the architect of these loggias would constantly have employed in their execution modules and accents not his own; critics of various eras, in accordance with the canons of their particular periods, have seen Palladio either as repeating Ser-

lio or as imitating Sansovino and Giulio Romano or as looking more or less to Bramante,[184] Sanmicheli,[185] and Antonio da Sangallo,[186] always on the basis of constant archaeological recapitulations.[187] By coincidence, all the architects mentioned (with the exceptions of Bramante and Sangallo) were personally occupied on their own account with the question of the loggias; but none came to any conclusion.

These references are in one way all equally valid, and in another way equally ineffective. It is clear that Palladio could not separate himself from any of the above-mentioned influences, as they were all immediate, fundamental, or simply obvious ones for that period and for someone who was born in Padua, lived in Vicenza, was educated in the Veneto, and matured in Rome. One might say that there was an implicit selectivity on the part of the architect regarding his sources of inspiration, but this is only minimally true.

The first great master that Palladio encountered was Sanmicheli, the tutelary deity of the Pedemuro studio. He saw Serlio and Sansovino later during their stays in Vicenza, as well as Giulio Romano. He knew the others or was informed about their work in Rome, at the same time that he encountered the much-admired antiquities. The exclusive circle under the aegis of Giangiorgio Trissino ceaselessly proposed to him the myth of an imperial and aulic classicism, an impossible dream to recover.

Therefore Palladio acquired a repertory of forms conditioned in an extremely precise way. The loggias—his first truly monumental work—illustrate the way in which he learned to profit from these forms: he avoided easy dogmatism and adapted them unhesitatingly to the precise function for which they were destined, creating at the same time a completion and a valid structural support for

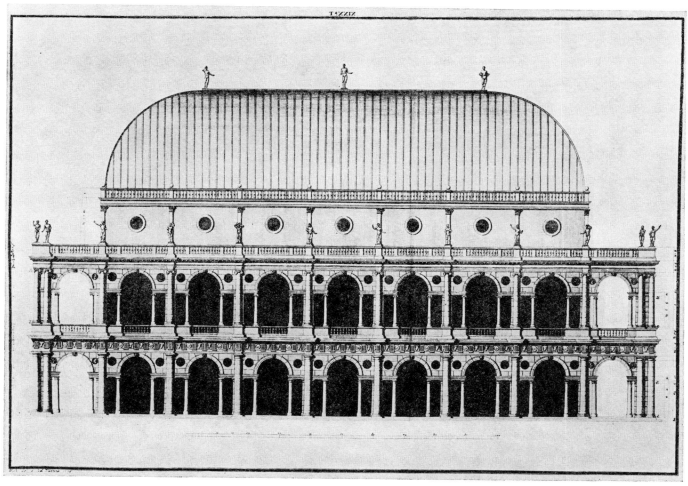

XXI - Ottavio Bertotti Scamozzi, *Palladio's " Basilica ": elevation.* From *Le Fabbriche e i Disegni di Andrea Palladio*, I, 1776, pl. xxix

a separate, earlier building. The loggias thus create a new context, unprecedented and capable of nullifying any proposed source—which in the very act of being adopted would have been surpassed. This is solely due to the tenacity and the ability with which every structural element is forcefully grasped—as if to refute any charge of a purposeless classicism or a specious formal elegance—and made to serve the structural needs of the building and of the precise situation.

We are, fortunately, dealing with a design very different from the senile and partially obscure one of the Teatro Olimpico, where academic erudition contributed to a compromise of archaeological inspiration.[188] The loggias were certainly not a renewal of the extremely modest example of the Formenton porticoes nor even less of the

Palazzo della Ragione in Padua,[189] but were instead a completely rethought addition to Domenico da Venezia's great structure. Unlike most structures, the loggias are an example of the professional honesty of an architect who was able to confer a dignity of form on an arid program by the humility of his efforts.

The Execution

Soon after his project had been definitively approved in April 1549, Palladio was appointed "*proto*" of the grandiose structure effective on May 1st, with a monthly compensation of five gold scudi.[190] This was a very modest sum, especially when compared to the difficulty of the charge, hardly corresponding to what a stonemason could earn at that time for about a month's work. However the artist must have had a real need of the money, since from the first payment of ten scudi on May 25, 1549, he began to get both large and small advances to cover his family's more immediate necessities.[191]

On the same date (May 25th) Maestro Martino "*marangon*" was paid for having made a model of the palace,[192] as was Maestro Alvise Sbari "*taiapria*,"[193] who had already made trips to the Piovene quarries to get material for the construction. The Piovene stone (which was white, compact, very hard, and easy to quarry in great blocks) had been used in Vicenza and in its surroundings since the beginnings of the Cinquecento,[194] although the results as far as durability was concerned had not been completely up to expectations. The stone was hard enough, but it had little resistance to the action of atmospheric agents.[195] However, it was capable of producing effects similar to those of the famous Istrian stone used in Venice, and it was available in a conveniently nearby area.[196]

The very precarious condition of the roads and of the available means of transportation soon created grave difficulties. Roads had to be repaired and bridges propped up, and special wagons, nicknamed "*carro matto*" and "*carro bastardo*," had to be made. Often these wagons broke down with loose wheels and broken axles during the journeys. Transportation was perhaps no less a job than the actual quarrying operation, and the expenditures for the two were equal.[197]

On August 13, 1549, workmen began digging the foundations for the northwest corner pier.[198] The placing of the first stone followed in the early part of September.[199] At the end of the month the architect himself began making trips to Piovene to select and measure the stone, as well as to speed up its delivery.[200] On November 5th the stone began to arrive at *Piazza dei Signori*, which was becoming transformed into a huge, noisy worksite.[201] Work was halted from the end of November through all of December because of Palladio's absence from Vicenza (perhaps for a brief trip to Rome); however, he returned by Christmas Eve.[202] Advantage may have been taken of the interval to level the ground and to knock down the five arches of the lower order on the western side, which had been re-erected in the sixteenth century according to the Rizzo-Spaventa project. Although propped up and damaged, the old Formenton loggias on the northern and southern sides of the palace still existed. They gradually disappeared as the Palladian structures advanced.[203]

Several out-of-town artisans chosen by Palladio in December 1549 in Venice and Padua were soon added to the local stonecutters.[204] Each group contracted to prepare the stones for one arch and at the same time to work at putting them in place, since in order to clear the public areas, this had to be done quickly.[205] Parts of some of the piers on the western side were ready as early as March 10, 1550. However, they were replaced after the middle of July, perhaps because some error of calculation had been made.[206] Also, the first two arches at the northwest corner (which Alvise Sbari supervised after August 9, 1550) were badly made and had to be demolished in June 1551.[207] They were completed anew on January 5, 1552.[208]

By June 24, 1553, three more arches of the lower gallery were erected (the second, third, and fourth on the western side, by Piazza dei Signori), but the cornice and steps were incomplete.[209] Sbari was now describing himself as "the most expert and also the most faithful of the artisans attached to the... loggias," [210] and Palladio begins to appear in the documents as the chief architect of the Commune of

Vicenza.[211] On May 27, 1553, a public donation of a thousand ducats annually was set aside for the grandiose undertaking.[212] From 1550 on three illustrious citizens were appointed every two years to serve as wardens of the construction.[213] The fifth arch, which was exactly in the center of the northern façade, was finished by September 4, 1554. Work quickly got underway on the fourth and the third on the left and progressed so well that on November 29th of the same year the relevant expenses were settled.[214]

At this point, the architect halted the sequence of arches and began work on the opposite pier at the northeast corner, the foundations of which were ready as early as July 8, 1556.[215] In this manner he framed the northern façade within distinct boundaries and clearly marked its separation from the nearby Torre Bissara. The brick vault by which the old loggias were linked to the tower of the podestà's palace was torn down.[216] The two arches at the northeast corner were completed on September 27, 1556, and by October 31 they were joined by vaults to the building within. Meanwhile, work continued on the western side. But in March 1558 attention had already turned to the southwest corner pier, the "*cantonale delle pescherie.*"[217]

This overriding concern to define at the vertices the exact planimetric progression of the loggias in their close relationship with the irregular, vaguely-trapezoidal configuration of the palace within confirms the function imposed by the Quattrocento palace on Palladio's design, as well as the artist's respect for the palace's structure. He wanted the three heavy piers to serve as the first structural reinforcements for the surround of porticoes, in a true integration of the old with the "modern." However, an examination of the plan (Scale drawings *j*, *k*) makes it clear that,

after the principal piers had been set in place, the positioning of the other piers was calculated in counterpoint both with the mass within the loggias and with the opening and course of the passageways from the two piazzas; there was no concern for symmetrical correspondence between the interaxes of the northern and southern sides of the loggias.[218]

The isolated building portrayed in the unfortunate illustration in the *Quattro Libri* (Fig. X, p. 50) is proven false on two counts: not just because the connection with the palace of the podestà is falsely presented, but even more because through this falsification the Palladian screen is deprived of its true *raison d'être* and is transformed from a completely thought-out construction *in situ* into a useless classicizing rehash. The structure was instead almost like an organism matured by age-old vicissitudes and nearing its definitive (and, one might say, "natural") conclusion. The Vicentine administrators could maintain with well-deserved pride from September of 1558 onward that there was not "*dubio alcuno che questo nostro palazzo di architettura e di bellezza non cede a qualunque altro edificio publico d'Italia, ed ogni di più si va riducendo ad una perfetta forma.*"[219]

Unfortunately, harder times were coming. In October of 1559, the Council of the Hundred, pressed by the impelling demands of a serious famine, was forced to halve the annual financing of 1,000 ducats (the sum that had been allocated for the work since 1553) for the following three years.[220] The choice was, however, justified by the circumstances.[221] Financing was again drastically reduced on May 20 of the following year (1560), forcing the work to a halt. Since Palladio, engaged in supervising his other projects, was often absent from Vicenza his provision was withheld, "*non esse honestum* [sic!] *sa-*

larium Andreae Palladii solvi debere"; on the 28th of the same month this decision was communicated to the *Provveditori alla fabbrica* so they could regulate things accordingly.[222]

Today the provision made to Palladio, which falls between the incredible and the ridiculous, amazes us. Considering the modesty of the sum withheld—but which the architect needed in order to maintain his family, especially when he was absent[223]—one's first spontaneous reaction is indignation, even admitting that the architect's frequent absences had become excessive.[224] Fortunately, there was no waste of time on the part of a certain individual in expressing his annoyance at this shabby miserliness, and on July 22, overcoming a compromise proposal advanced by Girolamo Ferramosca, the architect's salary was restored. However, when this honorable and fair decision was made, particular note was taken that the said compensation was not a right acquired by the effort and trustworthiness of the master but an approbation that the top administrators of public affairs could confer or take away according to their own judgment.[225] At the same time, although the decision had not provided for this, back payment for the two unfortunate months of June and July was made to Palladio, and he never had the heart to return to such a wretched and painful subject.[226]

Two documents indicate the state of the work in the meantime. A little before November 20, 1559, we learn from a memorandum by Antonio Maria Revese, *Provveditore alla fabbrica*, that on the Piazza dei Signori side only one arch of the lower gallery was still lacking (the second one from the northeast corner). On the western side four arches had been erected, including the one at the northwest corner; this in substance included all of the arches of the lower gallery, except the last one on

the left.[227] Revese, together with Alvise Sbari, took advantage of the occasion for a general check of all the accounts, which up until then had been rather confused. He organized the results in a notarized document of July 23, 1561.[228] On that date, the lower gallery facing the great piazza was finished; thus in all there were fourteen arches in operation. They were: the single one on the east facing the palace of the podestà; the nine on the northern side; and the four on the west facing the present-day Piazzetta Palladio, beginning at the northwest pier. The document specifies that none of the cornices and steps had been completed.[229] On November 16th the *Provveditori alla fabbrica* were reduced to two instead of three.[230]

The problem of the necessary money, however, was still very serious. On April 18, 1563, barely two months after contracts were drawn up for an additional supply of 5,000 feet of Piovene stone,[231] there was discussion in the Council of the Hundred as to whether to suspend the work or look for new sources of revenue.[232] The following day, the annual subvention was fortunately increased from 500 to 700 ducats for a three-year period.[233] However, this was not enough to initiate new work, but simply to settle the numerous debts and to complete the work already begun.[234] From 1561 to 1564, therefore, very little was done with the exception of work on the two arches adjacent to the southwest corner pier facing Piazza delle Erbe and Piazzetta Palladio: these arches were finished in the early months of 1564.[235] In the meantime, on October 14, 1562, agreement was reached with Pietro da Nanto to *"mudar la scala e porta che va su in salone e do scale vano in Torre."* [236] On March 6, 1564, it was finally decided to take up the work again with the necessary energy. However, the lower gallery of the loggias was put aside, and

XXII - OTTAVIO BERTOTTI SCAMOZZI, *Palladio's " Basilica ": transverse section.* From *Le Fabbriche e i Disegni di Andrea Palladio*, I, 1776, pl. xxx

it was decided to pass on to the upper gallery and to erect the two pairs of arches corresponding to the northwest corner, after a model prepared for that purpose by the architect had been approved.[237] (Evidently there was a hurry to be able to admire the two elevations most exposed to the public view.)[238] It is likely that the London drawing (Fig. XVI, p. 65; R.I.B.A. XIII, 8) refers to this event, although it has been interpreted as one of the four designs prepared after September 6, 1548, and paid for on the following October 27th;[239] it is, however, finished with such precision and detail that it must respond to the specific request of the March 6th decision. The drawing accurately portrays one of the arches of the upper gallery (specifically the one at the extreme northwest, which was perhaps the first to

be erected). It appears to be too minutely related to a single constituent element of the design to belong to the overall view which in all probability shaped the preliminary drawing of September-October 1548.[240]

In any event, it is important to observe (Plate 45) that in the course of the execution a slightly projecting fascia was placed under the base of the piers.[241] This fascia was later also run under the balustrade of the arcade, which is formed of columns and not made into the solid parapet indicated in the drawing. The two variants are indicative of the alert prudence with which the artist closely followed the work.[242] The "open" balustrades, set slightly back, accentuate the hollowness of the arch and augment its apparent height;[243] at the same time, they mark the boundaries and the organic structure of the piers. The fascia at the base is sufficient (and necessary) to raise the Ionic order the proper amount needed to counteract the visual encumbrance of the Doric cornice's strong projection, as seen in the fore-shortened view from below.

In the analogous case of the Chiericati façade more than ten years earlier (1551-52), the architect had used the normal method of placing the Ionic bases directly on the cornice of the order below; here the slight projection of the cornice detracted little, and it was always possible to see the palace comprehensively in a distant view of its façade from the large Piazza dell' Isola. But in the piazzas around the Basilica, the space was short and narrow in comparison to the mass of the loggias and the effect was crowded. Thus the need arose to ease the spatial tension, resulting in Palladio's deft adaptation to the actual situation.[244]

The four upper arches ordered in March 1564 were, as usual, entrusted to Alvise Sbari.[245] When Sbari died in the early months of 1566, he was replaced by Pasqualino da Venezia as *capomaestro della fabbrica*. A regular allocation was arranged for the latter on April 18th of the same year.[246] In April of 1570 the four arches —two facing Piazza dei Signori and two on the western side, starting from the northwest corner—were finished.[247] This was fortunate, as in that year the work was suspended a second time,[248] because the city gave 36,000 ducats in successive stages for the war against the Turks and set aside notable sums for the restoration of the Loggia del Capitaniato.[249] Consequently, the annual allocation for the loggias came to only 300 ducats on June 29th.[250]

The interruption lasted in effect until February of 1584. From 1570 to 1584 there were provisions only for the construction according to Palladio's precise di-

rections of the vaults connecting the arches of the loggias to the walls of the Quattrocento palace (with Domenico Raffioli as overseer),[251] as well as for a few other embellishments.[252] When later (on March 25, 1583) the Council of the Hundred finally decided to take up the work again,[253] Palladio had been dead for almost three years (since August 19, 1580).

By then, however, the positioning of the loggias was established down to the smallest detail, at least in regard to the northern and western sides. Thus on February 20, 1584, Maestro Giovanni Antonio Grazioli *"spezzaprede"* was able to undertake the construction of two arches of the upper gallery on the western side;[254] on November 21, 1585, having almost finished them, he took on the task of two new arches in continuation of the earlier ones: one facing Piazza delle Erbe and still another on the western side. He also agreed in principle to construct all the remaining ones.[255] Evidently he continued to follow the method which Palladio used, which was to start from the corners and work toward the center of each side, resolving problems of possible disparities in the measurements of the piers' interaxes as he went.

Meanwhile, on February 12, 1587, the clearing of the shops and storage areas encumbering the western side of the palace was decided upon, probably in preparation for the foundations of the new loggias to be erected on Piazza delle Erbe.[256] However, disagreements subsequently arose between the *Provveditori* and Grazioli. By June 27, 1597, the latter had executed twelve arches during the thirteen years that had elapsed since 1584, although they were not completely finished.[257] The arches on the northern and western sides and the short turn on the east seem to have been finished in both galleries, and the first two arches were erected in both galleries on the southern side, starting from the south-west corner.

Giannantonio Grazioli, after having been engaged on September 30, 1597, to construct all the arches still lacking on Piazza delle Erbe with their relative foundations,[258] subsequently died, and the contract was renewed with his brother Giovanni on January 23, 1599.[259] Nevertheless, the responsibility for the placement of the loggias facing Piazza delle Erbe must still rest with Giannantonio. The problem there was to raise the two orders on a high podium because of the notable disparity in level (circa 2.5 meters) existing between the Piazza delle Erbe and Piazza dei Signori.[260] It is almost certain that Palladio, who was surely aware of the difficulty, had done nothing about it other than to give a summary hint (if he ever touched on the question) in his projects of 1546 and 1548; he always trusted his empirical nature to come up with the most opportune solution on the spot.

The actual solution (Plates 31, 33, 34) is decidedly controversial in several aspects. The plinth, composed of great blocks of stone, assumes a heavy compactness and its excessive heaviness is not in any way "visually" obviated.[261] The large half-column and the smaller columns are placed very near the extreme edge of the plinth (Plates 31, 33) and therefore lack sufficient "breathing space" at the base. The massive loggias seem pushed almost to the point of leaping off the plinth, to the detriment of the apparent structural security.[262] In addition, the undeniably paltry buttresses shaped like truncated pyramids which rise under the half-columns are not very attractive.

However, on November 15, 1605, Giovanni Grazioli had already executed five arches on the southern side and had the material ready for a sixth.[263] Another three arches were finished by April 2, 1610.[264]

On July 1st of the same year Grazioli, together with Antonio Benetello, agreed to execute by Easter of 1612 the new south stairway of the palace (exactly corresponding to the Quattrocento one on the northern side) and to arrange six new shops under the same stairway.[265] A year earlier, on June 11, 1609, the great polygonal stair which leads from the loggias to the Piazza delle Erbe had been completed after the design of Giambattista Albanese.[266]

The last five arches of the southern façade (which consists of sixteen arches as opposed to eighteen on the north side, since there are two arches less on the right where the loggias join the Arco degli Zavatteri) were finished in 1614,[267] but payment was not made until March 14, 1617, to the procurator of the Confraternita della Santissima Concezione, the heir of the late Giovanni Grazioli.[268]

The city was still at that time rather small and had only modest resources (in 1557 there were 19,899 inhabitants),[269] so it had really accomplished an enormous task, devoting 60,000 ducats to the loggias in about seventy years, according to the sources.[270] The cost actually had probably been even more; but the result, even apart from the formal aspect, is reliable from the technical and structural point of view and justifies Palladio's foresight,[271] even in a close and accurate inspection.[272] Palladio was architect, master builder, and stonemason together, and he followed the construction with loving vigilance; the disciplined skill with which the workers had applied themselves confirms the fact that the building may, as Palladio himself said, "*esser comparata a gli edifici antichi e annoverata tra le maggiori, e le più belle fabbriche, che siano state fatte dagli antichi in qua, si per la grandezza, e per gli ornamenti suoi: come anco per la materia, che è tutta di pietra viva durissima: e sono state tutte le pietre commesse, e legate in-*

XXIII - OTTAVIO BERTOTTI SCAMOZZI, *Palladio's "Basilica": structural details of the loggias.*
From *Le Fabbriche e i Disegni di Andrea Palladio*, I, 1776, pl. xxxi

sieme con somma diligenza."[273] The most demanding modern "inspector" must acknowledge that even contemporary Rome, at the time so much richer and more prestigious, did not boast a single work that was built with such scrupulous rigor.[247]

The aulic name "Basilica," which was inflicted on the monument by Palladio himself, falsifies history in homage to classicizing rhetoric;[275] but not even the more pompous title "*Basilica palladiana*" can obscure the masterful integrity with which three generations of artisans fitted the stones and laid out the arches and vaults, in accordance with the terse, concrete clarity of form which the artist desired.

NOTES TO CHAPTER IV

[1] This was the project approved on March 5, 1546. The expression " *novissime presentatum* " with which the related resolution of the Council (Chapter III, n. 62) describes it has been interpreted by ARNALDI (1767, p. xl) as indicating that it had been worked up shortly before. Cf. ZORZI, 1958 (II), p. 17, who says we can be certain that Palladio returned to Vicenza to present a design for the Basilica's loggias sometime during February 1546.

[2] ZORZI, 1958 (II), p. 17.

[3] ZORZI, 1958 (II), p. 17; LAVAGNINO, 1962, p. 37.

[4] ZORZI, 1958 (II), pp. 18-20.

[5] LAVAGNINO, 1962, pp. 7-8, 22-42; 1962 (II).

[6] For a discussion of this ciborium, see especially: PANE, 1961, pp. 114-115; ZORZI, 1966, pp. 24-26; BARBIERI, 1966, pp. 338-339.

[7] Cf. DALLA POZZA, 1943, pp. 90-91; 1965 (II), pp. 45, 57.

[8] BARBIERI, 1967.

[9] BARBIERI, 1967, pp. 28-33.

[10] ZORZI, 1949 (II); 1964, pp. 183-187; DALLA POZZA, 1963, pp. 102-105.

[11] DALLA POZZA, 1963, pp. 105-118; ACKERMAN, 1967, pp. 40-41. The idea that Domenico Groppino designed the Palazzetto Da Monte (advanced by ZORZI, 1963, p. 128) collapses in the light of MANTESE's clarifications (1967).

[12] DALLA POZZA, 1965, pp. 203-216; 1965 (II), p. 57; ACKERMAN, 1967, pp. 38-40.

[13] DALLA POZZA, 1965, pp. 229-238.

[14] PANE, 1961, pp. 104-105; ROSCI, 1966, p. 130; ACKERMAN, 1967, pp. 59-60.

[15] This date, proposed by Pane (1961, pp. 111-112), seems to me more convincing than that of 1559 suggested by ACKERMAN, 1967, p. 76.

[16] See FORSSMAN, 1965, pp. 34 ff., on Cevese's proposal (1952); also BARBIERI, 1964, pp. 325-326. MAGAGNATO, summarizing the various opinions on the question, considers the decade between 1545 and 1555 as the period when Palazzo Thiene was designed and constructed and construes this as manifest proof of Palladio's complete adherence to the currents of the mannerist culture maturing in the Veneto in the decade after 1540 (1966, p. 16). His observation—along with his dating to about 1543 Palladio's point of greatest contact with contemporary events in Mantua (p. 20), an influence clearly seen in the Vicentine building—still permits the hypothesis that the conception of Palazzo Thiene preceded the Basilica projects. This idea is not contradicted by the suggestions of PANE (1961, p. 165) and ZORZI (1964, pp. 208-209) that date the effective beginning of work on Palazzo Thiene to around 1550. For GLOTON (1966, pp. 90-91), the references to Vignola are so plain in Palazzo Thiene as to suggest, at least at for the final stages, a date subsequent to Palladio's encounter with Vignola in Rome.

[17] ZORZI, 1964, pp. 187-195.

[18] ZORZI, 1966, p. 14.

[19] MAGRINI, 1845, pp. 12-13; PANE, 1961, p. 20.

[20] ZORZI, 1954 and 1954 (II); PANE, 1961, pp. 105-110; FORSSMAN, 1965, pp. 26 ff.

[21] DALLA POZZA, 1943, pp. 62-63.

[22] Cf. ARGAN, 1956.

[23] BARBIERI, 1952, pp. 34-35 (his list of Palladio's works, up-to-date until 1952, can be supplemented by ZORZI, 1954, pp. 106-107); PANE, 1961, pp. 73, 99-100; WITTKOWER, 1964, pp. 63-64 (esp. n. 2); FORSSMAN, 1965, pp. 14-17; ACKERMAN, 1966, p. 20 and 1967, p. 3. All these authors are more or less convinced of the attribution of the Villa Cricolo to Trissino. On the other hand, PALLUCCHINI (1958, p. 235 and 1959, p. 40), FIOCCO (1961, pp. 170-171), and FRANCO (1962, pp. 205-206) consider it an early work by Palladio. PUPPI, 1966 (II), p. 3 and IVANOFF, 1967, p. 15, more prudently consider it a collaborative effort of Trissino and Palladio, while FORSSMAN, 1966, p. 55, suggests that it is by an unknown architect.

[24] Book IV of the *Regole Generali di Architettura* was published in Venice in 1537; it was followed by Book III, Venice, 1540 (see WILINSKI, 1965 [II], p. 105).

[25] See Chapter III, nn. 41-43.

[26] BARBIERI, 1952, pp. 22-23; PANE, 1961, p. 46, n. 7.

[27] PANE, 1961, p. 103.

[28] Cf. BONELLI, 1960; ROSCI, 1966, p. 129.

[29] ROSCI, 1966, p. 130.

[30] ZORZI, 1958 (II), pp. 15-16. Zorzi does not expressly allude to any visit by Palladio to Venice before 1548; he refers only to a later documented trip between September 10th and 20th, 1548 (1950; 1954, p. 120, nn. 47 and 51; 1960, p. 90). However, such a delay on the part of the architect in visiting the capital of the Veneto is hardly likely.

[31] See Chapter III and cf. PANE, 1961, p. 144: " Throughout these years Palladio's attitude is like that of a person witnessing a dispute between individuals more authoritative than he is; in the guise of a discreet and attentive spectator, he takes advantage of the conflicts of others.... " We might add that he also took advantage of learning from any qualified source that could reach him, which was natural.

The credit for having investigated and selected the formative elements of Palladio's style belongs to modern art historians. The long undertaking was initiated by FIOCCO (1933 and 1935); PALLUCCHINI offers a valid synthesis (1959, p. 40), supplemented by FIOCCO (1965) and FORSSMAN (1966). However, the one-sidedness of the research itself, as well as the enthusiasm over the consequent discoveries, have at times exalted one component or another of Palladio's style at the expense of the others—a misrepresentation, even if an understandable one. To quote PANE (1963, p. 54), " A coordinated and general consideration of all the master's buidings clearly justifies the inevitable... perplexity which derives from assuming that any one of the [following] influences was prevalent ": i.e., Sanmicheli, Serlio, Sansovino, Falconetto-Cornaro or Giulio Romano. " This explains that sense of vague approximation which is implicit in greater or lesser proportions. "

[32] On Vitruvius, Trissino, and Palladio, see ZORZI, 1958 (II), pp. 111-112, and WITTKOWER, 1964, pp. 63-65. This first encounter with Vitruvius (the other took place with the publication of Daniele Barbaro's edition of Vitruvius in 1556; cf. FORSSMAN, 1962, p. 33 and 1966 [II]) had, according to ZORZI (1958 [II], p. 19), been effected with " humanistic and dilettantish sentiment"—characteristics which were transmitted to Palladio's participation in the vast undertaking of 1556. Perhaps it was a question for Palladio of a frank empiricism; but cf. PANE's acute observations on the subject (1961, p. 75), as well as POLACCO (1965, pp. 65-66) and TAFURI (1966, p. 207). On the contacts between Palladio and the Roman milieu of the Cinquecento, see especially the contributions of BRIZIO, DE ANGELIS D'OSSAT, and GLOTON (all in 1966).

33 BECHERUCCI, 1964, col. 457.

34 PALLADIO, 1570, Bk. IV, Ch. xvii.

35 Cf. BONELLI, 1960, pp. 19 ff.

36 PRAZ, 1961, pp. 161-162. Moreover, " Trissino was not a mediocre intellect. On the contrary, he was aristocratic and elevated by great literary ideals, although these were hatched in a kind of metaphysical presumptuousness. The latter cost dearly, as it removed all real capacity from the distinguished reformer to communicate with others or to find support. Speroni, who indeed considered him ' a miracle among fine intellects ' wrote of him... [that] he believed himself to be the most learned man in the world; he never showed his works in order to instruct those who saw them, but in order to arouse their admiration " (FLORA, 1941, p. 109). See also PANE, 1961, pp. 43, 73.

37 ZORZI, 1922, informs us that the name " Palladio " is found for the first time in two documents dated February 25 and March 10, 1540, and that this follows from a certificate of February 9, 1538, drawn up in Trissino's house at the " Pozzo Rosso " (the first documentation of the intimacy between the artist and his patron). We may recall that the "buon Angel Palladio " in Trissino's poem *Italia liberata dai Goti* who helps the Byzantine armies was trained in the rules of architecture; in the poem, this Palladio descends from the sky to defend a palace constructed in accordance with Vitruvian rules (cf. PRAZ, 1961, p. 161; PIOVENE, 1963, p. 19). The architect's new name derived from this. For a different but less likely hypothesis, see BATTISTI, 1962, p. 477, n. 18.

38 See the portal of S. M. dei Servi (1531) and the Dall'Acqua altar (1534-35).

39 Cf. BARBIERI, 1964 (II).

40 As LAVAGNINO seems to admit (1962, pp. 7, 42).

41 Cf. PANE, 1961, p. 111; 1963, p. 60.

42 PANE, 1964, p. 125. This position is shared, although with different emphases, by FORSSMAN (1965, esp. pp. 177 ff. and 1967), ACKERMAN (1966, esp. pp. 109, 159), and DE ANGELIS D'OSSAT (1966, p. 41). For an interpretation of Palladio from a decisively mannerist viewpoint, see PALLUCCHINI, 1958-59, and the stimulating studies by ZEVI (1963 and 1964), MAGAGNATO (1966, pp. 16 ff.), TAFURI (1966, pp. 80-93), PEVSNER (1967), and HAGER (1967). Nevertheless, MAGAGNATO (1966, p. 22) admits that Giulio Romano, while remaining a stimulating cultural precedent for Palladio, was still nothing more than a cardinal factor in the latter's *formation*. PEVSNER (1967, p. 309) justly confirmed that Palladio cannot be fully appreciated if mannerist elements are not accepted as part of his style; he concluded that if there was any sympathy on Palladio's part for the ambiguities of this style, it was accentuated around 1560-70. One must still examine the buildings of those years and their details closely in order to find such ambiguities, which never appear to be dominant. Similarly, HAUSER (1967, pp. 189-190) recognized that "the classical vein is stronger in him [Palladio] than in any other mannerist of note"; this among other things explains the architect's success during the ages of Rationalism and Enlightenment.

While remaining " grateful to the historian who has given us a better understanding of the mannerist side of Palladio " (SEMENZATO, 1967, p. 352), one must like Battisti (1967, p. 210) drive home the point that in no way is the term ' mannerism,' however enlarged, capable of covering all the artistic phenomena involved. For that reason the definition *tout court* of Palladio as a mannerist architect remains unsatisfactory: it could not be otherwise, after the recent investigations of the Venetian situation in the Cinquecento (SEMENZATO and FAGGIN, 1967). Later the term lost a large part of its original meaning (SEMENZATO, 1967, p. 352) and was enlarged to the point that it now encompasses the third and perhaps even the second decade of the Cinquecento, a period once customarily considered to be part of the Renaissance. However, the difficulties perceptively noted by BRIZIO (1967) should be mentioned: the new " category " must be accepted as a consequence of the fact that the study of cultural history has never been able to resist period and style classifications such as " Gothic," " Renaissance," and " Baroque " (PALLUCCHINI, 1967, p. 450). This does not preclude but rather polemically stimulates the " necessity to historicize " the

personal affairs of an artist within the context of the culture and society of his times; meanwhile, we must admit the unquestionable usefulness of this new historiographical tool (PALLUCCHINI, 1967, p. 451).

43 PANE, 1963, p. 58; see also p. 59 and 1961, pp. 78-79.

44 Cf. BECHERUCCI, 1964, col. 454.

45 BARBIERI, 1952, Ch. iii.

46 PANE, 1961, p. 82; see also 1963, p. 62.

47 POLACCO, 1965, p. 68.

48 Cf. PANE, 1963, p. 60.

49 As defined by PANE, 1961, p. 57.

50 POLACCO, 1965, p. 69.

51 BETTINI, 1961, p. 10; see also BETTINI, 1961 (II).

52 ARGAN, 1930; FIOCCO, 1933, 1935, 1942; BECHERUCCI, 1936, p. 55, and 1964.

53 ZEVI, 1959, p. 70.

54 FIOCCO, 1930; BETTINI, 1943.

55 See esp. the drawings (ZORZI, 1954 [II]), and the various stages of the plan for Palazzo Civena (ZORZI, 1949 [II]).

56 BARBIERI, 1967.

57 ZORZI, 1954 (II), figs. 1, 2, 3, 4, 9, 11, 16.

58 ZORZI, 1954 (II), figs. 5, 10, 15, 18.

59 BARBIERI, 1962 (II), Ch. ii.

60 Cf. BETTINI, 1961 and 1961 (II).

61 Cf. CEVESE, 1967.

62 Already noted by BÜRGER (1909) and examined thoroughly by MARIANI (1935) and by PANE (1953, pp. 24, 33; 1961, p. 192, n. 10). This element of Palladio's style, without detracting from Bernini's originality or from that of the famous " generation of the thirties " in Rome (BRIGANTI, 1960), nevertheless remains a component of major importance in Bernini's architectural culture (WITTKOWER, 1966, p. 23) and can no longer be neglected without resulting in a certain historical distortion (cf. FORMAGGIO, 1960, p. 38).

63 See Chapter III.

64 PANE, 1963, p. 59.

65 ZORZI, 1954 and 1954 (II).

66 DALLA POZZA, 1943, pp. 95-96.

67 See Chapter III, n. 62.

68 PIOVENE, Inaugural lecture for the fifth annual course of the Centro Internazionale di Studi di Architettura "Andrea Palladio," Teatro Olimpico, September 1963; PIOVENE, 1963 and 1964.

69 VENTURA, 1964, p. 170.

70 VENTURA, 1964, p. 344.

71 MURARO, 1967, p. 117.

72 MURARO, 1967, p. 116.

73 MANTESE, 1955, pp. 323-362 (343 and 345); 1964, passim.

74 Cf. VENTURA, 1964, pp. 344-345.

75 VENTURA, 1964, p. 345.

76 See n. 68 and TOFFANIN, 1965, pp. 478-479.

77 Cf. MORSOLIN, 1878.

78 FAGGIN, 1967, p. 50.

79 FAGGIN, 1967, p. 52.

80 FAGGIN, 1967, pp. 53-54.

81 Cf. PUPPI, 1963 (II), pp. 29-31.

82 See n. 68. DALLA POZZA, 1963, p. 117, verifies that during the Cinquecento the revenue of dominial buildings around Vicenza did not surpass 1.8 per cent; consequently investments of large amounts of capital in not-very-profitable or even unprofitable forms created imbalances in the domestic economy that could not be sustained for long. Thus Palladio's buildings, which were conceived on a grand scale with the costs of the projects probably not precisely calculated, imposed a commitment of liquid capital on a scale surpassing its availability and the patrons' normal incomes.

83 ZEVI, 1966, col. 61.

84 In 1546; cf. FIOCCO, 1961, p. 173 and ZEVI, 1966, col. 65.

85 Concerning Giovanni da Pedemuro, see the imposing documentation compiled by ZORZI, 1937, pp. 66-87 (followed on pp. 87-104 by the documentation for his associate, Girolamo Pittoni), as well as the additions and clarifications by DALLA POZZA (1943, pp. 146-148), BARBIERI (1954), ARSLAN (1956), and the *Guida di Vicenza* (1953 and 1956). For a broader discussion of the question, see PUPPI (1958 and 1965), BARBIERI (1967), and MANTESE (1967 [II]).

Leaving aside Master Giovanni, it is interesting to note that Palladio might have had a second adviser in the person of the Vicentine nobleman Stefano Gualdo (MAGRINI, 1845, *Annotazioni*, p. 11, n. 12; 1845 [II]; miscellaneous ms. on Vicentine artists, based on the ancient *Memorie mss. di casa Gualdo*). Gualdo is a rather indistinct figure to whom CEVESE (1956 [IV], pp. 194-195, 210-211) tried to give substance by associating at least three buildings with his name: the Villa Gualdo at the " Gualda " of Montecchio Maggiore (assigned to Stefano previously by MAGRINI, 1845, pp. 9-10), the western elevation of the courtyard of the first Palazzo Gualdo in Vicenza, and the Casa Dal Toso (now Polazzo) in Contrà Piancoli. By extension, we might perhaps add the portal of the Casa Thiene (now Da Schio) in Borgo S. Lucia (cf. *Guida di Vicenza*, 1956, pp. 321-322). These works are all in effect tied together by clear analogies based on a taste which oscillates between Serlian " picturesqueness " (the Gualdo courtyard) and evocations of Ammannati (the Casa Dal Toso). However, before assigning them to Stefano we must recall that at least two of the structures (the Villa Gualdo and the Casa Dal Toso) seem to belong to an artist of some stature rather than to an amateur, a personality not unlike Ammannati—who was in Vicenza precisely from 1546 to 1550 and who was a guest of the Gualdi family in their house in Borgo di Pusterla (BETTINI, 1941, pp. 22-23 and n. 10).

86 See Chapter III, n. 62.

87 See Chapter III, n. 70.

88 See Chapter III, n. 63.

89 See Chapter III, n. 68.

90 Cf. DALLA POZZA, 1943, p. 115.

91 ZORZI, 1964, pp. 247-248.

92 See Chapter III, n. 14.

93 ZORZI, 1950. For a different interpretation—which, however, is no longer accepted (cf. FORSSMAN, 1965, pp. 39 ff.; ACKERMAN, 1967, p. 90; IVANOFF, 1967, p. 26)—see PANE, 1961, p. 141, n. 6, who in substance takes up the position of DALLA POZZA, 1943, pp. 96-97; see also WITTKOWER, 1964, p. 77, n. 5. The rather modest compensations paid for these new designs might be explained by the fact that they were considered as simple modifications, at least from the administrative point of view. This and other factors permitted Palladio to overcome more easily the hindrance of his old master's presence, which had by then become cumbersome (Giovanni died between October and November of 1550, having made his will on August 28th of that year; DALLA POZZA, 1943, p. 92, and ZORZI, 1937).

94 See DALLA POZZA, 1965.

95 PANE, 1961, p. 159.

96 MANTESE, 1964, pp. 82 ff., 98-108; see also PIOVENE, 1963, pp. 20-23.

97 PANE, 1961, p. 63.

98 ZEVI, 1966, cols. 60, 64-65.

99 MAGAGNATO, 1967, p. 28.

100 ZEVI, 1966, col. 65. On the other hand, PANE (1961, p. 62), emphasizes in Palladio " the absence of any dissension," which was so marked that it appears " that no other great master was so immune from inner conflicts "; BATTISTI (1960, p. 71), while confirming his isolation, places the architect among the " rare... moments of equilibrium " noticeable in Italian art. Nevertheless PANE (1961, pp. 82-83), observes that some variations in the text of Palladio's treatise between the preliminary fragments in Venice (Codex Cicogna) and in London (R.I.B.A.; see ZORZI, 1958, [II], pp. 163-193) and the definitive edition of 1570 must have been suggested to the artist precisely because of a " prudent respect " for his patrons, indicating a " somewhat

pathetic " psychological state. One might say that the latter was more than pathetic if, for example, we consider the preliminary draft of the " *Scompartimento delle stanze ed altri luoghi alla commodità pertinenti* " published by ZORZI (1958, [II], pp. 181-184) and written (p. 153) between 1561 and 1566. In an addition to the second paragraph (p. 183, n. 281) Palladio observes sadly: " *in molte... fabriche mi è stato bisogno obedire non tanto alla natura de i siti quanto alla volontà de i padroni, i quali* [for their own personal motives] *mi hanno sforzato* "; later he corrects himself: " *hanno fatto ch'io mi sia partito.* " Even the more cautious version was not permitted in the 1570 treatise (Bk. II, Ch. ii, pp. 3-4); not only is the incriminating phrase gone, but the whole paragraph has vanished. The need for watchful prudence was so great that Palladio's desire to express his thoughts fully was stifled.

101 Cf. PRAZ, 1961, p. 161.

102 FLORA, 1941, p. 110.

103 The first nine cantos appeared in 1547 in Rome, the other eighteen in Venice in 1548 (SCARPA, 1950, p. 22).

104 MORSOLIN, 1894, p. 279.

105 ZORZI, 1954, pp. 105-106; 1958 (II), pp. 129-130. PANE, 1961, p. 110, acknowledges that it contains " some timid allusions to possible solutions for the arches of the Basilica."

106 PANE, 1961, p. 110.

107 ZORZI, 1964, pp. 90-91, 189.

108 PANE, 1961, pp. 144-145.

109 SERLIO, 1540, c. 17 a.

110 ZORZI, 1958, (II), pp. 58-59, figs. 54-56; SPIELMANN, 1966, pp. 137-138 (NN. 11-12). DALLA POZZA (1943, pp. 99-102, fig. 23) considered one of these drawings (the elevation) as an unpublished first study for the Basilica; this is an error, as its caption clearly indicates. LOTZ (1967, p. 14 and fig. 5) published the drawing as one of Palladio's projects for the loggias, along with R.I.B.A., X, 9. Zorzi does not mention it (1958 [II]); SPIELMANN (1966, pp. 140-141, N. 27), classifies it as a colonnade and arcade of the Doric order and interprets it as a preliminary study for Bk. I, Ch. xv of the 1570 treatise: more precisely, for the plates on pp. 23 and 24 of Book I. Again according to SPIELMANN, it is a drawing by Palladio or from his workshop dating between 1562 and 1570.

111 Cf. LOTZ, 1961, pp. 82-85.

112 For the references to the earlier interior structure, see Chapter II.

113 Cf. the precise verification of COGO, 1900, pp. 19-20, 29, 33.

114 Cf. DALLA POZZA, 1943, p. 102, fig. 24; PANE, 1961, pp. 145 and 152, fig. 6. However ZORZI (1964, p. 45) and DALLA POZZA (1965, p. 238, having changed his earlier opinion) date it before R.I.B.A. XVII, 22 (Fig. XV, p. 62), which suggests a somewhat different development of Palladio's "*invenzione.*" Zorzi proposes a lapse of at least four years between the two drawings; he places the one which he considers earlier around 1542, under the influence of Sanmicheli (in Vicenza between November 1541 and January 1542), and the later one in the early months of 1546 because of the strong influences from ancient Roman art. However, it is more logical to place them together and to date them at the latest between the last months of 1545 and the early months of 1546, as they mark the artist's progress toward formalizing his first project. On the other hand, ZORZI (1958 [II], p. 133 and 1964 [II], pp. 106-107) suggests yet another hypothesis concerning the chronology of these drawings.

115 PEE, 1939, pp. 15 ff.

116 PALLADIO, 1570, Bk. III, p. 38. The frieze and the cornice of the Basilica Aemilia, taken up again in the drawing in question and (still more emphatically) in the definitive solution for the loggias as executed, are reproduced in a drawing (Fig. XVII, p. 68) in the Museo Civico in Vicenza. ZORZI (1958 [II], p. 104, fig. 259) attributes the latter to Falconetto, with notations and measurements by Palladio (see also SPIELMANN, 1966, p. 145, N. 55).

117 A comparison which is all the more evident when we recall that the upper loggia of the Odeon was originally open (SEMENZATO, 1961, p. 77).

[118] Cf. r.i.b.a., XII, 4 r.; Zorzi, 1958 (II), p. 57, fig. 50 a; Spielmann, 1966, p. 169 (N. 205).

[119] The references to Serlio mentioned by Dalla Pozza seem rather general (1943, p. 102). Lotz (1967, p. 17) insists on a derivation exclusively from Giulio Romano for this drawing as well as for r.i.b.a. XVII, 22; but for the hypothesis that these drawings reflect the rejected project for the loggias, see n. 125. See also De Angelis d'Ossat, 1960, p. 30.

[120] *Michele Sanmicheli* (exhibition catalogue), 1960, pp. 160-161.

[121] Zorzi, 1964, p. 46.

[122] Barbieri, 1967, p. 29.

[123] Puppi, 1958.

[124] Marchini, 1966, pp. 10-11.

[125] Marchini's supposition (1966, p. 14, n. 12) that the fresco might reflect the projected reconstruction presented by Giulio Romano collapses of its own accord, as Giulio Romano never considered demolishing and reconstructing the old loggias in another form (see Chapter III).

[126] Marchini, 1966, pp. 6-7; Puppi, 1966, pp. 50, 58.

[127] Cf. Pane, 1961, p. 145. Which of Palladio's designs the author is referring to is not clear; the citation in n. 7 is obviously incorrect. Perhaps he had r.i.b.a. X, 15 in mind, which shows the niche in the pier at the upper left. However, see the reservations expressed above in regard to this drawing.

[128] Cf. Lotz, 1967, pp. 14-15.

[129] Cf. Pane, 1961, p. 146. r.i.b.a. XIII, 8, referring to a corner arch of the upper gallery and the two flanking piers, does not seem to me to pertain to this moment of the project's development; moreover, Dalla Pozza (1943, p. 106) considers it doubtful, and Pane (1961, p. 146, n. 8) attributes to it only the character of a summary scheme and not that of a variant in the group of drawings for the definitive project. It is in fact probably a later study, datable to March 1564 when the decision to put up the upper gallery of loggias called for a detailed model of the new arrangement (see below, pp. 80 ff.).

[130] Cf. Pane, 1948, pp. 77 ff.; also (but less critically controlled) Venturi, 1940, p. 332.

[131] Cf. Bettini, 1953, pp. xxiv-xxvii; 1961 (II), p. 95.

[132] Bettini, 1961, (II), pp. 95-96.

[133] Cf. Marini, 1944, pp. 75-77: " The *numerus clausus* of the intercolumniations... of Palladio's elevation is a completely different thing from the continuous rhythm... of the Roman [type of] perimeter." Moreover, as Haupt (1907, p. 15) guessed, the loggias were " the work in which Palladio least imitated ancient Roman art," although in fact they were " spiritually closer." See also Burckhardt, 1855 (1952 edition, p. 388).

[134] Besides the abovementioned portico of the Theatre of Pompey, we are reminded of the corner columns of the arches of Titus, of the Sergi in Pula, and of Augustus in Susa, to such an extent that we recall the ancient monuments which Palladio had studied in his own drawings or in those in his possession (Zorzi, 1958 [II], figs. 39, 72, 79, 80; pp. 55-56, 61-63). An allusion to corner column shafts seems to be taken up, albeit timidly, in an early Palladian project of about 1540 or even before for Palazzo Civena (r.i.b.a. XIII, 10; cf. Zorzi, 1964, p. 184, fig. 146). But certainly the closest solution to what was later executed in Vicenza is seen in the corner of the upper storey of the destroyed " House of Raphael " in the Borgo, a building begun by Bramante and finished by Raphael (cf. Bonelli, 1960, p. 25, n. 16); Palladio sketched it (Fig. XVIII, p. 71) probably as early as his first trip to Rome in 1541, emphasizing the corner view (Zorzi, 1958 [II], pp. 5, 132 and p. 137, n. 34; fig. 305).

[135] Since in the plan the angles formed by the external surfaces of the corner piers correspond exactly to those of the Quattrocento palace within (see Chapter II, n. 26).

[136] See below, p. 78.

[137] Even a purist like Bertotti-Scamozzi (1776, pp. 61 ff.) held the corners adorned with half columns to be worthy of consideration, since " con elegante robustezza dimostrano la solidità."

[138] Fiocco, 1958, p. xii.

[139] Boito, 1883, pp. 290-292.

[140] Palladio, 1570, Bk. III, pp. 42-43.

[141] Zorzi, 1961; 1961 (II), p. 147: " The drawings in the *Quattro Libri* consist of re-workings done at the time of the publication of the treatise according to the tastes of an unknown draftsman (or draftsmen), against which the architect did not consider opposing himself..."; p. 148: " It can be confirmed that all the drawings [in the treatise] are at the very least inexact, unfinished, or incorrect." In regard to the plate showing the loggias, Zorzi (1952; 1961, p. 16; 1964, p. 52) emphasizes their purely imaginary nature. Moreover, Palladio himself (1570, Bk. II, p. 4) seems to disavow the absurdity of these drawings, realistically admitting that " *nelle città quasi sempre o i muri dei vicini o le strade o le piazze pubbliche, assegnano certi termini oltre i quali non si può l'architetto estendere* "; and therefore " *fa di bisogno accomodarsi secondo l'occasione de' siti.* " Concerning the beauty of Palladio's treatise as a graphic work, see Pane, 1961, pp. 85-86. For the specialist (see also Pane, pp. 146-147), the alterations proposed for the Quattrocento palace in the treatise represent the completion of the work by a thorough transformation of the earlier structure; the failure to carry out these changes allows us to consider the Basilica as an unfinished building (an opinion shared in part by Zevi, 1966, cols. 65-66). However, Zevi notes that the modifications of the upper part of the late Gothic structure assume " strong value in the engravings of elevations of the building, but they are much less significant in an actual perspective view, since the depth of the loggias obscures the Gothic wall within."

[142] Scamozzi, 1615, pt. II, Bk. VI, Ch. vii, p. 20, r. 40. Three centuries later Cogo (1900, p. 36) took the trouble to verify that the height of the Doric arcades is in fact only 1.8 times the width, rather than twice the latter as required by the rules.

[143] We are reminded of the plates in Arnaldi (1767) and the excellent plates in Bertotti Scamozzi, 1776, pls. xxix-xxxi (Figs. XXI, XXII, XXIII, pp. 77, 81, 84). Earlier, see Leoni (1715 and 1721, III, pls. xx, xxi; Fig. XXVI, p. 102) and Muttoni (1740, pl. vii; 1744, pls. xix, xx; Fig. XX, p. 74). Goethe's admiration in 1786 (*Italienische Reise*, 1st ed. 1816-17; cf. 1948 ed., p. 482 and 1957 ed., pp. 66-67, 69) was completely generic.

[144] Boito, 1883, p. 320.

[145] Milizia, 1785, II, p. 34; Rigato, 1811, p. 22.

[146] Selvatico, 1859: he adds a lament over the excessive width of the Ionic intercolumniation and the consequent squat form of the whole corresponding space.

[147] Temenza, 1762, pp. xiii-xiv; Lodoli, 1786, p. 188.

[148] Fiocco, 1959, pp. 11-12. The same author in 1949 described the loggias as " more academic than practical," and in 1961 (pp. 173-175) he criticized their "modest, if not awkward" arrangement. Cf. also Pallucchini, 1936, p. 11.

[149] Zevi, 1966, col. 66.

[150] Lodoli, 1786, p. 188: " *E che male vi sarebbe stato ad ammettere le basi* [of the minor orders]? *La practica avrebbe corrisposto alla... teoria.* "

[151] Some reservations are expressed by Cevese, 1964 (II), p. 335.

[152] Cf. Dalla Pozza, 1965, p. 238; 1965 (II), p. 58.

[153] Pane, 1961, p. 145, considers this the most interesting drawing of the few related to the loggias that have come down to us; but he concludes: " Here we have only a timid statement.... The phase in which the Serlian aperture furnishes the key to the whole composition is still distant." Dalla Pozza, 1943, pp. 103-104, although maintaining that the earlier idea (r.i.b.a. XIII, 9) was " notably improved," admits that a satisfactory solution was still far off and did not even seem obtainable by that method. For a different dating of this drawing in the preparatory stages of the loggias (proposed by Zorzi), see n. 114. Lotz (1967, p. 17) emphasizes the derivation from Giulio Romano (also for r.i.b.a. XIII, 9).

[154] Gromort as early as 1922 (pp. 155-156) noted that doubling the columns of the smaller order in depth gives a perspective effect which is surprising in such a simple elevation.

[155] CEVESE (1962, p. 289, n. 1) notes that the compositional scheme of the loggias places the important structural emphasis on the piers, which allows the loggias to appear to be independent of any walls and instead to be standing free between the exterior space of the three piazzas and the interior space of the portico and gallery (see also 1967, p. 123).

[156] Cf. PANE, 1961 (II), p. 120: " It does not appear that we can evaluate the difference between the two [types of] articulation in a strict positive sense, as they face each other and share the same space."

[157] ZEVI, 1966, col. 66.

[158] SERLIO, 1537, cc. 33 v., 34 r. (on this, see also Chapter III, n. 43). The first citation of Serlio's design as a precedent for the Palladian loggias is by DALLA POZZA, 1943, p. 104; PANE, 1961, p. 145, considers that it " intervenes... by proposing the possibility of an absolutely new rhythm "; see also FORSSMAN, 1965, pp. 39 ff., and DE FUSCO, 1968, p. 608 and n. 29.

[159] ROSCI, 1967, p. 335. However, Serlio's design presents a solution using oculi in the spandrels of the arches, which was later taken up in the Palladian loggias. Palladio—who had already experimented with this in the Serliana at Palazzo Civena (1540) and also at the Villa Valmarana in Vigardolo (1541-44)— must have been aware of the harmony this offered with the pre-existing oculi in the upper part of the Quattrocento structure. ZORZI (1964, p. 53, n. 78) considers that the Palladian oculi in the loggias might have been derived from the analogous detail in the ground-floor arcade of the Palazzo della Ragione in Padua (concerning this hypothesis, see n. 189).

[160] CABIATI, 1945, p. 10; ZORZI, 1950; 1954, p. 120; 1958 (II), p. 5; 1960, p. 90; 1964, pp. 47, 53-54; LOTZ, 1961, p. 87; 1967 (however, here Lotz sharply reveals the diversities between the two buildings).

[161] ZORZI, 1950; 1964, pp. 46-47.

[162] Cf. LOTZ, 1967, pp. 15, 20.

[163] PALLADIO, 1570, Bk. I, *Proemio*, p. 5: " *... Messere Giacomo Sansovino scultore et architetto di nome celebre cominciò primo a far conoscere la bella maniera* [in the Veneto], *come si vede (per lasciare a dietro molte altre sue belle opere) nella Procuratia nova, la quale è il più ricco et ornato edificio che forse sia stato fatto da gli antichi in qua.*"

[164] Cf. PANE, 1948, pp. 77 ff.; HAUPT, 1907, pp. 14-15 had already noted differences, even in the analogies.

[165] LOTZ, 1961, pp. 83-84.

[166] CEVESE, 1964 (II), p. 335.

[167] LOTZ, 1967, p. 17.

[168] PANE, 1961, p. 145; see also p. 144, n. 6.

[169] Cf. LOTZ, 1967.

[170] Cf. PANE, 1960, pp. 57 ff.: " [the] composition... is at the same time an *ex-novo* creation, a remodeling, and a structural restoration "; WITTKOWER, 1962, p. 76: " Palladio's first great public success was the commission given him to support the mediaeval Palazzo della Ragione at Vicenza with a surrounding structure." PEROGALLI, 1954, p. 28, associates two unusual and similarly-conceived cases of restoration: the Tempio Malatestiano in Rimini and Palladio's loggias in Vicenza (an analogous idea was suggested by PORTALUPPI, 1955, p. 109).

[171] See Chapter II.

[172] PALLADIO, 1570, Bk. III, p. 43.

[173] PANE, 1961, p. 120. Cf. also ROGERS, 1959, p. 60: " Palladio's lesson is of an extraordinary immediacy in seeking a cultural continuity in the rapport between old and new. The Basilica... is the most outstanding example [of this], both as a work of architecture and as a cultural action. In creating his design ... Palladio acted with a subtle dialectic intent (much more so than Alberti did in the Tempio Malatestiano), as in designing an autonomous structure he nevertheless established a relationship between the old mediaeval façade and the new shape of its screen." Even ALGAROTTI (1781, p. 225) admired the Vicentine structure because of the close ties of the old with the new. Only recently IVANOFF (1967, pp. 28-29), on the basis of observations by CHASTEL (1960) and CHASTEL-KLEIN (1963, p. 168), criticized the Palladian loggias for " disguising a Gothic structure

in the ancient Roman style " according to the fashion of temporary wood and stucco festive decorations. This distorts the most profound sense of Chastel's comments: " *Palladio semble avoir exploité à sa convenance des données de l'architecture des fêtes.... Mais Palladio a manifestement résisté à l'impulsion générale qui tendait à confondre les genres; les ouvrages de l'époque doivent souvent à cette confusion un aspect trouble, amusant mais un peu faux. C'est contre quoi a finalment réagi Palladio* " (1960, pp. 32-33).

[174] Cf. ZORZI, 1953, pp. 84-85.

[175] See Chapter V.

[176] PANE, 1961, p. 364. Note, moreover, how the motif of the Palladian loggias when uprooted from the special circumstances that had determined it becomes transformed into a conventional solution. We may recall both Italian and foreign derivations (cf., for example, the use Aleotti made of it in the Teatro Farnese in Parma in 1618). See KOZAKIEWICZ (1960), HUBALA (1961), and DE AZEVEDO (1964).

[177] LOTZ, 1961, p. 86; see also 1966 (II).

[178] Cf. GALLIMBERTI, 1938, pp. 259-260: " the tall, very slender tower and the backdrop of mediaeval tower-houses [preserved in Piazza dei Signori] a scenographic rhythm in which Palladio's work [gained] monumentality but [was] unable to disrupt the mediaeval plan... The Basilica [was] set into a typically mediaeval perspective."

[179] Cf. FRANCO, 1959, p. 20 and 1959 (II), p. 22.

[180] ZEVI, 1966, col. 66.

[181] Cf. BETTINI, 1949, p. 65: " No architect ever succeeded in transforming exterior space like Palladio... focusing, so to speak, on the mysterious isolation of [a] building which reshapes the space around itself by the miraculous power of its form alone." As MARIANI (1943) had already observed rather blandly, the Vicentine loggias are an " intelligent taking-possession of a pre-existing ambience "; see also GIOVANNONI, 1943, p. 113. ZEVI likewise (1966, col. 456) sees the loggias as " a dominant and isolated personage," and LOTZ (1966, p. 123) emphasizes an analogous concept. Only ZORZI (1967, p. 170) finds that Palladio in conceiving the loggias " had perfectly understood the necessity of conditioning his imagination... to the magical circle of the great piazza... [and of establishing] a harmony with all the other earlier structures, which determined the particular conditions of mutual... coexistence."

[182] Cf. GOMBRICH, 1935, p. 138, n. 70; HARTT, 1958, p. 101. The latter, however, observes that the motif derives from Peruzzi's painted architecture in the large first-floor room of the Farnesina. See also CHASTEL, 1958, pp. 113-114.

[183] FIOCCO, 1961, pp. 173-175.

[184] WITTKOWER, 1959, p. 61; 1962, p. 77.

[185] DE ANGELIS D'OSSAT, 1960.

[186] According to MICHEL (1909, pp. 64-65), whose suggestion was repeated by GURLITT, 1921, p. x. For some formal details common also to Vignola (the combination of arched and rectangular bays), see GLOTON, 1966, p. 90.

[187] Besides the traditional precedents of the Colosseum, the Theatre of Marcellus, and the Basilica Aemilia (PEE, 1939, pp. 11 ff.), BANNISTER FLETCHER (1902, p. 18) recalls the colonnades of the Palace of Diocletian in Split; SERRA (1911, p. 355) mentions the Basilica Julia; and CREMA (1961, p. 22) also recalls the Basilica Julia and connections with Roman architecture in the eastern provinces (the arcades of the Basilica in Smyrna).

[188] PANE, 1961, p. 365.

[189] ZORZI (1964, p. 53) emphasizes the importance of both these models; regarding the second, see LOTZ, 1940, p. 217, and especially FIOCCO, 1961, p. 173, who confirms the example of the Palazzo della Ragione in Padua as the point of departure for Palladio's design. This hypothesis, refuted by CEVESE (1964 [II], p. 336), contradicts the bases and the very genesis of the Palladian project.

[190] DALLA POZZA, 1943, pp. 120-121. For the course of the construction, the fundamental source is the *Summarii delle spese per le logge* (see Manuscript Sources in the Bibliography). See in addition DALLA POZZA, 1943, pp. 117-142, and ZORZI, 1964,

pp. 48-51; 56-75, Docs. 6-52; and 323-346 (a long extract from the *Summarii*). See also Zorzi, 1958 (II), pp. 25-26 and 1962, pp. 17-19.

191 According to Magrini, 1845, pp. 88-90, Palladio was compelled to ask for money not just from month to month, but even from week to week and often for one or two days, just like any of the humblest artisans. Concerning the artist's compensation, see Dalla Pozza, 1943, p. 120. On his extreme poverty and that of his family, see Zorzi, 1962; 1964, pp. 308-309. Only after 1570, when he became the official architect of the Venetian Republic and lived with his family in Venice, did his economic situation become more respectable (Zorzi, 1953 [II], p. 124, and 1960 [II], pp. 109-110).

192 This concerns the model made from Palladio's final designs of October 1548 (see Chapter III, n. 71). Regarding the modest compensation allotted for this model (seven gold scudi), see the observations in n. 93 above concerning the related designs.

193 Dalla Pozza, 1943, p. 121. Sbari was a master builder and contractor who was approximately twenty years older than Palladio. He was affiliated with the Pedemuro studio and was enrolled in the Vicentine guild of masons and laborers from 1499 on; he died in the early months of 1566 (see Dalla Pozza, 1943, pp. 121-122, 126-129, 130-136, passim; also Zorzi, 1937, pp. 61-65; 1964, pp. 48-50, 56 ff.). It appears from the *Summarii* that he often served as intermediary between the *Provveditori alla fabbrica* and Palladio, and did not disdain to carry the architect's monthly salary to him, or to his wife or family, himself (Zorzi, 1937, p. 63).

194 Pozza, 1952, p. 30; see also Pigafetta, *Descrizione del Territorio e Contado di Vicenza*, cc. 54b-55a.

195 Pozza, 1957, and a half-century earlier, Cogo, 1900, p. 22.

196 Piovene is 27 kilometers from Vicenza, or about 18 miles as counted at that time.

197 Dalla Pozza, 1943, pp. 124-127 (includes other interesting details on the subject).

198 Dalla Pozza, 1943, p. 123.

199 Dalla Pozza, 1943, pp. 123-124 (also for other events up to November 1549).

200 On September 25, two troni, sixteen marchetti were paid to him " *per pagar uno cavallo da nollo et altre spese per andare a Piovene* " (Zorzi, 1964, p. 323 [from the *Summarii*]; p. 48).

201 Zorzi, 1964, p. 324 (from the *Summarii*); Dalla Pozza, 1943, p. 126.

202 Zorzi, 1958 (II), pp. 20-21.

203 Zorzi, 1937, p. 12. The dispersal of the material (columns, capitals, balusters, etc.) began in this way: it was partly broken up and used in the new foundations and perhaps partly re-employed. Attempts have been made to find traces of the material in other buildings in the city (see Chapter II, n. 58, second paragraph).

204 The architect was paid twenty troni for his transfer to Venice on December 24th (Zorzi, 1958 [II], p. 21). The contracts with the Venetian stonemasons were entered into about the middle of January 1550 (Dalla Pozza, 1943, p. 127).

205 Dalla Pozza, 1943, pp. 127, 129.

206 Dalla Pozza, 1943, p. 130.

207 Dalla Pozza, 1943, p. 131. Zorzi, 1964, p. 48, and Lotz, 1967, n. 19, think instead that the two corresponding corner arches of the old Formenton loggias were demolished in June 1551. But we may recall that the western side of the Formenton loggias had been pulled down as early as the beginning of August 1496, at the time of the Rizzo-Spaventa modifications.

208 Dalla Pozza, 1943, p. 131; the relevant document of payment is published in the Appendix (pp. 206-207) and in Zorzi (1964, pp. 56-57; see also p. 331 and n. 1). Note that these corner arches ended up costing twenty ducats more than had been envisaged because of the greater amount of work involved; in fact, according to Lotz (1967, pp. 19-21), Palladio was not satisfied with the early estimates and must have insisted on a more solid construction of the corner. It is worth noting that the incorrect calculation was pinpointed and corrected as soon

as the construction started. Palladio reveals himself here as a technician who had acquired during years of apprenticeship a fundamental knowledge of structural details. This is another important point demonstrating the difference between Palladio's training, which took place directly on the construction site, and that of Sansovino, who had more the sculptor's approach.

209 Dalla Pozza, 1943, p. 131.

210 Dalla Pozza, 1943, pp. 130-131.

211 Zorzi (1922, pp. 14-15) publishes a document of February 8, 1552, which offers a decisive confirmation of the architect's activity at the Palazzo della Ragione; this was so constant as to qualify him from that time onward as undisputed city architect. See also Dalla Pozza, 1943, p. 131.

212 Zorzi, 1964, p. 57, Doc. 7.

213 Arnaldi, 1767, pp. xlv ff.

214 Dalla Pozza, 1943, p. 132.

215 Ibid.

216 Dalla Pozza, 1943, p. 133; concerning this vault, see Chapter II.

217 Dalla Pozza, 1943, p. 133. Contemporaneously, all the old Formenton loggias on the northern side were torn down (by the end of 1557).

218 Cogo, 1900, p. 28, pointed out, in a hypothetical completion of the Palladian loggias, that along the fourth (eastern) side a projection in line with the single existing arch on that side would have to meet up with the corner of the Basilica which had been completed at the side opposite (i. e., on the south, where an arch is missing and the loggias join to the Arco degli Zavatteri), but that this line would be at least 1.8 meters off.

219 Magrini, 1845, p. 23; Zorzi, 1964, p. 58, Doc. 11.

220 Dalla Pozza, 1943, pp. 133-134; Zorzi, 1964, p. 58, Doc. 12.

221 Cf. Magrini, 1845, pp. 80-81.

222 Magrini, 1845, p. 81; Zorzi, 1964, pp. 309-312.

223 Zorzi, 1964, p. 309.

224 Cf. Dalla Pozza, 1943, pp. 135-136.

225 Magrini, 1845, pp. 82-83; Zorzi, 1964, p. 310. Ferramosca's compromise consisted of a proposal to halve Palladio's salary for as long as the public subvention for the loggias remained halved. Magrini verifies that only Ferramosca (who was custodian of the loggias and legal consultant to the Commune) and a few others were opposed to Palladio on this occasion. He suggests that Ferramosca's ill-will derived from his intimacy with Giandomenico Scamozzi, who built the Villa at Barbano for him around 1568 (Barbieri, 1952, pp. 49-50). This hypothesis, confirmed by Zorzi (1964, pp. 310-312), provides the first inklings of the " new directions " which were destined to triumph in little more than twenty years with the youthful works of Vincenzo Scamozzi.

226 Dalla Pozza, 1943, p. 136.

227 Dalla Pozza, 1943, p. 133. The first Doric arch facing Piazza delle Erbe, which vaulted the " *cantonale delle pescherie*," was begun in March 1558 but was still " *non fato mezzo.*"

228 Dalla Pozza, 1943, p. 134; Zorzi, 1964, pp. 58-59, Doc. 14.

229 Cf. Dalla Pozza, 1943, p. 134-135. It appears from the document that two columns and some parts of the pilasters and capitals for a new arch facing Piazza delle Erbe were also prepared; but the document states that " *al presente non si farà ditto volto.*"

230 Zorzi, 1964, p. 60, Doc. 16.

231 Zorzi, 1964, pp. 60-61, Doc. 17.

232 Monza, *Cronaca*, 1888 edition, p. 10, 18 aprile 1563: " *Fui in Consiglio per agiutar Palladio, che li Deputati metteano parte di sospender la fabrica del Palazzo; et parlò contro la parte Nicola di Negri, et cascò di largo.*" Zorzi, 1964, p. 311, raises the suspicion that also at this time the *longa manus* of Girolamo Ferramosca was secretly at work. Fabio Monza, author of the *Cronaca*, was reported by Palladio himself (1570, Bk I, *Proemio*, P. 5) to be " *intelligente di assaissime cose.*"

233 Zorzi, 1964, p. 61, Doc. 18.

234 Dalla Pozza, 1943, p. 136.

[235] DALLA POZZA, 1943, p. 136: The relative payments were in April and May. Cf. also ZORZI, 1951, p. 151, n. 6 (provides some clarifications, which are perhaps not completely accurate, on the state of the work at that time).

[236] ZORZI, 1961 (III), p. 204. The expression is not very clear, but in all likelihood it concerned modifications of the northern stair (built in 1495-96 by Bernardino da Milano; see Chapter II) and of the door nearest the same stair leading to the Hall. We are not concerned here with the two stairs that "vano in Torre" (dei Bissara, or del Girone?).

[237] ZORZI, 1964, pp. 50 and 61, Doc. 19.

[238] DALLA POZZA, 1943, p. 137.

[239] ZORZI, 1950; 1964, p. 47, n. 34; see also n. 129.

[240] ZORZI observed (1958 [II], p. 126) that Palladio had already designed the Ionic volute in the form indicated in Barbaro's description (in the 1556 edition of Vitruvius) much earlier than his intimacy with Barbaro, i. e., as early as the time of his first studies of Vitruvius. Actually, he used this form as far back as 1549, in a preparatory design for the upper gallery of the loggias which dates a good three years before the publication in 1552 of Giuseppe Salviati's pamphlet on the subject. In this pamphlet, Salviati attributes to himself the invention of the means for arriving at the exact Ionic volute according to Vitruvius, and he dedicated the work to Daniele Barbaro. The latter seems to have believed Salviati and almost accuses Palladio of plagiarism in connection with Salviati (1556). Even if the date of the design for the Ionic order is moved from 1549 (which is wrong in any case; if anything, it would refer to September-October 1548) to 1564, Zorzi's clarification remains valid: the drawings of the Ionic volute made by Palladio during his studies of Roman antiquities from 1545 to 1547 certainly precede Salviati's work (see ZORZI, 1958 [II]), p. 135 and the drawings in figs. 170, 285, 287, 308, 309 [Fig. XIX, p. 73]).

[241] From the executory contract of April 18, 1566 (see n. 246) it appears clear that " la bassa del quarisello [pedestal]... è stata da poi agionta par miser Andrea Palladio architetto " and did not figure in the first such agreement entered into with Alvise Sbari.

[242] Cf. DALLA POZZA, 1943, p. 138. MAGRINI, 1845, p. 85, observes that this indication reveals to us the way in which, in the process of executing his designs, Palladio varied his original concept according to circumstances that arose during the work.

[243] COGO (1900, p. 36) notes that the Ionic arcade achieves the appropriate height (double the width) only when the height of the balustrade is included; in any case, if the balustrade were not open, one would not visually relate it to the void of the arch.

[244] Cf. DALLA POZZA, 1943, p. 139.

[245] With the agreement of February 25, 1565 (see ZORZI, 1964, pp. 50 and 61, Doc. 20. Also DALLA POZZA, 1943, p. 137).

[246] ZORZI, 1964, pp. 50 and 61, Doc. 21. Also DALLA POZZA, 1943, p. 138. The new contract provides an increase of thirteen ducats in the compensation to the stonemasons, to cover the addition of the " bassa del quarisello."

[247] ZORZI, 1964, p. 62, Doc. 25; DALLA POZZA, 1943, p. 139. An indirect confirmation derives from two sources: VASARI in his life of Sansovino (second edition of 1568) describes the Palladian loggias as " con due portici di compartimento dorico, fatti con bellissime colonne " (ed. Milanesi, 1881, VII, p. 527); this is quite accurate, since at that time only the two lower porticoes on Piazza dei Signori and on the western side had been built. But cf. SANSOVINO (1575, c. 116 a): " Il palazzo publico [of Vicenza] è... di fuori ornato con architettura dorica et ionica et molto bene inteso."

[248] ZORZI, 1964, pp. 50 and 62, Doc. 24.

[249] DALLA POZZA, 1943, p. 139; PANE, 1961, pp. 30, 32: see 21 marzo 1570 and 26 ottobre 1571.

[250] ZORZI, 1964, pp. 50 and 62, Doc. 26.

[251] The contract is dated July 25, 1570; there are payments on August 19 and September 6 (ZORZI, 1964, pp. 63-64, Docs. 27, 28, 29; pp. 50, 304). Contemporaneously Raffioli had also to see to the arrangement of the " tromba " through which the north

stair of the building passed (Plate 43), cutting through the pavement of the upper loggias. The carpenter Battista Marchesi, always " iuxta il dessegno et ordine che li darà Miser Andrea Paladio," undertook to roof the four new arches of the just-completed upper gallery with larch wood (See also DALLA POZZA, 1943, p. 139).

[252] It should be recalled that shortly after 1570, when Palladio moved to Venice in the service of the Venetian Republic (ZORZI, 1964, pp. 130-136), his assistance with the work on the loggias and also his visits to Vicenza became rather intermittent. Thus we can understand why the deliberation of May 5, 1572, and the subsequent agreements were ineffectual: i. e., the agreement of June 6, 1572, with the carpenter Battista Marchesi (concerning Marchesi, see ZORZI, 1964, p. 50, n. 55) for the erection of " sei archi... quatro di sopra et doi di sotto verso le pescarie, et voltando il canton verso la Piazza dele herbe " and the other decisions in this regard of July 12, 1572, and January 4, 1573 (ZORZI, 1964, pp. 64-65, Docs. 30, 31, 32, 33). The whole resulted in the building of one arch, agreed to on August 29, 1573 (ZORZI, 1964, pp. 66-67, Doc. 37) and under construction in 1574 (ZORZI, 1964, pp. 50; DALLA POZZA, 1943, pp. 139-140). This is substantiated by a view of Vicenza dated around 1571 (now in the Biblioteca Angelica in Rome; published by Ackerman, 1967 [II]), in which the northern side of the loggias — finished only between 1585 and 1597 — is shown as completed, even in the upper gallery. Actually, " sixteenth-century cartographers frequently completed structures in progress when this could be done simply by carrying on motives already initiated. The draftsman here finished the Basilica because there was no question of how construction would continue, and because it would be impossible at this scale convincingly to draw partly-built arches and vaults hidden by scaffolding " (ACKERMAN, art. cit., p. 58).

On February 25, 1574, it was decided to renew the interior plastering and the pavement of the Hall of Palazzo della Ragione. The agreement for the plastering was entered into March 15th; here, too, the masons were committed to follow Palladio's directions. The architect for his part undertook to find suitable workers in Venice and to obtain a special rope from the Venetian Arsenal, useful for hauling stones up to the second gallery of loggias (ZORZI, 1964, pp. 67-68, Docs. 38-39; pp. 50, 304; FASOLO, 1938, pp. 261-262).

We might mention here that the new plastering of the Hall did not in fact destroy hypothetical paintings by Paris Bordone and Titian presumed to have been there (RIDOLFI, 1648 [1914 edition, I, p. 230]; followed by ALVERA, Notizie sulla Basilica). Paintings by Bordone (The Drunkenness of Noah) and by Titian (The Judgement of Solomon), on the contrary, were executed in 1521 for the old Loggia del Capitaniato (BORTOLAN, 1892, pp. 15-16), which was replaced after 1570 by Palladio's new Loggia. Titian's painting disappeared at that time, and only Bordone's work remained (this was visible up until the end of the Settecento). See MAGRINI, 1845, Annotazioni, p. xxxiv and MORSOLIN, 1892; also PUPPI, 1963, pp. 415-416, n. 44.

On April 16, 1581, fifty ducats were allotted to erect an altar dedicated to St. Vincent, the patron saint of the city, in the Hall, with an appropriate altarpiece (ARNALDI, 1767, pp. liv-lv).

[253] DALLA POZZA, 1943, p. 140.

[254] ZORZI, 1964, pp. 51 and 68-69, Doc. 42. See also DALLA POZZA, 1943, p. 140. It is likely that Grazioli was a descendant or a relative of the Francesco Grazioli (d. circa 1536) mentioned in Thieme-Becker Künstlerlexicon (1921). Francesco and his son Bartolomeo were stonemasons and architects of Lombard origin; they were active in Asolo, where they were the authors of various works including the famous " palazzina longobarda. " Francesco may have been responsible for the " Barco della Regina Cornaro " in Altivole (PUPPI, 1962 [II]). Another native of Asolo, Francesco Albanese, worked in Vicenza on the keystones of the loggias from 1564 on (see Chapter VI).

[255] ZORZI, 1964, pp. 51 and 69-70, Doc. 43. See also DALLA POZZA, 1943, pp. 140-141.

[256] Cf. ARNALDI, 1767, pp. lvi-lvii. For the February 12th document, see ZORZI, 1964, pp. 51 and 70, Doc. 44. On that date

it was also decided to construct a new stair at the south corner of the building, corresponding to the already-existing one at the north; this was to be " *in quella forma e dissegno che sarà presentato e approbato per questo Consiglio.* " But nothing was done about it before 1610 (see below, n. 265).

257 ZORZI, 1964, pp. 70-71, Doc. 45; DALLA POZZA, 1943, pp. 141-142. Grazioli had also made " *la porta da meza scala del palazzo di tutto punto con legnami prede figure serramenti e con il pozzo* [railing] *intorno* "; that is to say, he had arranged the arch and the well of the north stairway (Plate 43), which mounts from the lower gallery to the upper one. For the " *figure,* " see Chapter VI.

258 ZORZI, 1964, pp. 71-72, Doc. 47.

259 ZORZI, 1964, p. 72, Doc. 49; DALLA POZZA, 1943, p. 142.

260 See COGO, 1900, p. 23.

261 Cf. DALLA POZZA, 1943, p. 107.

262 This is the side which leans most dangerously (see Chapter V).

263 ZORZI, 1964, pp. 72-73, Doc. 50; DALLA POZZA, 1943, p. 142.

264 DALLA POZZA, 1943, p. 142.

265 ZORZI, 1964, pp. 73-75, Doc. 52. The resolution of February 12, 1587, come to nothing (see n. 256). Only on June 12, 1609, did the Council of the Hundred approve a design for the south stairs, prepared by Grazioli and Benetello and presented by Leonardo Valmarana (ZORZI, 1964, p. 73, Doc. 51). The relevant model made from this design must have been followed in the execution (see also ZORZI, 1964, p. 51). The exact chronology is set out by MAGRINI (1845, p. 87), but there are strange errors concerning this stairway: MAGRINI (loc. cit.) states that the model was made by Giovanni Grazioli in 1587, and this date is repeated by COGO (1900, p. 23) and by the author of the pamphlet *Il Palazzo della Ragione in Vicenza* (1875, p. 72). The latter claims that the stair was constructed in 1598 and this error is retained in the *Guida di Vicenza* (1953 and 1956, p. 91), where the termination date is given as 1610, which is actually the date when it was begun.

266 *Il Palazzo della Ragione in Vicenza*, 1875, p. 75; ZANELLA, 1880, p. 33. There are six drawings in the Museo Civico in Vicenza related to this stairway (Inv. D 50, 51 and 551-554). Two of these (50-51) are signed with the name of Giambattista Albanese; one sheet (50) corresponds to the project later executed.

On the basis of a passage in the contract of September 30, 1597 (ZORZI, 1964, pp. 71-72, Doc. 47), ZORZI, 1964, p. 51, states that the stair was designed and executed by Giovanni Antonio Grazioli. This not only distorts the sense of the document but also contradicts the fact that the stairway, which was adapted to the Palladian arch at its foot — as the preparatory drawings in the museum demonstrate — cannot have preceded but must rather have followed the erection of this arch, which dates back to about 1605. Similarly, the *Guida di Vicenza* (1953 and 1956, p. 106) assigns the stairway to Francesco Albanese, as does PAVAN TADDEI (1960). However, the document of September 30, 1597, confirms the logical suggestion that at that point there was an earlier stairway which had to be demolished, as it was not suitable for the new loggias.

SELVATICO (1859, p. 14) maintains that since the work on this stairway was badly executed, it had damaged the foundation of the arch to which it was joined. In 1778 the stairway was " *rimessa tutta di nuovo... di pietra viva* " (DIAN, *Notizie*, II, pp. 447-448; LAVANELLO-CORONA, *Memorie*, under 1778; FAVETTA, *Fatti successi in Vicenza*, entry dated March 12, 1778). In 1846, Berti — continuing an undertaking that had been commissioned to Malacarne five years earlier — planned to demolish the stair and replace it with a wider one embracing three arches. But the idea was turned down, and in 1855 the original stair was renovated (see also FORMENTON, 1867, p. 605 and 1870, pp. 33-34; BORTOLAN, 1885, p. 8).

267 CASTELLINI, *Descrizione della città di Vicenza*, I, cc. 276 ff.; ARNALDI, 1767, pp. xlv ff. confirms this and cites another manuscript source by Castellini; cf. also MAGRINI, 1845, pp. 23, 86, and ALVERA, *Notizie sulla Basilica*. Only CASTELLINI, *Storia della città di Vicenza*, Bk. XVIII, 1821-22 edition, p. 167, publishes the date 1630.

268 DALLA POZZA, 1943, p. 142.

269 MANTESE, 1964, pp. 1076-77.

270 CASTELLINI, *Descrizione della città di Vicenza*, I, cc. 276 ff.

271 Certain inevitable inaccuracies and " slips " pointed out by COGO (1900, p. 38) in this regard seem very insignificant.

272 Cf. PANE, 1960, pp. 57-58 and 1961, p. 148; only here can the examination of the question be considered profound.

273 PALLADIO, 1570, Bk. III, p. 42; see also the two earlier readings in the *Frammenti Correr*, in the Codex Cicogna (ZORZI, 1958 [II], p. 191).

274 PANE, 1961, p. 148.

275 PALLADIO, 1570, Bk, III, p. 42: " *Si come gli antichi fecero le lor Basiliche, acciò che il verno e la state gli uomini avessero ove raunarsi a trattar commodamente le lor cause et i lor negocii: così a tempi nostri in ciascuna città d'Italia e fuori si hanno alcune sale publiche, le quali si possono chiamar meritamente Basiliche: percio che lor presso è l'abitazione del supremo magistrato, onde vengono a esser parte di quella; e propriamente questo nome, Basilica, significa casa regale: et anco perché vi stanno i giudici a render ragione al popolo.* " With the Romanesque-Gothic building tradition here supplanted, the structure was joined to the mainstream of Roman architecture. Palladio the theoretician betrayed Palladio the constructor, who fortunately had had a very different attitude in regard to the old Vicentine building.

For a refutation of the hypothesis that the name recalls an analogous Roman building existing on the site in ancient times and partially incorporated in the present building, see GIRARDI, 1924, p. 40. SETTI's curious opinion (1902) is contradicted by the architect's statement quoted above; however, it is worth recalling, as it suggests a certain basic truth: " Just as the side aisles with their projecting buttresses served to secure the great vaults of the ancient basilicas, so likewise these loggias [function]; and the whole building was called [the] ' Basilica ' by Palladio, because of the structural principle that gave form to his project. "

V

THE LATER HISTORY OF THE LOGGIAS

Only a little more than fifty years after Vicenza's Palazzo della Ragione had been perfected by the construction of the Palladian loggias, which were completed in 1614, the city was already considering the necessity for certain restorations. On June 12, 1670, the Council of the Hundred found the great structure in need of being brought back to a "*stato lodabile*,"[1] and 1,000 ducats were earmarked for that purpose on June 13, 1674. On the 16th of the same month the sum was augmented by another 1,000 ducats.[2] Interventions were necessary in 1681 for repairs to the leading of the roof and to the gutters, again in 1691 and after the earthquake of 1695, and in 1697, 1704, and 1736.[3]

The earthquake of February 25, 1695, was particularly serious. The vaults of the loggias were damaged "*a segno talle che minacciando precipitosa caduta si è dovuto farl[e] puntellare*." As the necessary money was lacking, application was made for a loan "*del denaro delle Regallie et intercessure del Santo Monte*." The work was entrusted to two entrepreneurs, the brothers Giacomo and Giuseppe Farini. Payments were made on May 31 and on July 17, 1695. We have an estimate of expenses drawn up on the 18th of April by the *capomaestro* Carlo Borella for the restoration of 1697.[4]

Much apprehension but little damage was caused on the other hand by a fire which broke out on the evening of Christmas Day, 1745, in an underground storage area of the palace facing Piazza dei Signori.[5] On February 27, 1752 it was decided to bar the windows of the Hall with iron rods "*perché ad ognuno altrimenti era lecito entrare in palazzo di giorno e di notte*."[6] Some years later a new door was opened in the Hall, and two windows in the Hall looking out on the southern loggia were renovated after designs by Ottone Calderari; these were carried out by a certain Angeli, a famous local stonecutter of the period.[7]

Notwithstanding all the care, by 1765 the palace appeared to be in disastrous condition, especially on the inside.[8] In that same year, aid having been requested of the Venetian government, a general restoration was ordered.[9] Due to unexpected impediments, however, the work was not begun before 1775-76,[10] after a new subvention of 2,000 ducats had been obtained (1775), as well as an assured annual contribution from Venice of 560 ducats for the next decade (to which the city later added 500 ducats of its own for a decade).[11] In 1778 the "external" restoration of the loggias was completed under the direction of Enea Arnaldi, with Ottone Calderari as consultant.[12] Between January and May of 1780 the "internal" work on the Quattrocento palace and roof was begun.[13]

In 1783 Enea Arnaldi in his role as

XXIV - ANDREA PALLADIO, *Loggias of the " Basilica " in Vicenza: detail of the northwest corner.*
From *I Quattro Libri dell'Architettura*, 1570, III, xx

Soprintendente alla fabbrica made a precise report of what had been done up until that time.[14] The stairs leading down toward Piazza delle Erbe had been completely renovated[15] and the balustrades of the loggias had been repaired, as well as the bases of the statues, missing sections of the friezes, and several beams (some of which were very worn or actually crumbling). Efforts were made to prevent further infiltration of moisture within the loggias and within the great roof, especially on the side facing Contrà Muschieria and the palace of the podestà. Also, the job of painting the interior of the Hall (done partly in blue with some decorations) had been begun.

Arnaldi concluded by indicating the direction which should be followed in order to complete the projected and prescribed restoration: the whole *carena* had to be fixed, both the leading and the framework; the interior had to be repainted, as they had begun to do; the intrados of the loggias all had to be plastered; and the floors of the loggias and Hall and the window-frames had to be redone, and the window-panes replaced.

In 1783, shortly after Arnaldi's recommendations were made, the work of preparing the lead slabs for repairs to the roof was begun at the convent of S. Biagio;[16] this was a large undertaking for that time and was not yet finished in 1791. Another three-year subvention was necessary in 1791, and yet others in 1792 and 1794.[17] By the end of 1793 the *carena* had been repaired, but contemporaries found that the work had been done quite poorly and this negative impression was quickly confirmed by subsequent events.[18]

In 1797 and 1798 the Hall was devastated by the occupation of French troops during the Invasion. From that time on it fell into progressive abandon, and after the suppression of the free civic judiciary offices which were located there it unfortunately became useless. The neglect reached such a state that on one morning in August of 1809 several dissolute youths armed with rifles went bird-hunting under the spacious vault.[19]

In September 1810 Giacomo Fontana and Bartolomeo Malacarne seem to have interested themselves again in the roof, which had not been well-repaired in the closing years of the Settecento;[20] in 1818 and 1819 a polemic on the subject flared up between some professors from the Accademia in Venice who had been consulted and Malacarne. The competent Venetians maintained that the covering of the *carena* ought to be redone in lead, but Malacarne insisted on copper as being both lighter and more resistant. On the basis of a detailed report by Malacarne himself, the *Congregazione Centrale Veneta* (which had been charged with the decision) chose copper. The plan of execution was presented on July 18, 1823, and was approved August 2, 1824.

When work was begun, it was noted that a large part of the timber constituting the framework of the *carena* was ruined and had to be replaced; however, everything was completed by 1828. To prevent oxidation, the copper sheets were covered with a special bond of tin, zinc, antimony, and bismuth;[21] this was a recent invention of Vincenzo Pepe, a Neapolitan chemistry professor, and had already been used on the cupola of the new Duomo in Brescia.[22]

In 1827 the central arch of the Basilica (i.e., the pedestrian passageway between Piazza dei Signori and Piazza delle Erbe) was modernized, and the shops underneath were rendered more uniform after a plan by Bartolomeo Malacarne.[23] This project had been formulated in 1825 and was very simple and modest, but perhaps not completely inappropriate.[24] However, some people would have unwisely preferred to imitate a fifteenth-century style, as that was the epoch to which the surviving shops under the loggias belonged.[25]

In 1830, when this time Cicognara desired "quick restorations" of the building,[26] it was decided to redo the floor of the upper northern loggia with large flat blocks of stone;[27] two years later, almost all the flooring of the second storey of loggias was renewed.[28] On July 20, 1831, Stefano Madonetta finished the job of "painting" at the Basilica; this probably involved decorating the inner walls of the Hall in the neo-Gothic taste of which that artist was particularly fond.[29]

In 1837, taking advantage of an 1836 plan by Zilio for the transformation of the remaining shops on ground level, Antonio Piovene and Luigi Loschi advised completely demolishing all the shops under the northern and southern loggias. Not satisfied with that, they also wanted to have the two stairs demolished (i.e., the Quattrocento stair on the northern side and the Seicento one on the southern side) and to replace them with a large stair to be built on the western side, between the Palazzo della Ragione and the palace of the podestà; thus the ancient access to the Hall would have been restored.

Fortunately, the ill-advised idea—which would at one stroke have canceled several pages of the complex history of the monument—was not accepted. However, in 1843 fruitless discussions were still going on about demolishing the stairs (or at least the one on the southern side),[30] and in 1893 some of the shops "cluttering" the southern loggia facing on Piazza delle Erbe (those counting eastward from the present Dal Monico shop) were demolished.[31]

Meanwhile efforts were made in two different stages to adapt the inside of the Hall to some sort of use. In 1832 Malacarne received a first commission to initiate studies on this question; after his death in 1842, the unfulfilled charge passed to the city engineer, Pietro Scaldaferro. Here also, hesitancies dragged on and due to the events of 1848 nothing was done in the end.[32] In the meantime, the ground floor was paved in 1841 with large flagstones; in 1843 the shops facing Piazzetta Palladio were made to match exactly those in the central passageway (Malacarne, 1827), and in 1846 the rest of the shops in the eastern passageway between Piazza dei Signori and Piazza delle Erbe received the same treatment.[33]

Soon after the middle of the nineteenth century grave concern arose about the structural condition of the building. Alarm about this question had been felt since 1836, especially in regard to the southern flank. However, an on-the-spot investigation in that year by the architects Bartolomeo Malacarne, Carlo Barrera, and Carlo Greco found the situation to be less serious than had been feared; it was observed that the bulge of the southern loggias was probably a centuries-old phenomenon and was not dangerously progressive. The consultants limited themselves to proposing that the pier on the right of the stairway leading down to the "Pescaria" be restored, and to advising that the Doric cornice be covered with metal sheets.[34]

Finally in 1858 a special commission was named to study the question and was charged with reporting to the Archduke Ferdinand Maxmilian, the Governor of Lombardy-Venetia, for the information of the Austrian Emperor.[35] We have an account of this drawn up in 1858 by Pietro Selvatico (one of the most authoritative members of the commission) and published in Milan in 1859; from it the necessity for a prompt and radical intervention can

XXV - CRISTOFORO DALL'ACQUA, *Piazza dei Signori and Piazzetta Palladio.* From the *Vedute vicentine* (1770-80)

be deduced.[36] But, as had so often happened, the work was put off: only in 1869 was it decided to begin, in view of the *Esposizione Regionale Veneta* which was to have been held in the Palazzo della Ragione in 1871.[37] At that time the pavements of the Hall and the loggias were redone with *pietre di macigno* from Monte Merlo and with white stones from S. Ambrogio in Verona. The vault over the large northern stairway was repaired, and fifteen small columns in the balustrade of the stairs which were very worn were replaced. The upper balustrade of the loggias, the pedestals of the statues, and the copper roofing (wherever necessary) were restored; the loggia vaults were plastered; and the Lion of St. Mark on the eastern side of the Hall was newly gilded. But the radical intervention that had been hoped for was not realized,[38] and a few years later a new cry of alarm was raised

for the still-disturbing structural condition of the building.[39]

In subsequent years a chorus of complaints arose, which broke out anew at the beginning of this century when the "technicians" descended to polemics, dividing into two camps. Some of them maintained that the instability came from the slipping of the Palladian loggias toward the outside, which was especially evident on the southern side facing Piazza delle Erbe and which consequently "pulled" on the Quattrocento palace.[40] Others held that the weak point was certainly to be sought on the south side, but within the construction of Domenico da Venezia's palace.[41] The controversy ended as could be foreseen, with everything at exactly the same point as when it had started.

The only thing gained was the incentive for a more exhaustive examination of the building's condition, extending to an investigation of the basement and the foundations.[42] It was ascertained that the most dangerous area of the foundations was in the middle, where the subsoil had been furrowed for ages by the drainage of filthy rain water from the high part of the city toward the Bacchiglione. The vestiges of a sewer with brick vaulting were found, the walls of which were disintegrating and which was undermined at the base, the pavement having been partially carried away. Thus, during periods of heavy rain the water had overflowed and spread over a vast area, with notable damage.

Nevertheless, these alarms must be at least partially exaggerated, as in practice the Basilica managed to survive without excessive difficulties until 1945. On the 18th of March of that year, just at the conclusion of World War II, an air raid hit the building with incendiary bombs causing a fire in the roof—which completely collapsed as a result—as well as a variety of serious damages to the masonry and to the three upper arches of the loggias in the northwest corner.[43]

However, as early as 1947 the work of restoration had been initiated by the Soprintendenza ai Monumenti in Venice, under the direction of the architect Ferdinando Forlati. Restoration consisted mainly of enclosing the shell of loggias at the top with a ring of reinforced concrete, which helped to consolidate the entire structure of the edifice; then the enormous *carena* was courageously rebuilt. However, it was necessary to replace the old wooden weight-carrying framework with a new framework strengthened by a core of reinforced concrete faced with oak. In this way, wood provided by the upland plain of the Sette Comuni was employed as in the old days for the inside facing, and copper for the roofing.[44] The result, which only the excessively scrupulous critic would condemn, is unobjectionable on the practical level;[45] moreover, it has restored equilibrium to the building and has given back to the piazza its own unforgettable physiognomy.[46]

The work was finished in September of 1949: the opportunity was taken to restore the floor of the Hall, and it was decided to lower all the pavement of Piazza dei Signori and of Piazzetta Palladio so that a three-step base could be constructed at the bottom of the Basilica.[47]

The controversy over the "three steps" was long and often heated.[48] In 1948 a competion on the subject was set up; it was won by the "Trevi" project (Cattaneo, Dalla Pozza, and Ortolani), which provided that the pavement of Piazza dei Signori and Piazzetta Palladio should be lowered about 30 centimeters. However the City Council turned the project down in April 1949, as they were unconvinced by an experiment that had been made and were afraid of compromising the other buildings surrounding the piazzas.

The Consiglio Superiore delle Belle Arti became concerned, as well as the Congresso Nazionale di Storia dell'Architettura, which was held in Vicenza in 1949. The project, subsequently re-examined after certain modifications, was approved in 1950 and executed. The discussion turned above all on the question of whether or not the steps were a part of Palladio's design, and why they had never been executed; for as far back as anyone could see, the bases of the lower order of half-columns had always been placed directly on the pavement of the piazzas.

The supporters of the hypothesis that the three steps were originally in Palladio's design based their argument on the illustration in the *Quattro Libri*,[49] where the Basilica is portrayed on a podium of precisely this type. This was easy to attack by stating that the value of the engraving as proof of the architect's genuine intent is slight indeed.[50] On the other hand, those who upheld a different hypothesis according to which the steps would never have existed[51] could also be refuted with valid arguments drawn from the related bibliography[52] as well as from documentary sources.[53] However, when the project was finished in 1950 the short podium unmistakably gave more proportion to the loggias, as well as providing a more appropriate separation from the vast space of the piazzas.[54]

NOTES TO CHAPTER V

[1] FORMENTON, 1870, pp. 29 ff.

[2] *Il Palazzo della Ragione in Vicenza*, 1875, pp. 82 ff.

[3] See n. 2.

[4] The accounts for 1695 and 1697 were brought to my attention by Giangiorgio Zorzi, who kindly furnished me with transcriptions of the relevant documents.

[5] F. ARNALDI, *Memorie*, cc. 15*b*-16*a*.

[6] F. ARNALDI, *Memorie*, c. 48*b*; ALVERA, *Notizie sulla Basilica*.

[7] ALVERA, *Notizie sulla Basilica*. An indication of the exact year is lacking; however, the work is recorded between 1752 and 1778. Judging from the quality of the mouldings, the door in question seems to be the one closest to the top of the southern stair. As for Angeli, Alvera records that " *per la prima volta fece vedere di sostenere in aria l'arco del Campo Marzo nella occasione di rimettere a quello il zoccolo di masegna.*" This work was finished on May 20, 1752, as F. ARNALDI indicates (*Memorie*, cc. 50*a*-50*b*). The arch had been erected in 1608 and was demolished in 1938 (cf. *Guida di Vicenza*, 1953 and 1956, pp. 12-13).

[8] F. ARNALDI, *Supplica ai Deputati del Comune.*

[9] *Il Palazzo della Ragione in Vicenza*, 1875, pp. 82 ff. Help was also requested from the Venetian government in 1760.

[10] ARNALDI-TORNIERI, *Memorie*, II, c. 86*b*: On June 9, 1775, he notes that " *in questi giorni* " restoration was begun on the palace, but the *Memorie* of LAVANELLO-CORONA date the start of the work in 1776.

[11] *Il Palazzo della Ragione in Vicenza*, 1875, pp. 82 ff.

[12] DIAN, *Notizie delli due secoli XVIII e XIX*, II, c. 448; LAVANELLO-CORONA, *Memorie*, anno 1778.

[13] FAVETTA, *Fatti successi in Vicenza*: On January 15, 1780, the work on the roof of the palace began; ARNALDI-TORNIERI, *Memorie*, III, c. 120*b*, states that the restoration of the Hall inside was then being started. LAVANELLO-CORONA, *Memorie*, notes that in 1780 the restoration of the lead roof was begun.

[14] E. ARNALDI, *Relazione sui restauri*. Concerning these restorations (begun in 1775), see also BALDARINI, 1779, II, pp. 3-8; DIAN, *Notizie delli due secoli XVIII e XIX*, III, cc. 466-474; ALVERA, *Notizie sulla Basilica*.

[15] See Chapter IV, n. 266, third paragraph.

[16] LAVANELLO-CORONA, *Memorie*, anno 1793.

[17] *Il Palazzo della Ragione in Vicenza*, 1875, pp. 82 ff.

[18] LAVANELLO-CORONA, *Memorie*, anno 1793.

[19] ARNALDI-TORNIERI, *Memorie*, V, cc. 312*b*-313*a*, 324*b*; VII, 624*b*; IX, 800*b*.

[20] *Il Palazzo della Ragione in Vicenza*, 1875, pp. 82 ff.

[21] ALVERA, 1834.

[22] *Il Palazzo della Ragione in Vicenza*, 1875, pp. 82 ff.

[23] ALVERA, *Notizie sulla Basilica.*

[24] *Il Palazzo della Ragione in Vicenza*, 1875, pp. 82 ff.

[25] ALVERA, 1834.

[26] CICOGNARA, 1830, p. 14.

[27] *Il Palazzo della Ragione in Vicenza*, 1875, pp. 82 ff.

[28] FORMENTON, 1870, pp. 39-41.

[29] TRISSINO, 1856, p. 22. According to Trissino, Stefano Madonetta (b. 1794 in Vicenza; d. 1865) had been the pupil of Francesco Bagnara and then from 1818 onward had studied under Bartolomeo Mezzetti in Venice. Several landscapes by him are recorded, but he is mainly remembered for his activity as a decorator, *quadraturista*, and scenographer. He was the author of garden and villa " perspectives, " executed in a climate of Neo-Gothicism diffused by Romanticism, and of scenery for the theatres of Vicenza, Venice, and Lonigo.

[30] *Il Palazzo della Ragione in Vicenza*, 1875, pp. 82 ff.

[31] COGO, 1900, pp. 25-32. Even Cogo, usually so perceptive, called for abandoning all the shops, shifting the stairs, and completely clearing out the ground floor in order to open up a great central gallery, which would have destroyed the existing " spine " of shops between the two pedestrian passageways.

[32] *Il Palazzo della Ragione in Vicenza*, 1875, pp. 82 ff.

[33] See n. 30.

[34] See n. 30.

[35] FORMENTON, 1870, p. 39.

[36] SELVATICO, 1859. The remedies suggested were substantially the following: 1) to reconstruct the arch through which the stairs descending to Piazza delle Erbe pass; 2) to reinforce the angle arches and the corresponding piers; 3) to reconstruct and reinforce the upper balustrades, which were all considered dangerous; 4) to remake the pavement of the upper loggias so that it would be impervious to the rainwater that was seeping in rather alarmingly, causing damage to the vaults beneath; 5) to replace many capitals and other deteriorating decorative elements, using Piovene stone.

[37] FORMENTON, 1869; *Il Palazzo della Ragione in Vicenza*, 1875, pp. 82 ff.

[38] Concerning these restorations, see FORMENTON, 1872 (II), pp. 23-24 and 1870, *Prefazione*; and *Il Palazzo della Ragione in Vicenza*, 1875, pp. 82 ff.

[39] BELLIO, 1875. As the bulge in the southern wall was considered very serious, and since radical restoration would per-

haps have cost too much, Bellio proposed that at least some buttresses be constructed on the inside of the northern wall of the
Hall, to which iron rods could be fixed to retain the opposite
(southern) wall. Other iron rods were to be fixed to the bases of
all the loggia's arches. However, shortly thereafter Bellio's suggestion was opposed by Barichella's more optimistic one (1878).

40 Cf. Morseletto, 1901.

41 Cf. Cogo, 1901, 1902, and 1903 (II, III, and IV). Note
that the supporters of both theses still proposed the use of iron
rods as the most effective remedy.

42 See esp. Anti, Bassani, Setti (all 1902); Beltrami-Bru-
sconi, 1903; De Filippi, 1903, pp. 232-234.

43 Forlati, 1947.

44 Forlati, 1952, p. 266. The reconstruction of the *carena*
was executed by the Vicentine firm of Giuseppe Maltauro (see
the long technical report by Maltauro, 1955). Particularly interesting is the comment on p. 276: " The mighty vaults [of the
new *carena*] are anchored onto the base from which they spring,
which is a reinforced-concrete stringcourse around the perimeter;
this is tied in turn to some stanchions within the walls... [These]
are tied at the base into an enormous horizontal reinforcing-slab
inserted into the pavement of the loggias..., [a slab] whose ancho-
rages are bound directly into the two transverse walls [of the
palace]: the one facing the Torre [di Piazza] and the one facing
Piazzetta Palladio. In this way, the upper part of the building...
has now been reinforced, perhaps definitively."

45 Cf. Zevi, 1959, col. 660.

46 Rosi (1949, p. 382), calls the restoration of the Vicentine
carena " one of the best results of the work done in the field
of post-war restoration of monuments," and Perogalli (1955,
p. 98) proposes it as a significant example of the excellence
and appropriateness displayed in certain cases by " integral "
restoration. Cevese (1958) criticizes certain details of the execution.

47 Forlati, 1952, p. 266.

48 Magagnato, 1949 (II) gives a synthesis of it (see also
Franco, 1951).

49 See esp. Bardella, 1948; Cevese, 1948; Magagnato,
1949 (II).

50 See Chapter IV, n. 141.

51 Zorzi is especially convinced of this.

52 Cogo, 1900, p. 23, states that " originally... there were
two more steps [besides the single one existing in 1900]... which
were done away with in the last century when the pavement was
restored. " Previously Bertotti Scamozzi (1796, I, pp. 91-100),
confirming Cogo's statement exactly, had observed that two of the
steps of the loggias " *furono ricoperti nel rimuovere il lastricato
della* [piazza] " (similarly in 1776, pp. 61-65 and in 1780, pp. 11-
16). In 1761 Bertotti Scamozzi explicitly stated that " [the
Basilica] *fu sopra tre* [steps] *fabbricata; ma dopo terminata questa
gran fabbrica, dovendosi porre il selciato della piazza, da questo
degli scalini due restarono coperti* " (pp. 13-18). This verifies
Arnaldi's analogous opinion (1767, pp. lxxxix-xc).

53 These are mainly several payments and contracts for the
loggia's execution during the years 1550-1614 in which explicit
reference is made to the construction of the steps (cf. Dalla
Pozza, 1943, pp. 134, 135; p. 219, Doc. XIII, paragraphs three
and four; p. 220).

54 Zorzi has always objected to the steps (1964, p. 52, n. 69).
As has already been noted (Barbieri, 1950), the solution adopted
repeats with a few variants the one shown in the two plates
in Bertotti Scamozzi (1776, pls. xxviii and xxix; Fig. XXI,
p. 77). This is formally a valid precedent, but in practice
it is not free from drawbacks: The main deficiency is the
lack of a distinct separation between the second step and the
plinths of the Doric half-columns attached to the piers. They
are only a few centimeters apart, and consequently at the
corners we see only one projecting step from which the columns
seem to rise—almost as if they were on a single too-high plinth,
double the normal height.

Minor restorations took place at the loggias in 1959-60 and
during 1964 (*Restauri palladiani*, 1959; Guiotto, 1964).

VI

THE SCULPTURAL DECORATION OF THE LOGGIAS

THE MASCHERONI AND FRIEZES

The *mascheroni* are located at the centers of the keystones, and therefore their placement would have coincided with the completion of the arches themselves. Their chronological sequence may thus be fixed with sufficient approximation to serve as a guide in determining their various authors.[1]

The first arches to be completed were those in the Doric order at the northwest corner of the loggias. They were begun in August of 1549 and were finished by January 5, 1552. The first decorative work was recorded at the same time, starting from November 15 and December 6, 1550, when the sculptor Girolamo Pittoni was paid for carving a mask and an ox-skull (usually recorded as " *teste di bove* " or "*testa de vacha*") and for other ornamentation of the cornice and the modillions.[2]

However, after the following January (1551) the name of Maestro Girolamo no longer appears in the expense accounts. As early as January 4, 1551, a "*testa umana*" is instead associated with the name of Lorenzo Rubini;[3] Rubini was paid again on November 27, together with Giuseppe di Girolamo Pittoni, for the carving of four leaf-ornaments and two roses in the frieze.[4] The following January 13th we find Palladio's nephew Marcantonio, who had executed two ox-skulls, on the list for the first time.[5]

The compensations stipulated were rather modest and differed in accordance with the importance of the sculptors. Girolamo Pittoni received 27 troni for his mask and 9 troni for each ox-skull. But in 1551 a reduction was made in the case of Rubini, which brought the compensation for each *testa umana* to 22 troni and to 8 troni for a *testa de vacha*.[6] Evidently it was necessary to proceed as economically as possible and to hire rather unpretentious artists, although with Pittoni gone the circle of Alessandro Vittoria, who was much better known, enters the picture.

Thus the keystones of the two lower arches at the northwest corner, which we know from the payments cited above to have been executed between November 1550 and January 1551, belong to Pittoni and Lorenzo Rubini. The corresponding ornamentations of the frieze and the cornice belong to Pittoni also, and to Marcantonio Palladio. Leaving aside these decorations—although they are undeniably fine works, they are anonymous products which could belong to any Cinquecento workshop (Plates 49, 50)—we can attempt a more precise discrimination regarding the masks. The *testa umana* on the arch at the west (Plate 51) has in respect to the one at the north an undeniably more rigid form and a drier modelling. It is therefore probably the one executed by Pittoni, as indicated by a comparison with the three statues by Pittoni in the

XXVI - GIACOMO LEONI, *Loggias of Palladio's "Basilica": detail of the northwest corner.*
From *The Architecture of A. Palladio*, 1721, III, pl. xxi

crypt of S. Corona [7] and his high-relief for the Dall'Acqua altar in the Cathedral.[8] Consequently, the date of execution can be fixed at the end of 1550. The other keystone—that of the first arch at the right on the north—is datable on or before January 4, 1551; it is softer in effect, with more chiaroscuro contrast, and is clearly reminiscent of Vittoria's style—as befits Rubini's work.[9]

As has been suggested,[10] the reduced compensation must have soon persuaded the elderly and established Girolamo Pittoni to abandon the execution of the work to the hands of younger and more enthusiastic sculptors. Throughout 1551 and 1552 we find payments to Lorenzo Rubini and to Palladio's nephew Marcantonio. In April 1551 Lorenzo prepared a "*testa humana*"; between January 30 and February 20, 1552, Marcantonio sculpted a head, and both artists worked on the various customary parts of the frieze.[11] These heads were used for the keystones of the arches in the Doric order, erected in sequence on the north side: that is, the eighth and seventh on the left, completed together with the sixth on June 24, 1553. It is very likely that Rubini was responsible for the keystone of the eighth arch,[12] which is analogous to the adjacent one of the first arch on the right. The one by Marcantonio, Palladio's nephew, would consequently be the seventh one, and perhaps the analogous sixth one might be his as well (Plate 52).

Lorenzo Rubini was in Venice from 1553 on, in Alessandro Vittoria's retinue.[13] Palladio's nephew Marcantonio, left in 1552 to work at Palazzo Chiericati;[14] and we find a first payment for a "*mascara*" made out on March 17, 1554 to another Marcantonio, Palladio's son.[15] From that year up to 1560 the latter worked as a sculptor on the loggias.[16] In the two-year period of 1556-58 he was assisted by a Master "Zuanantonio *intagiador milanese*,"

who is not further identified but whose work in all likelihood was limited to simple cornices.[17]

In 1555-56, the work at Palazzo Chiericati finished, Palladio's nephew Marcantonio returned to work on the loggias.[18] During those years the fifth arch on the left on the northern side (Plate 53) was erected; it was completed on September 4, 1554. The fourth and third arches (Plate 54) were finished about November of 1554, and—putting aside for the present the second arch, which was executed later—the two arches at the northeast corner were completed on or about September 27, 1556. These keystones must therefore all be by Palladio's son Marcantonio, except for those of the two corner arches, which were executed in 1555-56 and for which we have precise documents of payment to Palladio's nephew Marcantonio.[19]

Three arches on the western side—the second, third, and fourth on the left—were completed on November 20, 1559. The second and third (Plate 56) have keystones very similar to those on the northern side which can be attributed to Marcantonio, Palladio's son (note especially the third to the left on that side; Plate 54). The same may be said of the "*testa di uomo*" of the second arch on the left on the northern side (Plate 55), which was put in position on or about July 23, 1561; it definitely seems to be the work of Palladio's son, Marcantonio, and to have been executed—but perhaps not put in place—before his departure for Venice in 1560.[20]

The group which includes the whole lower order on the northern side extending to the three arches of the western side on the left (excluding the first, which represents the work of Girolamo Pittoni) indicates, despite the inevitable variety of hands, a common stylistic matrix; without doubt the latter is to be sought in the influence that Alessandro Vittoria exercised

XXVII - MARCO MORO, *Piazza dei Signori*. From Giulio Pullè, *Album di gemme architettoniche*, 1847

on the Vicentine situation in the middle of the century.[21] One of the high points of the series is undoubtedly the fifth northern keystone on the left (Plate 53), where Palladio's son, Marcantonio, almost equals Vittoria in the tempestuous pictorial vitality that he imparts to his material. We can date the third mask (Plate 54) on the left on the same side slightly after it. In this work, however, one notes a more academic rigidity and a less happy recapitulation of Vittoria's manner.

The fourth keystone on the left of the western side (Plate 57), which was placed in position in 1559, is somewhat removed from the preceding ones. Angular and hard, the face is enclosed in an approximately rectangular scheme from which rigid and symmetrical locks of hair project. The ex-

pression is also different, not grotesque like the others but rather expressive of the suffering of a tragic mask. For these reasons it seems to have been differently inspired from the rest.[22]

There are payments on account in April of 1564 for the heads in the arches of the lower gallery at the southwest corner (Plate 58), and on May 31st Francesco Albanese the Elder—who at that time was not yet thirty—was paid in full.[23] Generally speaking, the first known work for reconstructing the activity of the elder Albanese —who was a diligent designer of tombs and altars in a correct, " archaizing " taste distantly reminiscent of Ammannati's work [24]—is the tomb of Gaetano Thiene, dated 1583, in the Cathedral of Vicenza.[25] This securely datable early work on the loggias is therefore quite important, as it anticipates by about twenty years our earliest knowledge of this *petit-maître*, who was actually a powerful influence in Vicenza in the late Cinquecento. It is very likely that the payment of 1564 marks the beginning of Albanese's uninterrupted collaboration on work on the loggias, which lasted until his death sometime before 1621.[26]

The northern and western sides of the upper gallery were put up between 1570 and June 27, 1597, and it is quite possible that the keystones (Plates 61, 62)—which are conceived in the rather cold and academic manner of the two masks below of 1564—were done by Francesco Albanese, or perhaps by his studio.[27] We should not forget that Francesco's son Giambattista, who was born in 1573, was then more than twenty years old. He had enrolled in the local guild as early as 1592 and had shown signs of expressing his own personality in more interesting tests than the sculpture of the loggias. He must have collaborated with his father for a certain period, from at least 1593 onward.[28]

From the last five years of the Cinquecento onward, the attention of the builders turned to the southern side of the loggias. There, near the "*teste umane*" executed in the manner of Francesco Albanese, we find two others which are more agitated and bold and are undoubtedly the product of a different, warmer sensibility. The chronology of the work clarifies the attribution by documenting that the arches on that side had been finished in three stages: around November 1605, six arches of the lower order were finished (the second, third, fourth, fifth, sixth, and seventh on the left); by April 28, 1610, another three arches had been done (the eighth in the Doric order and the second and third in the Ionic order on the left); and by 1614 the last five arches in the Ionic order were completed.

In the first and second groups we may assume the continuing collaboration of Francesco (then seventy years old, but perhaps still active) and his son Giambattista, who was in his full maturity; the last group, with the father dead, is a matter of the work of Giambattista alone. As proof, several masks of the lower southern portico may be considered: for example, the fifth (Plate 59), the seventh, and the eighth (Plate 60) on the left. The fifth, more rigid with its sharply simplified planes, recalls the manner of Francesco Albanese. The other two, which are executed with an energetic pictorial vigor, easily approach Giambattista's best works, from the statues of the Oratorio del Gonfalone (1596, and slightly later)[29] to those for the Capra altar in S. Lorenzo (c. 1605).[30] Moreover, Giambattista's masterpiece, the *Pietà* on the façade of S. Vincenzo, was commissioned in 1614,[31] just when the work on the keystones ended.

THE STATUES ON THE NORTHERN AND WESTERN SIDES

On June 27, 1597, a statement of accounts for the work executed up until that time at the palace, under the supervision of Giannantonio Grazioli, was drawn up.[32] It states expressly that by that date, with the conclusion of the upper gallery of loggias on the northern and western sides, Grazioli had "*anco messo a tutte sue spese sopra li quareselli* [the rectangular pedestals placed at intervals between the small columns of the upper balustrade, corresponding to the half-columns of the piers underneath] *et archi predetti sedici figure di preda viva.*" For his labor, he received five ducats per statue for a total of eighty ducats, evidently more than had been foreseen in the contract. Two other statues were then ready but had not yet been raised onto their pedestals. Grazioli, having anticipated an expenditure of fifty ducats per statue (including the honorarium for the sculptors and the acquisition of the stone), must have also been refunded nine hundred ducats.[33] In addition, he collected a debt of twenty ducats paid " *al q. Augustin Rubin scultore per caparra il quale essendo morto non ha potuto fare le figure.*" [34]

This very clear document thus convinces us that in June of 1597 eighteen statues were already set up, or had at least been executed (two were still on the ground, but this would have been for only a short period). These must have been the eighteen statues on the northern and western sides, excluding only the group of three figures on the southwest angle pier.[35] The question of authorship remains open, however, since no mention is made of any names in regard to them and all we have to work from is information concerning the sculptors active in Vicenza at the close of the Cinquecento.

First of all, the statues were not all in position in June of 1597 and those of them which, as is explicitly stated, were still being made had probably not been commissioned more than a few years earlier, when the work on the arcades was nearly completed. Although carved from the hard Piovene stone, the statues are not really large,[36] and the 1597 document speaks precisely of agreements made with more than one sculptor, which surely must have been done in order to hurry the work along.[37] Lorenzo Rubini, who died in 1574,[38] was not involved;[39] his son Agostino was invited to participate, but as far as we know he did not do anything.[40] Lorenzo's other son, Vigilio, remained after 1587 in Venice in the house of his famous uncle, Vittoria; therefore only in that city can possible evidence of

his work be sought, at least up until the year of Vittoria's death in 1608.[41]

Vittoria's name has been suggested for at least one of the loggia statues, the figure of the old man above the third pier on the left on the northern side (Plate 73). The attribution is based on the undeniable ease of the figure's execution and on its similarity to three other works by Vittoria in S. Francesco della Vigna in Venice.[42] In order to be able to accept the hypothesis, however, it is necessary to verify it chronologically. Vittoria lived in Vicenza during two different periods: in 1547-48, when he was working on the Arnaldi house, and in 1552-53, when he was involved with the decoration of Palazzo Thiene; and about twenty-three years later, in 1576-77, when he came back with his family in hopes of escaping a plague (which, however, also reached Vicenza).[43]

Logically eliminating the first period, there is only the sojourn of 1576-77 to consider.[44] At that time the four upper arches in the northwest corner were completed, and the idea of commissioning a crowning statue from Vittoria could somehow have sprung up. But such a commission at that date seems extremely improbable, inasmuch as we know that the statue was only placed in position some twenty years later. The decade from 1570 to 1580 and thereafter was, on the other hand, a period of almost complete inactivity in the work on the loggias because of the lack of funds, which were diverted to the war against the Turks and to work on the Loggia del Capitaniato.[45] It is difficult to believe that in such a situation someone like Alessandro Vittoria would have been engaged, who was already famous and who consequently would have had to be paid accordingly.[46]

Therefore, having eliminated the Rubini and probably Vittoria, too, we are left

XXVIII - MARCO MORO, *Piazza dei Signori and Piazza delle Erbe*. From *Vicenza e suoi dintorni*, 1850

with the elder Francesco Albanese. He was at least sixty years old[47] and had been engaged, as we have noted, to work on the keystones from 1564 onward; therefore he was already involved in work on the loggias. His older son, Giambattista, was about twenty-five, but his younger son Girolamo was still an adolescent in 1597 and can be excluded.[48]

An unsuspected source, somehow overlooked in this particular instance, indicates the presence of Camillio Mariani among the sculptors of the statues.[49] He was born in 1567 and was then just thirty years old, and he was on the verge of departing (in 1597) for a long period in Rome.[50] The dates consequently are not contradictory, and the name of Mariani is actually very useful in explaining certain passages of open chromaticism in the works.

These areas undeniably echo the language of Alessandro Vittoria, but they are not sufficient to suggest an attribution to the master; on the other hand, they are well above the known or documented capabilities of an artist like Francesco Albanese, or the briefly-revealed ones of Giambattista. It would have been, moreover, rather strange if an artist of the calibre of Camillo Mariani—who was later capable of directly influencing the Roman situation of the early Seicento[51]—had been left out of an undertaking like the decoration of the loggias in his own native city.

Unfortunately today our knowledge of Mariani's Veneto period and pre-Roman activity hinges on only a few sure works. The *Pietà* once in the Church of S. Bortolo is lost,[52] and the intervention of the sculptor in the decoration of the Olimpico is problematic and, moreover, is yet to be studied.[53] Hence we have just the two figures of Aeolus and Persephone (1588-89) crowning the Library of St. Mark's in Venice,[54] along with the pediment statues and the two allegorical figures with a coat-of-arms in the tympanum of the façade of S. Pietro in Vicenza (renovated in 1597),[55] as securely documented works. However, there are various other attributions: the statues in the atrium of the Villa Cornaro at Piombino Dese;[56] several of the statues in the Church of S. Gaetano in Padua, completed after 1586;[57] and the bust of Giambattista Gualdo (c. 1588) in the Gualdo monument in the Cathedral.[58]

The statues on the loggias were evidently conceived, despite the variety of sculptors involved, in accordance with a uniform scheme of poses and were made to conform to an overall decorative effect,[59] which makes the task of distinguishing the various authors more difficult. We may, however, at least formulate some hypotheses concerning the workmanship. The two corner groups at the north (Plates 64, 65), especially the one at the northwest,[60] undeniably recall the style of Giambattista Albanese as exemplified in the statues on the attic of the Arco delle Scalette and on the façade of the presbytery of S. Pietro: works which are approximately contemporary, dating between 1595 and 1596.[61] All have the same elongated forms, almost Tintorettesque in the slight mannerism of the slender bodies, the long curved lines, and the long flexible arms. There is a clear presentiment in these nude figures of Giambattista's beautiful allegories in the Capra altar in S. Lorenzo of 1605.[62]

The three figures on the sixth (Plate 67), seventh (Plate 66), and ninth piers on the northern side at the left seem very similar to the abovementioned corner groups, in conception, in plastic structure, and in the twisting of the poses. They are

decidedly close to Vittoria but only in a superficial sense, with clear anticipations of the later production of the Albanese studio, which led to Girolamo's work in the Cappella del Rosario in S. Corona (after 1619) and in the Chapel of St. Joseph in the Cathedral (c. 1650).[63] This is a clear sign both of the continuity and the restrictions of a provincial tradition.

Thus, the hand of Francesco Albanese senior is not clearly apparent in any of the loggia statues. If, in fact, the already-elderly sculptor did collaborate on the work, his intervention probably came through the medium of his youngest son, Giambattista. Giambattista probably did the fine male nude on the eighth pier at the north on the left (Plate 68), which is comparable to the *Adam* of the Capra altar (c. 1605) but is more alive and spontaneous.[64] For analogous reasons, the still-more-successful figure holding a book on the second pier to the left on the western side may also belong to him.

The final autograph work by Giambattista is probably the figure of a youth holding a sack on the fifth pier on the northern side.[65] This is perhaps the finest piece of the whole Albanese contribution to the loggias: an interesting ensemble which, passing from the " archaizing " corner groups to the freer and more open figures, has the undeniable merit of marking a critical moment in Giambattista's development; his work here emerges from academic paternal restraints vaguely reminiscent of Ammannati and assumes a wider significance for the Veneto.

It is quite likely that this impulse toward renewal, the fruits of which are seen in the stupendous *Deposition* of the façade of S. Vincenzo (1614-17),[66] came to the young artist (he was then about twenty-four) through his association around 1597 with the more mature Camillo Mariani. Mariani was present in Vicenza in order to execute some of the statues, one of which might certainly be the famous figure of the old man (Plate 73) above the third pier at the north, which was previously attributed to Vittoria. It almost constitutes a connecting link between earlier Venetian sculptures—especially those by Vittoria in S. Francesco della Vigna, or those by Danese Cattaneo in S. Salvatore, cited by Venturi in this connection[67]—and the logical consequences later drawn from them by Mariani in his *St. Jerome* in S. Bernardo alle Terme.

Mariani, interpreting Vittoria in a masterly fashion, created in the two powerful figures of old men in Vicenza and Rome works of fluent plasticity and intense painterliness. Considering the scarcity of information and the bad state of preservation of the figures on the acroteria of S. Pietro, the statue of the loggias takes on an exceptional importance.

The figure of a youth on the left (above the second northern pier to the left; Plate 74), as well as the adjacent statue of another old man on the right (above the fourth northern pier to the left; Plate 72), seems to belong with the figure of the old man sleeping. The modelling is of very high quality, and the agitated and open treatment of the figures recalls the observation—made in a different context but applicable in this instance—that Mariani used a rhythm based principally on having the figures bear more weight on one leg than the other, with the corresponding arm hanging loose on the side opposite to that thrust forward; this recalls the "serpentine movement" preferred by Francesco Segala and provides a series of elegant, spirited figures with intensely expressive heads.[68]

The plastic energy of this "serpentine movement" becomes peremptory in the two statues above the third and fifth piers to the left on the western side. In the statue above the fifth pier (Plate 70), the spiral pose of the body is reinforced by the uncoiling of a snake between the legs and at one side of the figure. The two male heads have a fiery proudness unknown in any of Albanese's figures. To see this again, we must go back to Mariani's work in the Cappella Paolina in S. Maria Maggiore and in S. Bernardo alle Terme in Rome. Several statues there have profiles almost identical to those in Vicenza: the same short strong nose, the mouth folded downward at the corners with two incised furrows leading from the nostrils, and deeply carved eye sockets.

If, as tradition indicates, Mariani's first apprenticeship was his admiration for the Rubini,[69] he achieved a stupendous interpretation of that style, filtered through a new sensibility which mitigated its harshness, smoothing the forms and immersing them in a cristalline Veronesque light—as in the female nude (Plate 71) on the fourth pedestal to the west. The reference to the *Persephone*—a secure and documented in work by Mariani on the balustrade of the Library of St. Mark's—is fitting. It seems clear that the sculptor obtained his result by starting out under the influence of the statues on the stairs of the Rotonda, Lorenzo Rubini's masterpieces. From that illustrious precedent, he completely embraced the "free adherence to the ideals of plastic synthesis and full pictorialism" characteristic of Vittoria's work.[70] However, he added masterly touches of a delicacy unthinkable in an artist like Rubini, such as the soft mass of the hair or the admirable detail of the grapes and pomegranates in which the faintly-suggested fingers are submerged.

A comparison with Albanese's *Eve* in the Capra altar in S. Lorenzo, on the other hand, demonstrates the distinct difference the level of quality between works by Giambattista and his circle and comparable ones by Camillo Mariani. Unfortunately, in the same year that the statues were erected on the loggias the artist left his native city without leaving behind anyone worthy of following and continuing his style—except Giambattista Albanese, who preserved certain elements of it.[71]

THE STATUES ON THE SOUTHERN SIDE

While the Palladian loggias on the southern side were being finished, Giambattista Albanese entered into an agreement on January 22, 1614,[72] specifying " *che far debbi de preda de Piovene bene et sufficientemente figure undese o quel più vero numero che occorrerà da metter su li pedestalli su in cima esso palazzo.*" The compensation arranged with the sculptor was 55 ducats for each statue, including the cost of the blocks of stone sent to Vicenza (12 ducats for each one) and the arrangement of the statues " *a drita linea del piedestile,*" where they had to be hoisted. Money was to be advanced gradually in convenient amounts as the work progressed. As far as the subjects were concerned, the artist was bound to follow precise directions given him by the *Presidente alla fabbrica*.

At the conclusion of the document, Giambattista " praised and affirmed " what had been agreed; however, in actuality, he must not have executed anything. The " *figure undese* " for which he had been so solemnly commissioned correspond exactly to all the statues then still lacking: three on the pier at the southwest corner and eight on the piers on the southern side, which was shorter because it was interrupted by the Arco degli Zavatteri.

With these done and placed in position the work would have been completed, and two days later on January 24th the sculptor received an advance of 50 ducats for

the work.[73] However, in August of 1637 we find that his brother Girolamo Albanese received 75 ducats as payment for " *tre statue di preda viva per la fabrica del palazzo della Ragione, in ragione di ducati 25 l'una,*"[74] and on June 2, 1655—well over forty years after the first agreement made with Giambattista—the Council of the Hundred was again forced to concern itself with the problem, so that the loggias could finally " *quanto prima perfettionarsi sino che vive anco scultore le cui opere sono tenute in grande stima.*"[75]

Evidently in 1614 the *Pietà* of S. Vincenzo (which was finished in 1617), had been entrusted to Giambattista, who soon after began work on the Cappella del Rosario in S. Corona;[76] in subsequent years he was busy with other undertakings and did not find time before his death in 1630 to concern himself with the loggia statues. His brother Girolamo, younger by about ten years (who is cited on his own in the documents only after 1630, since earlier he was probably always in the shadow of the older Giambattista),[77] must have assumed the task at that time. The payment made to him in 1637 is the proof of his good intentions.

It is logical that the three figures sculpted by Girolamo are those above the pier at the southwest corner, as they were the first to be put in position after the more-than-twenty-year interruption. They represent three female figures (Plate 63) and are rather weak and mannered, which would be proper for this " traditionalist " sculptor.[78] Moreover, they fit easily into his chronology at that date. After the statues on the façade of S. Vincenzo and the work for S. Corona[79] comes the beautiful *St. John* in the Baptistery of the Cathedral, which is very interesting in its open "Maffeiesque" theatricality. It immediately precedes the loggia statues,[80] after which comes *Christ the Redeemer* on the southern col-

XXIX - MARCO MORO, *Piazza dei Signori, seen from the west.* From *Vicenza e suoi dintorni,* 1850

umn in Piazza dei Signori, for which Girolamo was paid on February 14, 1643[81] and which is considered his masterpiece.[82]

However, after 1637 Girolamo—possibly because of the burden of work, or for some other reason which we do not know[83]—must also in his turn have neglected the loggia statues and thus have justified the concern of the Council in 1655 to get them finished while the sculptor, then more than seventy years old, was still living.[84] He probably replied in 1655 with excuses to the pressures, suggesting substitutes in the persons of Bartolomeo Muggini[85] and Francesco Albanese the Younger.[86] Eight years later, on January 4, 1663, the latter received fifteen ducats as partial payment of his compensation for having executed several statues.[87] In the same year he worked with Muggini,[88] who later received

forty ducats on August 31, 1664, and sixty more on January 22, 1665, for the statues he had completed.[89]

With all this, by about 1665 there should have been statues on the southern side just as on the two preceding sides. If we consider that several had been made by Francesco Albanese the younger and at least two by Muggini (judging from the amount of the latter's compensation),[90] it is strange that today of the eight possible statues there are only two on that side. Moreover, they are illogically situated as they do not form a continuation with the three which were placed at the southwest corner in 1637, but are at the opposite end.

If we can believe Arnaldi, some statues on the southern side were missing as early as the end of the eighteenth century;[91]

certainly in 1845 the situation was already as it is today.[92] Cogo's observations at the beginning of the century are interesting in this respect: " It cannot be ruled out that at one time... those statues on the southern side existed... and that they were removed from their position either because of possible danger of falling as a consequence of the bulge which existed in that façade, ... or for other reasons." One of these reasons was the visit of Ferdinand I, Emperor of Austria, to Vicenza. There is actually information concerning "three statues which in order to solemnize the visit of the monarch... were taken from the loggias in 1838... with the idea of forming an allegorical group, ... without its being noted whether or not they were put back in place."[93]

The only two surviving statues clearly seem to be by different hands: the male figure (Plate 75) on the seventh pedestal on the left still recalls the nude figures on the northern and western sides but is much more feeble and academic; the female figure above the eighth pier is a cold, rigid schematization of motifs from the Rubini and Giambattista Albanese. As we lack information about Muggini and Francesco Albanese the Younger with which to compare these figures, a precise discrimination is impossible. Here, while the last gleams of the glorious Vicentine sculptural tradition of the sixteenth and seventeenth centuries faded away, the re-energizing arrival of Valsoldan and Lombard sculptors and stucco-workers was imminent[94]—and Orazio Marinali (b. 1643), the noblest voice of the new era, was already twenty years old.

MEMORIAL TO A PRAETOR

This imposing trophy (Plate 77) on the northern wall of the palace encompasses the sixth abutment from the left of the corresponding upper order of loggias. A male figure (Plate 78) standing on the surviving polygonal pilaster of the Quattrocento loggias is inserted between the archway of the door and the arch of the adjacent window. Four paired female figures (Plate 79) lie on the mouldings of the two arches, the keystones of which are replaced by brackets which support a curved tympanum. In the middle of the tympanum is a coat-of-arms, flanked by two smaller figures. The figures, which are unfortunately in a poor state of preservation except for the male figure, are in terracotta plastered to simulate stone.[95] Soft stone was used for the coat-of-arms and for some of the architectural mouldings. The whole complex is so darkened that, considering the scarcity of light beneath the vault, it is difficult to read.[96]

An attribution to Giambattista Albanese has been suggested by the eighteenth-century guidebooks and by other contemporary texts,[97] as well as by the few texts that deal with the monument during the nineteenth century.[98] Later, the splendid work is scarcely mentioned;[99] the latest *Guida di Vicenza* (in the two editions of 1953 and 1956) refers to it only in an extremely general way.[100] However, as early as 1939 Silvagni had established its attribution to the most important of the Albanese family, and had dated its execution to 1598-1600;[101] this was exactly the moment when Giambattista, then almost thirty, began a more mature phase which was decisively closer to Vittoria.

Only Zorzi rejected the attribution, assigning it to Lorenzo Rubini and noting analogies with the figures of Fame and the festoons on the façade of the Palazzo Iseppo Porto, which are also given to Lorenzo.[102] He suggests a date of about 1571-72, the period during which Rubini was executing the stuccoes for the Loggia del Capitaniato

XXX - Marco Moro, *Piazza delle Erbe, seen from the west.* From *Vicenza e suoi dintorni,* 1850

and the Palazzo di Montano Barbarano.[103] Unfortunately, a secure dating is not possible, as the inscription on the shield has been cancelled and is no longer identifiable even using Faccioli's *Lapidarium*.[104]

Alessandro Vittoria's influence is very plain here and is even recognized by Zorzi, who almost suggests the name of the Venetian master next to that of Rubini. The level of work is actually so high as to surpass any known work by Lorenzo Rubini, starting with those which Zorzi considers to be contemporary at the Capitaniato and Palazzo Porto Barbarano.

However, to resolve the question by advancing the hypothesis of an attribution to Vittoria as others have done[105] does not seem possible to me. This would oblige dating the work between 1576 and 1577, i.e., to the years of the artist's

second stay in Vicenza. But it is necessary to remember that in exactly those years the upper arcade under which the trophy was later placed was not yet constructed, as it was part of a group begun after 1585. The old Formenton loggias had been demolished in that area ever since 1553,[106] so that that side of the palace was not closed off by vaulting above. Yet it is evident that in conceiving the trophy the sculptor took into consideration the vault which was erected between 1585 and 1597,[107] placing the figures and architectural elements under it in such a way that they obviously occupy a space already arranged.[108] It should also be borne in mind that the nearby door at the midway-point of the north stairway and the balustrade around the well of the stair itself had also been put in place in 1597.[109] Therefore the date proposed by Silvagni for the execution of the work—i. e., the end of the century—does not seem far from correct. Excluding Lorenzo Rubini, who died in 1574, the name of Giambattista Albanese remains the most reasonable and convincing. It is sufficient to compare the trophy with the angels executed by Giambattista, using the same technique and material, over the door of the Oratorio del Gonfalone, which was erected in 1596.[110] The decided reminiscences of Vittoria in the work may well be explained at that date by the influence exercised for some years on Albanese by Camillo Mariani,[111] who had collaborated with Albanese on the upper statues and who left at the loggias examples of a cool Venetian chromaticism.[112]

Niche for a Coat-of-arms

This niche (Plate 82) is located on the northern wall of the Quattrocento palace, in the first arch of the upper gallery counting from the northeast corner, up under the Late Gothic spiral moulding. The central shield is gone and the inscription in the scroll is cancelled, so there is therefore no possibility of dating the work on a documentary basis.[113] The bibliography is completely silent on the problem: the single very brief mention is in the latest *Guida di Vicenza*.[114]

The niche is composed of a broken tympanum supported on two composite pilasters to which two female figures are attached. Under the figure at the right the word CHARITAS is still visible. A third female figure is within the tympanum, standing on a lion's head in the center of the architrave. At the sides are volutes and festoons; two curious masks flank the tympanum, and underneath is a scroll between two curved brackets. The niche is made of

soft stone and is in a fair state of preservation except for the figures, which unfortunately have deep abrasions and missing parts. The whole work is very darkened.

Actually, the agitated and scenographic architectural structure seems almost to be the product of two different interventions: the elements of the composite pilasters with female figures, the architrave with the lion's head, and the female figure placed in the opening of the tympanum seem to have been superimposed at some undetermined time on a niche in the shape of a broken tympanum, probably of seventeenth-century craftsmanship (ca. 1610-20) and similar to those in the Oratorio di S. Nicola. At that time the side volutes must have been executed and the masks set in. However, the masks, the pilasters, and the female figures have all the appearances of ornaments whose execution predates the workmanship of the early Seicento niche. They may be dated to the late Cinquecento and placed within the range of forms current in the studio of the Albanese. The lion's head and the whole architrave of which it is a part refer directly back to early Cinquecento forms in the manner of the Pedemuro. The same can be said of the masks.

Moreover, the curving brackets are not aligned on the same axis as the elements above, and the scroll is badly proportioned for the space above meant for the coat-of-arms. The whole bears out the hypothesis of an ensemble put together by different hands at two different periods, with material from different sources.

Niche with a Tablet of the Emperor Gordian III

This niche (Plate 84) is in the center of the wall, under the previously described piece. It was inserted in 1586, as is stated in the inscription at the bottom,[115] in order to frame a Roman tablet from the middle of the third century dedicated to the Emperor Gordian III;[116] the tablet was probably found in 1540 under the houses then belonging to the Castelli family on the north side of Piazza delle Biade.[117]

The work, executed under the aegis of the same Castelli heirs,[118] is very simple although not entirely devoid of elegance. A typical late-Cinquecento frame holds the tablet, which is split in many places but is still complete. Above in the triangular tympanum is the coat-of-arms of Vicenza, the city decemviri having urged that the ancient object be placed in the *palazzo pubblico.*

The niche is the work of Giannantonio Grazioli, under whose direction the Palladian arcades on that side were constructed; he was paid for it on September 18, 1586.[119]

FRAMING OF A TABLET OF 1261

The tablet (Plate 81) is set into the southern wall of Palazzo della Ragione, within the first arcade of the upper gallery counting from the southwest corner. The framing is dated by the inscription to 1584.[120] It consists of a simple cyma moulding: a narrow, unified cordon placed around a tablet of 1261 that came from the city gate called " di Pusterla " and which was set into the wall in 1584, an interesting document of Vicenza's mediaeval history.[121] Underneath is a Cinquecento cartouche, smooth and outlined by two faintly-incised volutes on the sides. The arrangement was probably by Giovanni Antonio Grazioli, who from February 20, 1584, was the contractor for the work on the loggias and who must certainly have served as supervisor of whatever stonecutters were working there.

FOUR FIGURES OF FAME AND TWO COATS-OF-ARMS OF VICENZA

The arch and gate located approximately in the center of the northern stairway of the palace (1495-96; Plate 43) had been made as early as June 27, 1597, " *di tutto punto con legnami prede figure serramenti,*" under the supervision of Giovanni Antonio Grazioli.[122] One has the impression that Grazioli reused the existing late Quattrocento mouldings for the extrados of the arch and similarly for the lintel above the arch itself, which was decorated on the outside with the characteristic convex mouldings. On the inside, on the other hand, is a Cinquecento moulding with a slight framing in relief. At the center is the coat-of-arms of Vicenza. In the spandrels at the sides are two reclining winged figures of Fame carrying wreaths of laurel.

The coat-of-arms and the figures show a close dependence on the style of the Albanese. The figures recall the analogous figures on the altars of S. Mauro and S. Giustina in the Church of S. Pietro; the latter are contemporary (1596) and are very probably by Giambattista Albanese,[123] and the figures of Fame in the loggias seem to be an interesting derivation from them.

Between 1610 and 1612, Giovanni Grazioli and Antonio Benetello erected the south stairs.[124] Therefore the arrangement of the gate in the middle of the flight must go back to those years. In the spandrels on the inside are two more reclining winged figures of Fame holding wreaths of laurel (Plate 80), and at the center is the coat-of-arms of Vicenza. But here the workmanship is much cruder; the drapery is hard and rigid and the limbs are rather awkward and clumsy. The work is perhaps by Grazioli and within the sphere of Albanese influence, but it retains the modest quality of studio execution.

THE LION OF ST. MARK

The symbol of Venice is located prominently inside the palace, more than halfway up the east wall of the Hall, within a niche. It was restored and regilded after World War II.

A comparison with the two other surviving lions which can be dated—the one on the northern column of Piazza dei Signori (Martin del Vedello, 1520)[125] and the one on the Arco delle Scalette (Giambattista Albanese, 1595)[126]—shows that the lion of the Palazzo della Ragione should be placed chronologically between the two. A possible date for it would be between 1530 and 1540.

Because of the typical form of the niche, it can probably be attributed to the Pedemuro sculptors, as has been suggested.[127] The head of the studio, Master Giovanni, was not new to works of this kind; he worked continuously in palaces on coats-of-arms and insignia (alone or with his associate Girolamo), especially in the years from 1520 to 1550.[128] Beneath the lion is a congratulatory inscription of 1486, dedicated to the prefect Antonio Bernardo. The two lateral coats-of-arms are now cancelled and unrecognizable.[129]

OTHER DECORATIVE ELEMENTS

In the upper gallery at the west (which joins the northern to the southern side of the loggias), over the door that leads into the Hall, is a small niche which today lacks a coat-of-arms. The finely-grooved pilaster strips and the delicacy of the whole are a remarkable example of the work of the Pedemuro studio (from the first half of the sixteenth century), always under the influence of graceful Sanmichelesque forms.

In front over the door which leads to the palace of the podestà are two other niches adorned with beautiful lions' heads. These are certainly by the same stonecutters and form an interesting comparison with the similar but finer motifs on the tomb of Lavinia Thiene (1542) in the Cathedral of Vicenza.[130]

For the other Quattrocento coats-of-arms in the lower and upper loggias, we must turn to the accurate survey by Magrini[131] and to the subsequent one in *Il Palazzo della Ragione in Vicenza*.[132] These studies are useful for detailed historical documentation but are of little significance on the formal level.

NOTES TO CHAPTER VI

[1] See Chapter IV.

[2] *Summarii delle spese per le logge*, L. 40, cc. 76 and 93 *b* (transcribed by ZORZI, 1964, pp. 326-327). Concerning Girolamo Pittoni, Giovanni di Giacomo da Porlezza's associate in the Pedemuro studio, see the bibliographical references in n. 85 to Chapter IV. The payments of 1550 partially correct ZORZI's opinion (1937, p. 92) that the sculptor had been away from Vicenza after 1547.

[3] *Summarii delle spese per le logge*, L. 40, c. 93 *b* (transcribed by ZORZI, 1964, p. 327). The fundamental source for Rubini (called in the documents " Lorenzo de M. Andrea Fornaro, *tagliapreda* ") is ZORZI (1951, 1965, and 1966 [II]); other references are in BRENZONI, 1953-1954.
Rubini came from a Valtellinese family (although Brenzoni says they were from Adria). He lived in Vicenza in Contra' S. Tommaso and was enrolled in the local guild of masons and stonecutters from 1549-50, after an apprenticeship with the stoneworkers of Pedemuro; he is recorded as an " *intagliatore* " of marble as early as 1553. In 1553 he followed Alessandro Vittoria to Venice, and in 1554 he married Vittoria's sister, Margherita; he returned to Vicenza before 1557 and carried on a vast activity, especially as a stucco decorator. He died shortly before the end of 1574 (see also L. TRISSINO, *Miscellanea di appunti su vari artisti vicentini*, in the section dealing with the life of Camillo Mariani; CESSI, 1960, p. 70).

[4] *Summarii delle spese per le logge*, L. 40, c. 167 *b* (transcribed by ZORZI, 1964, p. 330). Giuseppe di Girolamo Pittoni was a modest stonecutter in his father's studio. A document of November 8, 1550, records his presence in the house of Giovanni da Pedemuro's heirs (ZORZI, 1937, p. 97), and in a contract of March 4, 1570 (DALLA POZZA, 1943, p. 178) he commits himself and his brother Vincenzo to construct an altar for Marcantonio Cogollo, still existing in S. Corona (BARBIERI, 1954).
Suggestions that Palladio's sons Silla and Leonida were also involved in the sculpture on the lower gallery of loggias (*Il Palazzo della Ragione in Vicenza*, 1875, pp. 73-74; ZANELLA, 1880, p. 33) are without foundation.

[5] *Summarii delle spese per le logge*, L. 40, c. 93 *b* (transcribed by ZORZI, 1964, p. 327). Concerning the two Marcantonios, Palladio's son and his nephew, see the bibliography brought up-to-date in 1962 by BARBIERI (1962 [II], pp. 43-44, n. 94) and the recent clarifications by ZORZI (1964, pp. 49-50, 305-306, 307-308). Palladio's nephew Marcantonio worked on the sculpture of the lower gallery during all of 1551 and up to February 1552 (*Summarii*, L. 40, cc. 93 *b* and 156 *a*; transcribed by ZORZI, 1964, pp. 327-328, 329). From 1552 to 1554 he worked on the frieze of Palazzo Chiericati (MAGRINI, 1855, pp. 68-70, n. 7; BARBIERI, 1962, [II], p. 43), and in 1555 his name reappears in the *Summarii* and is found there until 1556 (L. 40, cc. 261 and 317; transcribed by ZORZI, 1964, pp. 332, 334). Subsequently, we have no further information concerning him.

[6] *Summarii delle spese per le logge*, L. 40, c. 94 *a* (transcribed by ZORZI, 1964, p. 328); DALLA POZZA, 1943, p. 128. The *Summarii* specifies moreover that eight troni were paid for each of the " *rose* " in the frieze and 5 marchetti for each of the " *bacinette* " (paterae); " *de le foglie non è fatto mercato nè pagata ancor alcuna.* "

[7] ARSLAN, 1956, p. 62, NN. 323-325.

[8] ARSLAN, 1956, pp. 29-30, n. 140; BABIERI, 1956 (II), pp. 134-141: cf. figs. on p. 137. ZORZI (1964, p. 49) attributes the keystone head to Palladio's son Marcantonio; however, Marcantonio was working there only after 1554 (see below).

[9] ZORZI (1965, fig. 99 and 1964, p. 49) attributes it instead to Girolamo Pittoni.

[10] DALLA POZZA, 1943, p. 128.

[11] *Summarii delle spese per le logge*, L. 40, c. 93 *b* (transcribed by ZORZI, 1964, pp. 327-328).

[12] Cf. ZORZI, 1965, fig. 100 and 1964, p. 49.

[13] ZORZI, 1951.

[14] See n. 5.

[15] *Summarii delle spese per le logge*, L. 40, c. 224 *a* (transcribed by ZORZI, 1964, p. 331). Note that from this time on the *Summarii* no longer speak of " *teste humane* " for the keystones, but of " *mascare.* "

[16] ZORZI, 1964, pp. 305-306, 307-308; also pp. 49-50. After 1560 Palladio's son Marcantonio (who was probably the second child born, after Leonida) transferred to Venice and Vittoria's studio, where he carried on various activities until about 1585. In 1588 he was still in Venice, but he returned to Vicenza a short time later. Notices of him and of some of his works survive up to 1600 (see also MAGRINI, 1845, p. 94 and 1855, pp. 69-71). *Il Palazzo della Ragione in Vicenza* (1875, p. 74) also contains references to Marcantonio's probable activity in Brescia and Padua. CESSI (1961) is useful for the Venetian period; on p. 37 Cessi suggests that perhaps this Marcantonio had assisted Vittoria at Maser. For further information, see ZORZI, 1916, p. 9.

[17] *Summarii delle spese per le logge*, L. 40, c. 341 *a*; L. 38, c. 22 *b* (transcribed by ZORZI, 1964, pp. 333, 336).

[18] See n. 5.

[19] *Summarii delle spese per le logge*, L. 40, cc. 261 (March 2, 1555), 317 (May 9, 1556) (transcribed by ZORZI, 1964, pp. 332-334).

[20] See n. 16.

[21] CEVESE, 1954. Vittoria was in Vicenza in 1547-48, working on the stuccoes in the hall of the Arnaldi house at S. Paolo, and again in 1552-53 to decorate rooms in Palazzo Thiene with Bartolomeo Ridolfi (see ZORZI, 1951). Cevese's suppositions that the creator of the heads was Vittoria and that the masks could have been executed directly after his designs are helpful as a stylistic orientation but are difficult to verify; it would be necessary to suppose that the master, who departed for Venice in 1553, left designs with the sculptors Lorenzo Rubini and Palladio's son Marcantonio for the keystones, which were subsequently executed between then and 1559. Unless Cevese is referring to general designs for masks circulating in Vittoria's studio (he has observed that there is considerable similarity between the loggia keystones and the masks that decorate the magnificent ceiling of the lower rotonda of Palazzo Thiene), this is somewhat of an overstatement. See also CESSI, 1961, pp. 16-27.

[22] We must remember that Palladio himself might have taken part in preparing the keystones of this group of arches on the western side (the second, third, and fourth on the left, erected between September 1556 and November 1559), if we accept ZORZI's interpretation (1964, p. 50) of a document of August 4, 1557 (transcribed p. 58, Doc. 10; see also CEVESE, 1964 [II], p. 336). Among the many other expenditures appear 30 troni " *A Paladio e Maestro Zanantonio Vinitiano per fatura dele teste.* " But it should be noted that no payment appears to Palladio for work in sculpture in the carefully-kept *Summarii*, and the wording " *tr. 30... per fatura dele teste* " is at the very least unclear, since we do not know whether this involved human heads or " *teste de vacha.* " In fact, since Palladio would probably have sculpted human heads for the keystones rather than the very modest ox-

skulls, 30 troni would have been payment for one human head plus part of another (as we have seen, 22 troni was the compensation for one head). This makes little sense; moreover, from November of 1556 to January of 1558, as far as we can tell from the *Summarii* (L. 40, cc. 340 *b*, 375 *a*; transcribed by ZORZI, 1964, pp. 335-336), Palladio must have hardly been in Vicenza, since his salary as superintendent of the work on the loggias was collected through the agency of his son Marcantonio for the whole of 1557. Therefore, it does not seem possible for the architect to have devoted himself to sculptural work in that year—a type of work that he had not done for at least twenty years. Either there is an involuntary error in the document (" Paladio " perhaps having been hastily written instead of " Marcantonio Paladio " his son, who was actually involved during that year in the sculpture for the loggias), or the document might signify that Palladio gave directions to the sculptors. In the latter event, could the fourth keystone on the west possibly reveal a different character in this regard?

23 *Summarii delle spese per le logge*, L. 38, cc. 107 *a* and 111 *a*; DALLA POZZA, 1943, p. 136. Francesco Albanese the elder, head of two generations of architects and sculptors, is certainly the " Francesco di Asolo " mentioned in the *Summarii*. This identification is also proposed by MAGRINI (1845, *Annotazioni*, p. viii, n. 19) and is commonly accepted (SILVAGNI, 1939, pp. 17, 50-51); the only dissident voice is that of BORTOLAN, 1885, p. 8. According to SILVAGNI, Francesco would have been born c. 1515-20; but this would have a man nearly in his fifties executing keystone masks, a work which usually seems to have been entrusted to more modest beginners. More important, Francesco Albanese executed the Rutilio monument in the Cathedral in 1593 (ARSLAN, 1956, p. 34, N. 158 and BARBIERI, 1956 [II], pp. 161-162), which would make him then almost eighty if we accepted Silvagni's birth dating; and three years later (in 1596) he collaborated on the group on the northern side of the Torre di Piazza. The two statues of Sts. Vincent and Stephen in that group are surely by him, as ARSLAN guessed (1596, p. 157, N. 1083). However, it would be more prudent to shift Francesco's birth date at least to c. 1535-40, especially if we agree with Silvagni that he died in the first decade of the seventeenth century (MAGRINI, loc. cit., states that was he still alive in 1597). Moreover, DA SCHIO, *Memorabili* (Appendix) placed the date 1539 by the name of Francesco Albanese (p. 174), evidently as the probable date of his birth.

24 For this important component of Albanese's style, see ARSLAN (1956, p. 48, N. 260); concerning the Vicentine period of Bartolomeo Ammannati (1546-50), see BETTINI, 1941, esp. pp. 23-24 and n. 10.

25 ARSLAN, 1956, p. 34, N. 157 and BARBIERI, 1956 (II), p. 170.

26 PUPPI, 1968, p. 74, n. 18.

27 The fact that no specific accounts of payment to Albanese (or to anyone else) exist for the upper keystones must be related to the reform recorded from 1572 onward in the contracts for the construction of the loggias: from that time on the contractor undertook to provide arches which were finished in every detail and to attend personally to the payment of everyone involved (cf. also MAGRINI, 1845, p. 94). We must remember that the Ionic keystones were necessarily handled differently from the Doric ones; they could not be grotesque masks, but had to harmonize with the supposed " feminine " aspect of the Ionic order and thus are more composed and formal female heads.

28 We are reminded of the statues on the Arco delle Scalette erected in 1595, as well as of those in the presbytery of S. Pietro (1596) and on the façade of the Oratorio del Gonfalone, built in 1596 (*Guida di Vicenza*, 1953 and 1956, p. 405; ARSLAN, 1956, pp. 141-142, N. 956 and 113-114, n. 766; SEMENZATO, 1966, pp. 79-81; BARBIERI, 1968). The statues on the Arco delle Scalette, notwithstanding some opinions to the contrary (SEMENZATO, loc. cit.), appear to be correctly attributed to Giambattista on the basis of style (cf. MAGRINI, 1845, p. 291 and esp. *Annotazioni*, p. lxxvii and *Guida di Vicenza*, loc. cit.).

29 ARSLAN, 1956, pp. 141-142, n. 956; SILVAGNI, 1939; SEMENZATO, 1966, pp. 79-81.

30 ARSLAN, 1956, pp. 122-123, N. 819 and p. 126, NN. 845-846; SEMENZATO, 1966, pp. 79-81.

31 ARSLAN, 1956, p. 169, N. 1166; SEMENZATO, 1966, pp. 79-81.

32 DALLA POZZA, 1943, pp. 235-237, Doc. XXV; ZORZI, 1964, pp. 70-71, Doc. 45.

33 This was the hard stone from the nearby Piovene quarries that was also used in the construction of the loggias. But the excessive hardness and the poor weather-resistance of this stone (especially if it has been worked in such a way that water is allowed to collect in folds of draperies or elsewhere; POZZA, 1952, p. 30) and its " crystalline fragility " (POZZA, 1957) explain the unfortunate state of preservation of many of these statues.

34 Agostino Rubini died shortly before 1595 (ZORZI, 1965. p. 90; 1966, p. 162).

35 For a different—and unlikely—interpretation of this document, see SILVAGNI, 1939, p. 42.

36 Each has a height of about 2.5 meters.

37 The text reads precisely: " *per l'accordo che già fu fatto con li scultori.* "

38 See n. 3.

39 VENTURI referred to his possible presence there (1937, p. 320).

40 MAGRINI's observation (1845, p. 87) that " Giovanni Antonio Grazioli received payment for eighteen statues at the rate of 50 ducats apiece, indicating that two of them, the work of Agostino Rubini, were unfinished, " contradicts both the tenor and the exact letter of the document of June 27, 1597. This ambiguity gives rise to two equally unfounded hypotheses: first, that Grazioli had completed two statues left unfinished by Agostino Rubini (*Il Palazzo della Ragione in Vicenza*, 1875, pp. 74-75), and second, that Grazioli, along with his brother, was among the possible authors of the statues crowning the loggias. They were actually only the contractors; nevertheless the misunderstanding, which began with historians of the last century, has continued up to the latest *Guida di Vicenza* (p. 92). ZORZI's hypothesis (1966 [II], p. 162) that the two statues which " *mancano a drizzarsi* " on June 27, 1597 (but which would today be in position) were executed by Agostino Rubini contradicts the sense and the letter of the document in question; the latter very precisely states that Rubini's work came to nothing. See n. 46 for the stylistic motifs that this hypothesis would have to support.

Interestingly enough, some writers give the statues crowning the Palladian loggias to De' Pieri, an important Vicentine painter of the first half of the Settecento (CISCATO, 1870, p. 43; BARICHELLA, 1878; MUNARETTO, 1933); but no one goes so far as VELO (1790, pp. 243, 252), who attributes the statues to Orazio Marinali!

41 ZORZI, 1965, p. 90.

42 VENTURI, 1937, p. 90, n. 1, fig. 66: this hypothesis is accepted by SILVAGNI, 1939, pp. 75-80. Vittoria's presence among the sculptors at the loggias was noted rather indiscriminately by nineteenth-century historians; the earliest sources (GUALDO, *Vicenza tamisata*, and CASTELLINI, *Descrizione della città di Vicenza*) are completely silent, while some Settecento texts (BALDARINI, 1779, II, pp. 8-9; CHIUSOLE, 1782, p. 52) more prudently refer to Vittoria's school (followed by ALVERA, 1834 and *Appunti mss. per una Guida di Vicenza*).

43 ZORZI, 1951; concerning Vittoria's second transfer to Vicenza, see also BARBIERI, 1952, p. 122; CESSI, 1960, p. 18.

44 As put forward by MORRESI, 1956, pp. 44, 47.

45 See Chapter IV.

46 ZORZI (1966 [II], p. 162) insists on maintaining the hypothesis set out in n. 40 and consequently endeavors to identify among the statues set up on or before June 27, 1597, the two which he says were done by Agostino Rubini. He suggests attributing the statue of the old man formerly given to Vittoria to Rubini, as it reflects " the style of the great master from Trent and the manner of other of Agostino Rubini's works. " Leaving aside every argument previously noted about the almost complete improbability that Agostino worked on these statues, Zorzi advances as evidence a comparison with the two allegories of the Retrone and Bacchiglione rivers, located at the western corner of the portico of Palazzo Trissino and attributed to Rubini by Zorzi himself (1966 [II], pp. 161-162). However, we can re-

assign these on a precise documentary basis (BARBIERI, 1967 [II])
to Giambattista Barberini, who was active in the palace in 1662-
64—almost a century later.

[47] See n. 23.

[48] Girolamo was born about 1580-84 (PUPPI, 1968, p. 74,
n. 18; SEMENZATO, 1966, p. 81). Therefore ARSLAN'S suggestion
(1956, p. 35, N. 163) that his work is prevalent in these statues
is to be discarded.

[49] CASTELLINI, Descrizione della città di Vicenza, I, c. 277 b
(ed. BORTOLAN, 1885, p. 121) states that these statues were " di
mano dei più celebri scultori di quei tempi, tra i quali Camillo
Mariani."

[50] FIOCCO (1940-41) is fundamental on Camillo Mariani, who
was a Vicentine follower of Vittoria. See also the ample note
by NAVA CELLINI, 1960 (cols. 314-315) and the citations by MAR-
TINELLI (1960) regarding the formation of Gian Lorenzo Bernini,
summarizing his previous research. Mariani's birth in 1567 was
recently confirmed by ZORZI (1960 [III], pp. 239-240) on a
documentary basis different from that of Fiocco's earlier study.

[51] Cf. MARTINELLI, 1960, cols. 460-461, 464.

[52] FIOCCO, 1940-41. Castellini also mentions this work: no
doubt it was lost in 1838 when the church was almost completely destroyed by Malacarne in order to build the city hospital
(ARSLAN, 1956, p. 5, N. 29).

[53] For the sources and texts which support the hypothesis
of Mariani's activity at the Teatro Olimpico, see FIOCCO, 1940-
41, pp. 77, 86. Valentino Martinelli (in several verbal com-
munications, for which I am very grateful) identifies Mariani's
hand in the stuccoes of the perspectives and in the second statue
in the bottom first row of the proscenium, counting from the right.
ZORZI, who at one time (1956, p. 195) considered that Camillo's
work in the Olimpico cannot be precisely identified, later denied
that the sculptor ever worked in the theatre, as it was officially
opened in 1585 when he was barely eighteen years old (1960 [III],
pp. 239-240); moreover, the proscenium was completed in March,
1583, when the artist was only sixteen (ZORZI, 1966 [II], p. 159).
Zorzi attributes the stuccoes of the perspectives to AGOSTINO
RUBINI (p. 160).

[54] IVANOFF, 1964, pp. 105, 108-109; figs. 4-5.

[55] ARSLAN, 1956, p. 142, NN. 957-960. This attribution, extended to the plan of the façade itself by some scholars (cf.
ARLSAN, N. 956, part c), is by Castellini (FASOLO, 1934). Regarding Sts. Peter, Paul, and Andrew on the façade, Arslan dis-
misses the figure of St. Andrew as the work of a mediocre
sculptor.

[56] According to a suggestion by Carlo Ludovico Ragghianti,
which was accepted by FIOCCO (1940-41).

[57] For the conclusion of work, see BARBIERI, 1952, p. 137.
The attribution to Mariani is by FIOCCO (1940-41) and is also
based on the sculptor's friendship with Scamozzi, the architect
of the church (cf. BARBIERI, 1952, p. 152).

[58] BARBIERI, 1956, p. 152; ARSLAN (1956, p. 33, N. 156)
suggests Alessandro Vittoria. The statues of Sts. Benedict and
Scholastica on either side of the second altar at the left in
S. Pietro were attributed to Mariani by FIOCCO (1940-41, p. 77;
however, the attribution was not accepted by ARSLAN (1956,
p. 142, NN. 957-960). The works are not by Mariani but are
undoubtedly by the brothers Tommaso and Matteo Allio about
1660-65 (see BARBIERI, 1968, pp. 22-23).

[59] It is difficult to decipher the iconography of these statues.
The subjects, which derive from contemporary mythological interests, would have been assigned to the sculptors by local human-
ists. We know for example that subsequently (in 1614) the
statues commissioned from Giambattista Albanese had to be
called by the names assigned to them by the Presidente alla fabbrica, Adriano Porto (see n. 72). RIPA (1764-67) might be useful
to consult, but it is much more important to note the statues'
architectonic significance as the necessary completion of the
loggias' structure and their function as the indispensable visual
connection between the projecting plane of the piers and the
receding plane of the great Quattrocento roof (see Chapter IV).
This recalls the function which sculpture was frequently required
to perform from the Cinquecento to the Settecento, as mediator

between the human presence and the abstraction of architecture
(cf. SEMENZATO, 1968, p. 36).

[60] We must remember that the northeast corner group now
appears as it was restored by the sculptor Neri Pozza after the
war.

[61] See n. 28.

[62] See n. 30.

[63] ARSLAN, 1956, pp. 26-27, N. 124 and p. 54, NN. 285-286;
concerning the Chapel of St. Joseph, see also BARBIERI, 1956 (II),
pp. 116-118.

[64] ARSLAN (1956, p. 127, NN. 845-846) doubts Giambattista's
authorship of the Adam and Eve of the Capra altar, as does MAGA-
GNATO (1953 and 1956, p. 63); SILVAGNI (1939, p. 72) suggests
Girolamo's intervention. However, it is necessary to take into
account the vicissitudes of the two statues; they were exposed
to the weather on the façade of the Ospizio Trento from
1838 onward, and they were much restored in 1952 when they
were returned to S. Lorenzo.

[65] Following BALDARINI (1779 [II], pp. 8-9) the statues on
the fifth and sixth piers on the north, counting from the left, have
traditionally been attributed to Giambattista Albanese (cf. CHIU-
SOLE, 1782, p. 52; ALVERA, Appunti mss. per una Guida di Vicenza, and 1834; FAVETTA, Picolo Regualgio; BERTI, 1822, p. 22).

[66] See n. 31.

[67] VENTURI, 1937, p. 90, n. 1.

[68] FIOCCO, 1940-41, p. 78.

[69] Discarding Trissino's hypothesis (Miscellanea di appunti
su varii artisti vicentini, Vita di Camillo Mariani) of Mariani's
(b. 1567) direct apprenticeship with Lorenzo Rubini (d. 1574),
the possibility remains that Agostino Rubini—who was very
active at the Teatro Olimpico from 1576 to 1583—may have
given Camillo some instruction (ZORZI, 1960 [III], pp. 239-240;
1962 [II]; 1965, p. 93; 1966 [II], pp. 157-160). Moreover,
during this important period in Mariani's youthful formation,
only the Rubini circle could have served as medium between the
sculptor and Vittoria's great achievements; the elegant, " archaiciz-
ing " manner of Francesco Albanese the elder was retardataire
(cf. the monument to Gaetano Thiene in the Cathedral, dated
1583, and the Trissino altar of 1587 in S. Maria dei Servi).

[70] MAGAGNATO, 1952, p. 23; see also SEMENZATO, 1966, pp. 34
and 42, n. 29.

[71] FIOCCO, 1940-41, p. 85.

[72] DALLA POZZA, 1943, p. 242, Doc. XXVIII. Through an
oversight the date is omitted; however it can be taken directly
from the source (Summarii delle spese per le logge, L. 41, c. 24).

[73] SILVAGNI, 1939, p. 75. The wording of the document of
January 22, 1614 (" che far debbi ... figure undese o quel più
vero numero che occorrerà ") may be interpreted as meaning that
perhaps there was uncertainty whether to place other figures on
the terminal pier at the east, which is partially incorporated in
the wall above the Arco degli Zavatteri. According to SILVAGNI
(loc. cit.) and SEMENZATO (1966, p. 80), the eleven statues commissioned from Giambattista were to have been placed seven on
the Piazza dei Signori side and four on the Piazzetta Palladio side;
but this contradicts what had already been done by 1597.

[74] VENTURI, 1937, p. 334; Venturi notes that the source of
his information was Giulio Fasolo. SILVAGNI (1939, pp. 131 and
143-144) has checked the sources.

[75] VENTURI, 1937, p. 335; for a check against the source,
see SILVAGNI, 1939, p. 147. The sculptor mentioned is Girolamo
Albanese, who was dead by 1663 (see n. 84).

[76] ARSLAN, 1956, p. 169, N. 1166 and p. 54, NN. 285-286;
SEMENZATO, 1966, pp. 13-14, 80.

[77] SILVAGNI, 1939.

[78] ARSLAN, 1956, p. 35, N. 163.

[79] According to SILVAGNI (1939), the statues at S. Vincenzo
are all by Girolamo; but ARSLAN (1956, p. 169, N. 1166) is
hesitant about the two at the sides. It is difficult to dis-
tinguish between the work of Girolamo and that of Giambattista
in the Cappella del Rosario in S. Corona; ARSLAN (1956, p. 54,
NN. 285-286) suggests that Girolamo was responsible for the

statues of Sts. Peter, Paul, Jerome, and John. See also Semenzato, 1966, pp. 80-81.

[80] For this attribution, see Barbieri, 1956 (II), pp. 110-111.

[81] Venturi, 1937, p. 334 (Silvagni, 1939, p. 132, verifies
this from the source); Semenzato, 1966, p. 81.

[82] Silvagni, 1939, pp. 145-146.

[83] We can only note that around 1650 he was working on
the statues for the Chapel of St. Joseph in the Cathedral of Vicenza (Arslan, 1956, pp. 26-27, N. 124; Barbieri, 1956, pp. 116-
118; Semenzato, 1966, pp. 14, 81).

[84] L. Trissino (*Miscellanea di appunti su varii artisti vicentini*) states that Girolamo died in 1660; this date is accepted
albeit with some reservations by Silvagni (1939) and by Semenzato (1966, p. 81). Timofiewitsch (1962, pp. 264 and 265,
n. 9) proposes 1663 (cf. *Lacrime di Parnaso*, 1663), but 1660 is
definitively confirmed by the documents (Puppi, 1968, p. 74,
n. 18).

[85] Cf. Silvagni, 1939, p. 147. I was unable to find any
information concerning Muggini apart from this indication of his
work on the loggia statues.

[86] Francesco is always identified with the son of Giambattista who was the heir of Vincenzo Scamozzi (Barbieri, 1952,
p. 182), and who consequently called himself Francesco Alba-
nese-Scamozzi. For this identification, see Da Schio (*I Memorabili*, pp. 174-178); it was accepted by Magrini (1845, p. 87 and
esp. p. 274), in *Il Palazzo della Ragione in Vicenza* (1875, p. 9),
and, finally, by Silvagni (1939).
However, Da Schio (loc. cit.) mentions another Francesco
Albanese, the brother of Giambattista and Girolamo; he states
that this Francesco worked with his brothers on the statues of the
Arco delle Scalette (1595). More important is the evidence in the
pamphlet *Lacrime di Parnaso in morte del Signor Girolamo Albanese*, Vicenza, 1663; here we learn that there was another
Francesco Albanese, who was Girolamo's son and the brother of
another Giambattista who was a writer. This Francesco Albanese was also a sculptor. In fact, the pamphlet records that he
carved a portrait of his father in stone and that in him "*spira
viva la paterna eccellenza.*" Marchi (*Memorie di famiglie vicentine*, I, p. 33) states that this Francesco di Girolamo was baptized
on March 7, 1643, with Antonio Pizzocaro and Francesco Maffei
as godfathers; Magrini later mentions him (1845, *Annotazioni*,
p. lxxvii), although with a certain confusion with Francesco di
Giambattista (see also Marasca, 1876). More recently, Ferro
(1907) has noted that this Francesco was active around 1665 (see
also Pavan Taddei, 1960).

[87] Magrini, 1845, pp. 82, 87; Bortolan, 1885, p. 9; Silvagni, 1939, pp. 75-80.

[88] Magrini, 1845, p. 87.

[89] Silvagni, 1939, pp. 75-80: includes citation of sources.

[90] Or maybe even three, considering that Muggini was not
a well-known sculptor and would not have received very high
payments; the 100 ducats did not include charges for materials,
for which Giacon Merlo "*priaro*" received exactly 30 ducats
(Silvagni, 1939, pp. 75-80).

[91] Arnaldi, 1767, p. lix; see also Venturi, 1937, p. 335.
Silvagni, 1939, p. 147, verifies this from the source.

[92] Magrini, p. 87.

[93] Cogo, 1900, p. 22. In April 1801 (Arnaldi-Tornieri,
Memorie, VII, c. 465/a, 21 Aprile 1801), when the lion was removed from the northern column in Piazza dei Signori in order
to substitute a statue of Liberty, the target of attack was "*quel
gruppo di tre statue che sta sull'angolo del Palazzo della Ragione
sulla ringhiera dei piombi*" (possibly the group on the northern
side, at the northeast corner?); one of the figures was to be
"lifted" to serve as the effigy of Liberty. Ottone Calderari
prevented this folly from being carried out.

[94] Cf. Barbieri, 1967 (II) and (III).

[95] Concerning this technique and its diffusion on the Venetian *terraferma*, see Arslan, 1956, p. 113, N. 766.

[96] Baldarini, 1779, II, p. 9, thus refers to it, identifying it
as a "*memoria di un patrizio che fu già Pretore, consistente in
un Ercole che sostiene lo stemma gentilizio con due amorini la-
terali, e a' fianchi quattro statue rappresentanti quattro virtù.*"

[97] Baldarini, 1779, II, p. 9; Chiusole, 1782, p. 52.

[98] Alvera, *Appunti per una Guida di Vicenza*; *Il Palazzo
della Ragione in Vicenza*, 1875, p. 20.

[99] Cogo, 1900, p. 24: as Baroque in style.

[100] *Guida di Vicenza*, 1953 and 1956, p. 91.

[101] Silvagni, 1939, pp. 3, 47, 62-63, observes that the distribution of mass, the articulation of movement, and the unusual wealth of decorative elements suggest the intervention of
a painter in the execution of the work. In fact, there are traces
of color in the surface depressions; this indicates that it was a
temporary display, created on the occasion of a distinguished visit
and not meant to last. However, this theory is difficult to accept
in the case of a work of this importance.

[102] Zorzi (1951, pp. 146-147) suggests that the male figure
represents Atlas rather than Hercules; he also records that there
were analogous statues in the corner lunettes of Palazzo della
Ragione, which were destroyed by incendiary bombs during the
air raid of March 18, 1945.

[103] Zorzi, 1951, pp. 152-153, 154; 1955, p. 104; 1965, pp. 87-
88, 92. See also Morresi, 1956, pp. 33-38, 51-53.

[104] Faccioli (1776, pp. 165-168) records—albeit with some
confusion and without precise locations—a whole series of inscriptions which no longer exist, but which at that time were
"*variis in locis*" in Palazzo della Ragione. Many of these refer
to praetors, but it is impossible to ascertain the one commemo-
rated in this trophy. Zorzi proposes (using Faccioli) the identification of the lost inscription with a celebratory inscription of 1567
honoring the Podestà Pietro Bon and Captain Niccolò Malipiero
(I am very grateful to him for giving me this information). For
Zorzi the identification serves to confirm the attribution to Lorenzo Rubini (d. 1574).

[105] Morresi, 1956, pp. 41-46.

[106] The new Palladian loggias advanced quickly along that
side of the palace from 1549 on. The sixth arch on the left in
the Doric order was part of a group finished June 24, 1553 (see
Chapter IV).

[107] See Chapter IV.

[108] On the other hand, Zorzi thinks that the complex might
have been executed independently of the construction of the loggia vaults and of the upper cross vaults (verbal communication;
see n. 104).

[109] See below.

[110] Arslan, 1956, pp. 113-114, N. 766.

[111] Cf. Silvagni, 1939, p. 18.

[112] See the section on the statues on the northern and western
sides.

[113] Insofar as Faccioli (1776) is concerned, the same difficulties exist as those mentioned in n. 104.

[114] *Guida di Vicenza*, 1953 and 1956, p. 92. For the sculpture
formerly existing in the other corner lunettes, see n. 102 and
Zorzi, 1952.

[115] Faccioli, 1776, p. 165, N. 3.

[116] Mommsen, 1872, p. 308, N. 3112. Gordian III held the
second consulship and was the fifth tribunal podestà in 242. The
Vicentine tablet dates back to that epoch (Girardi, 1924, pp. 40-
41), and perhaps even more precisely to July of 242, when Gordian
probably passed through Vicenza on his way to the Thracian war
(Da Schio, 1850, pp. 44-45). The tablet proves that the magistracy of the Decurions existed in Vicenza, as well as the benefits
received from the "*Matidie*" (Barichella, 1891, p. 47, N. 28).
In fact, a building erected in the city approximately a century
earlier with donations from the "*Matidie*" (the descendants of
Trajan) was dedicated to the Emperor Gordian (Da Schio, 1850,
pp. 20, 44-45; *Le antiche iscrizioni*, section entitled *Monumenti
anepigrafici*, p. xxiv bis). See also Lampertico, 1884, pp. 45-47,
for the interpretation of the term "Respublica" on the tablet.

[117] The date 1540 is the one most commonly accepted (Da
Schio, 1850, pp. 44-45; Formenton, 1867, pp. 22-23; Formenton, 1870, pp. 36-37). However Marzari (1591, pp. 21-22),
writing close to the time of the discovery, says that it was found
in "*i mesi passati,*" and Barbarano (1649, pp. 32-33) mentions
1586. In regard to the exact location of the discovery, Marzari

speaks of "*scavando una cantina nelle case dei Castelli mercanti di lana vicino alla piazza delle Biade e alla chiesa di S. Eleuterio, dieci piedi entro le viscere della terra*"; according to DA SCHIO (loc. cit.) the Castelli house would be Palazzetto Valeri (formerly Colonnese) at S. Barbara (*Guida di Vicenza*, 1953 and 1956, p. 130); but BRESSAN (*Studi sulle iscrizioni vicentine*) identifies it more convincingly with the porticoed building that still occupies almost all the northern side of Piazza Biade at the corner of Contrà S. Barbara and which at that time belonged to the Marasca.

[118] As indicated by the inscription under the niche: ANT[O-NIUS] ET FRANC[ISCUS] CASTELLORUM M[ISERUNT].

[119] I am grateful to Giangiorgio Zorzi for providing me with the information regarding the relative document from the *Libri Provisionum*, XIV, 18 Sett. 1586. This confirms his own observation (1952, p. 156).

[120] FACCIOLI, 1776, p. 165, N. 4.

[121] See BORTOLAN, 1910, pp. 4-5: the inscription refers to a decision made in 1261 by Bishop Bartolomeo da Breganze concerning the tithes to be allotted to the Chapter of the Cathedral from lands surrounding the city (the "*Colture*"). Five identical examples of this decision were incised and were placed as a perpetual record on the five gates of the pre-Scaligeri city wall. The tablet in the loggias is the only one surviving today. It was transported there from the tower "*in capite pontis Pusterlae prope segam*" (BRESSAN, 1878, p. 27; also, *Studi sopra iscrizioni moderne e medioevali vicentine*, fasc. *Iscrizioni gotiche*, N. 41), perhaps at the time when the tower and the tower gate were demolished (*Il Palazzo della Ragione in Vicenza*, 1875, pp. 117-118). The latter had become useless after the Venetians extended the city walls during the first half of the fifteenth century. See also BARBARANO, 1649, p. 10; 1761, pp. 229-230; FACCIOLI, 1776, p. 165, N. 4).

[122] DALLA POZZA, 1943, pp. 234-237, Doc. XXV (p. 236). See also Chapter IV.

[123] ARSLAN, 1956, p. 143, NN. 965-966; BARBIERI, 1968.

[124] DALLA POZZA, 1943, pp. 237-242; see also Chapter IV.

[125] BARICHELLA, 1878 (II); FASOLO, 1932.

[126] *Guida di Vicenza*, 1953 and 1956, p. 405; see also n. 28.

[127] *Guida di Vicenza*, 1953 and 1956, p. 91.

[128] ZORZI, 1937, pp. 66 ff.

[129] FACCIOLI, 1776, p. 168, N. 28. An undertaking involving the regilding of the lion also occurred during the general restoration of the palace in 1869-71 (see Chapter V).

[130] Cf. BARBIERI, 1956 (II), p. 173, n. 15.

[131] MAGRINI, 1845, *Annotazioni*, pp. iii-iv, n. 15.

[132] *Il Palazzo della Ragione in Vicenza*, 1875, p. 51 (for the lower loggias and consequently for the ground floor); p. 58 (for the upper loggias); pp. 72-73 (for the Hall).

BIBLIOGRAPHY

MANUSCRIPTS (PUBLISHED AND UNPUBLISHED) FROM THE 13TH TO THE 18TH CENTURY

Regestum Possessionum Communis Vincentiae [16 January 1262], parchment ms. in folio, Vicenza, Biblioteca Bertoliana, Archivio di Torre, A, N. 762.

Statuti del Comune di Vicenza [1264], ed. F. Lampertico, Venice, 1886.

N. Smereglo, *Annales Civitatis Vicentiae* [1200-1312], ed. F. Lampertico, in *Scritti storici e letterari*, II, Florence, 1883, pp. 270 ff.

C. Da Costozza, *Frammenti della cronaca* [1372-87], ed. Rumor, Vicenza, 1886.

G. B. Paglierini, *Croniche di Vicenza... dal principio di questa Città fino al tempo ch'ella si diede sotto al Serenissimo Dominio Veneto* [1404], ed. G. G. Alcaini, Vicenza, 1663.

M. Sanuto, *Itinerario per la terraferma veneziana nell'anno MCCCCLXXXIII*, Padua, 1847.

Z. Lilio (Lilio Vicentino), *Breve descrittione del mondo*, transl. F. Baldelli, from the first Latin edition of 1493, Venice, 1551.

Cronica ad memoriam praeteriti temporis praesentis atque futuri [1237-1524], Vicenza, 1884.

Cronicha che comenza dall'anno 1400 [up to 1524], ed. D. Bortolan, Vicenza, 1889.

B. Baretaro, *Chronica ab anno 1444 usque ad annum 1552*, ed. G. Curti, Vicenza, 1890.

F. Monza, *Cronaca* [1548-92], ed. D. Bortolan, Vicenza, 1888.

Summarii delle spese per le logge del Palazzo della Ragione [16 th-17 th centuries], ms., Vicenza, Biblioteca Bertoliana, Archivio di Torre, Vols. Marked 37-41, NN. 763-767; see also the unmarked *Sommario* by Francesco Trissino.

S. Castellini, *Descrizione della città di Vicenza dentro dalle mura e delli borghi della medesima*, Vols. I-II [c. 1628], ms. Vicenza, Biblioteca Bertoliana, Libreria Gonzati, 22.11.15/16.

S. Castellini, *Descrizione della città di Vicenza dentro dalle mura* [c. 1628], ed. D. Bortolan, Vicenza, 1885.

S. Castellini, *Storia della città di Vicenza* [first decades of the 17 th century], Vicenza, Bks. I-XII (pt. 1), 1783-85; Bks. XII (pt. 2)-XIX, 1821-22.

G. Gualdo, *La Vicenza tamisata (del 1639; et hora con poche aggionte del 1647)*, ms., Venice, Biblioteca Nazionale Marciana, Cl. VI, n. 141 b.

F. Pigafetta, *Descrizione del Territorio e Contado di Vicenza* [c. 1680], ms. copy of 1747, Vicenza, Biblioteca Bertoliana, Libreria Gonzati, 25.8.3., fasc. I.

G. Favetta, *Fatti successi in Vicenza dall'anno 1704 sino al 1814 diligentemente raccolti*, ms., Vicenza, Biblioteca Bertoliana, Libreria Gonzati, 22.9.42.

F. Arnaldi, *Memorie dall'anno 1740 sino al 1762*, Gonzati ms. copy, Vicenza, Biblioteca Bertoliana, Libreria Gonzati, 21.10.26.

M. Lavanello - G. Corona, *Memorie dal 1750 a tutto 1783, continuate dallo stesso Corona sino al 18 maggio 1814*, Gonzati ms. copy, Vicenza, Biblioteca Bertoliana, Libreria Gonzati, 21.10.26.

E. Arnaldi, *Supplica ai Deputati del Comune* [of Vicenza] *estesa dal Co. Enea Arnaldi nel maggio MDCCLXV in nome anche de' suoi colleghi presidenti al Palazzo della Ragione sull'urgente bisogno di riparazione del palazzo stesso*, Vicenza, 1869.

A. (I) Arnaldi-Tornieri, *Memorie di Vicenza che cominciano dall'anno 1767, 18 giugno e terminano nel 1822*, Bks. I-XII, ms. copy by Arnaldo III, called "Muzio Tornieri", Vicenza, Biblioteca Bertoliana, Libreria Gonzati, 22.10.10/13.

E. Arnaldi, *Relazione sui restauri fatti e da farsi al Palazzo della Ragione in Vicenza* [8 September 1783], Vicenza, 1904.

G. Dian, *Notizie delli due secoli XVIII e XIX spettanti alla città di Vicenza*, ms., Vicenza, Biblioteca Bertoliana, Libreria Gonzati, 20.10.1/7.

Additional sources which were consulted are the Libri Partium *and the* Libri Provisionum *of the Commune of Vicenza* (Vicenza, Biblioteca Bertoliana, Archivio di Torre).

NINETEENTH-CENTURY MANUSCRIPTS (all of the following are located in the Biblioteca Bertoliana in Vicenza, Libreria Gonzaga; therefore only the inventory number is given for each, in parentheses).

A. Alvera, *Appunti per una Guida di Vicenza* (21.11.20).

A. Alvera, *Notizie sulla Basilica, la Torre di Piazza, il Palazzo del Podestà di Vicenza* (25.9.4).

B. Bressan, *Studi sopra iscrizioni moderne e medievali vicentine* (G. 22.9.39).

B. Bressan, *Studi sulle iscrizioni vicentine* (22.9.38).

G. Da Schio, *I Memorabili* (G. 5.9.5-16; G. 6.10.1-11).

G. Da Schio, *Le antiche iscrizioni che si dicono essere state in Vicenza e che più non vi sono, raccolte... ed illustrate, Venezia, Febbraio 1850, con Appendice delle iscrizioni che vi sono e non vi furono trovate e, di più, di quelle straniere che parlano di Vicenza; aggiungansi i monumenti anepigrafici della stessa città* (22.9.20).

G. Favetta, *Piccolo Regualgio su le chiese di Vicenza (con altre indicazioni su le architetture, pitture e sculture di Vicenza)* [c. 1830] (21.11.26).

A. Magrini, *Miscellanea di scritti su artisti vicentini* (3314).

G. Marchi, *Memori di famiglie vicentine*, Vols. I-VII (26.7.1/7).

L. Trissino, *Miscellanea di appunti su varii artisti vicentini* (3154-55).

PUBLISHED WORKS

1525 G. B. Dragonzino da Fano, *Nobilità di Vicenza*, Venice.

1537 S. Serlio, *Regole generali di Architettura*, Bk. IV, Venice.

1540 S. Serlio, *Regole generali di Architettura*, Bk. III, Venice.

1555 A. F. Doni, *Seconda Libraria*, Venice.

1568 G. Vasari, *Le vite de' più eccellenti pittori, scultori ed architettori*, ed. G. Milanesi, Vol. VII, 1881, Florence.

1570 A. Palladio, *I Quattro Libri dell'Architettura*, Venice.

1575 F. Sansovino, *Ritratto delle più nobili et famose città d'Italia*, Venice.

1591 G. Marzari, *La Historia di Vicenza*, Venice.

1615 V. Scamozzi, *L'Idea dell'Architettura universale*, Venice.

1648 C. Ridolfi, *Le meraviglie dell'Arte overo le vite de gl'illustri pittori veneti e dello stato*, Vols. I-II; ed. D. F. von Hadeln, Berlin, 1914.

1649 F. Barbarano, *Historia ecclesiastica della Città Territorio e Diocese di Vicenza*, Vol. I, Vicenza.
A. Scoto, *Itinerario overo nova descrittione de' viaggi principali d'Italia*, Padua.

1663 *Lacrime di Parnaso in morte del Signor Girolamo Alba-
      nese*, Vicenza.

1715 G. LEONI, *L'Architettura di Andrea Palladio in inglese,
      italiano e francese, con note ed osservazioni d'Inigo Jones,
      riveduta disegnata e pubblicata da Giacomo Leoni*, London.

1721 G. LEONI, *The Architecture of A. Palladio in four books...
      revis'd, design'd and publish'd by Giacomo Leoni*, London.

1740 [F. MUTTONI], *Architettura di Andrea Palladio vicentino...
      con le osservazioni dell'architetto N.N.*, Vol. I, Venice.

1744 [F. MUTTONI], *Architettura di Andrea Palladio vicen-
      tino... con le osservazioni dell'architetto N.N.*, Vol. V,
      Venice.

1761 F. BARBARANO, *Historia ecclesiastica della Città Territorio
      e Diocese di Vicenza*, Vol. V, Vicenza.
      O. BERTOTTI SCAMOZZI, *Il Forestiere istruito delle cose
      più rare di architettura e di alcune pitture della città di
      Vicenza*, Vicenza (1st ed.).

1762 T. TEMANZA, *Vita di Andrea Palladio*, Venice.

1764-67 C. RIPA, *Iconologia... notabilmente accresciuta... dal-
      l'Abate Cesare Orlandi*, Perugia.

1767 E. ARNALDI, *Delle Basiliche antiche e specialmente di
      quella di Vicenza*, Vicenza.

1769 M. COCHIN, *Voyage d'Italie ou recueil de notes*, Vol. III,
      Paris.

1776 O. BERTOTTI SCAMOZZI, *Le Fabbriche e i Disegni di Andrea
      Palladio raccolti ed illustrati*, Vol. I, Vicenza.
      J. T. FACCIOLI, *Musaeum Lapidarium Vicentinum*, Vol. I,
      Vicenza.

1778 P. CALVI (ANGIOLGABRIELLO DI S. MARIA), *Biblioteca e
      storia... di scrittori così della Città come del Territorio di
      Vicenza*, Vol. IV, Vicenza.
      T. TEMANZA, *Vite dei più celebri Architetti e Scultori ve-
      neziani che fiorirono nel secolo decimosesto*, Venice.

1779 P. BALDARINI, *Descrizione delle architetture, pitture e scul-
      ture in Vicenza* (ed. E. Arnaldi, O. Vecchia, L. Buffetti),
      Vols. I-II, Vicenza.

1780 O. BERTOTTI SCAMOZZI, *Il Forestiere istruito delle cose
      più rare di architetture e di alcune pitture della città di
      Vicenza*, Vicenza (2 nd ed.).

1781 F. ALGAROTTI, *Opere*, Vol. VII, Cremona.

1782 A. CHIUSOLE, *Itinerario delle pitture, sculture ed archi-
      tetture più rare di molte città d'Italia*, Vicenza.

1785 F. MILIZIA, *Memorie degli architetti antichi e moderni*,
      Vols. I-II, Bassano.

1786 W. GOETHE, *Giornale del Viaggio in Italia per la signora
      von Stein*, ed. Dario De Tuoni, Turin, 1957.
      [C. LODOLI], *Elementi dell'architettura lodoliana o sia
      l'Arte del fabricare con solidità scientifica e con eleganza
      non capricciosa*, Vol. I, Rome.

1790 G. B. VELO, *Poemetti e versi*, Vicenza.

1796 O. BERTOTTI SCAMOZZI, *Le Fabbriche e i Disegni di Andrea
      Palladio raccolti ed illustrati*, Vols. I-IV, Vicenza (posthu-
      mous ed.).

1804 O. BERTOTTI SCAMOZZI, *Il Forestiere istruito delle cose più
      rare di architettura e di alcune pitture della città di Vi-
      cenza*, Vicenza (posthumous ed.).

1811 A. RIGATO, *Osservazioni sopra Palladio*, Padua.

1816-29 W. GOETHE, *Il viaggio in Italia* [*Italienische Reise*],
      in *Opere di W. Goethe*, ed. L. Mazzucchetti, Vol. II, Flo-
      rence, 1948, pp. 423 ff. (Italian transl. by E. Zaniboni).

1822 G. B. BERTI, *Guida per Vicenza*, Venice.

1825 L. CICOGNARA, *Storia della scultura dal suo risorgimento in
      Italia fino al secolo di Canova*, Vol. V, Prato.

1830 L. CICOGNARA, " Elogio di Andrea Palladio, " in *Atti
      della Regia Accademia di Belle Arti di Venezia per l'anno
      1830*, Venice, pp. 3-51.

1834 A. ALVERA, *Le principali vedute di Vicenza e suoi dintorni
      con illustrazioni storiche*, Vicenza.

1845 A. MAGRINI, *Memorie intorno la vita e le opere di Andrea
      Palladio*, Padua.

      A. MAGRINI (II), *Dell'Architettura in Vicenza: Discorso
      con Appendice critico-cronologica delle principali sue fab-
      briche negli ultimi otto secoli*, Padua.

1847 G. PULLÉ, *Album di gemme architettoniche, ossia gli edi-
      fizii più rimarchevoli di Vicenza e del suo territorio, rile-
      vati da Giuseppe Zanetti, disegnati da Marco Moro e con
      cenni illustrativi dimostrati da Giulio co. Pullé*, Venice.

1848 A. MAGRINI, *Notizie storico-descrittive della Chiesa Cat-
      tedrale di Vicenza*, Vicenza.

1850 G. DA SCHIO, *Le antiche iscrizioni che furono trovate a
      Vicenza e che vi sono*, Bassano.
      M. MORO, *Vicenza e suoi dintorni*, Vicenza-Venice.

1855 J. BURCKHARDT, *Der Cicerone*, ed. P. Mingazzini and F.
      Pfister, Florence, 1952.
      A. MAGRINI, *Il Palazzo del Museo Civico in Vicenza de-
      scritto ed illustrato*, Vicenza.

1856 F. TRISSINO, *Vita di Stefano Madonetta pittore vicen-
      tino*, Vicenza.

1859 P. SELVATICO, " Vicenza: Palazzo della Ragione detto la
      Basilica, " in *Monumenti artistici e storici delle Provincie
      Venete descritti dalla Commissione istituita da Sua Al-
      tezza I. R... Ferdinando Massimiliano Governatore Ge-
      nerale*, Milan.

1861 J. CABIANCA-F. LAMPERTICO, *Vicenza e il suo territorio*,
      Milan.

1863 F. FORMENTON, *Tomaso Formenton ingegnere del Comune
      di Vicenza nel secolo XV*, Vicenza.

1867 J. BURCKHARDT-W. LÜBKE, " Geschichte der neueren Bau-
      kunst, " in Franz Kugler, *Geschichte der Baukunst*,
      Stuttgart.
      F. FORMENTON, *Memorie storiche della Città di Vicenza
      dalla sua origine fino l'anno 1867*, Vicenza.

1869 F. FORMENTON, *Il salone della Basilica*, Vicenza.

1870 A. CISCATO, *Guida di Vicenza*, Vicenza.
      F. FORMENTON, *Storia e illustrazione della Basilica di Pal-
      ladio in Vicenza*, Vicenza.

1872 F. FORMENTON, *Confutazione ad una memoria dell'Abate
      Magrini intorno a Tommaso Formenton*, Vicenza.
      F. FORMENTON (II), *Vicenza e sue gemme artistiche*, Vi-
      cenza.
      A. MAGRINI, " Intorno a Tomaso Formenton ingegnere
      vicentino nel secolo XV, " in *Archivio Veneto*, VI, pt. 1,
      pp. 38-59.
      T. MOMMSEN, *Corpus Inscriptionum Latinarum*, Vol. V,
      pt. 1, Berlin.

1875 G. BELLIO, " Sullo stato attuale della Basilica, sulla ne-
      cessità di riparazioni alla medesima e parere relativo in
      argomento, " in *Il Palazzo della Ragione in Vicenza*, Vi-
      cenza, pp. 93-101.
      *Il Palazzo della Ragione in Vicenza: Rivista tratta da
      memorie inedite dell'Abate Antonio Magrini con quattro
      tavole di Giovanni Bellio ed un capitolo dello stesso, a
      cura di Giuseppe Bacco*, Vicenza.

1876 P. MARASCA, *Cenni biografici di alcuni celebri artisti vi-
      centini*, Vicenza.

1878 V. BARICHELLA, " Il Palazzo della Ragione, " in *Il Berico*,
      7 February, no. 6.
      V. BARICHELLA (II), *Le colonne di S. Marco e del Re-
      dentore nella piazza dei Signori*, Vicenza.
      B. BRESSAN, *Torri della città di Vicenza nel Medio Evo:
      Memoria storica*, Vicenza.
      B. MORSOLIN, *Giangiorgio Trissino: Monografia di un
      gentiluomo letterato nel secolo XVI*, Florence (1 st ed.).

1880 V. BARICHELLA, *Andrea Palladio e la sua scuola: Cenni*,
      Lonigo.
      C. BOITO, *Terzo centenario di Andrea Palladio: Di-
      scorso letto nell'aula del Civico Museo il XXIX agosto
      MDCCCLXXX*, Vicenza.
      F. LAMPERTICO, *Discorso su Andrea Palladio*, Florence.
      G. ZANELLA, *Vita di Andrea Palladio*, Milan.
      G. ZANELLA (II), *Parole lette nella chiesa di S. Corona
      in Vicenza nel terzo centenario della morte di Andrea
      Palladio*, Vicenza.

1881 *Elenco dei principali monumenti e oggetti d'arte esistenti nella Provincia di Vicenza soggetti alla sorveglianza della Commissione Conservatrice di Antichità e Belle Arti: Monumenti architettonici*, Vicenza.

1883 C. BOITO, "Andrea Palladio," in *Leonardo, Michelangelo, Andrea Palladio*, Milan, pp. 228-325.

1884 F. LAMPERTICO, "Vicenza e le leggi patrie." Letter appended to the text of B. Morsolin's study on the odes of Parini, "La Magistratura," in *Atti dell'Istituto Veneto di Scienze, Lettere e Arti*, s. 6, Vol. II, pp. 891-914.
     A. SASSELLA, *Il Palazzo della Ragione o Basilica di Palladio in Vicenza*, Marcerata.

1885 D. BORTOLAN, *Saggio di un Dizionario biografico di artisti vicentini: Lettera A*, Vicenza.

1886 D. BORTOLAN, *Supplizi e Prigioni*, Vicenza.
     D. BORTOLAN (II), *Il Castello dell'Isola*, Vicenza.
     D. BORTOLAN (III), *Saggio di un Dizionario biografico di artisti vicentini: Lettera B*, Vicenza.

1887 G. HOWELEY, "Impressioni di un americano a Vicenza" (from the *Italian Journeys* of G. Howeley, Leipzig, 1883), in *La Provincia di Vicenza*, 6-7 and 7-8 December.

1889 D. BORTOLAN - F. LAMPERTICO, *Dei nomi delle Contrade nella città di Vicenza*, Vicenza.

1891 V. BARICHELLA, *Vicenza del terzo secolo: Visione*, Vicenza.

1892 D. BORTOLAN, *L'antica Loggia del Palazzo del Capitanio in Vicenza*, Vicenza.
     J. BURCKHARDT, *Le Cicerone: Guide de L'Art Antique et de l'Art Moderne en Italie. Traduit par Auguste Gérard sur la cinquième édition, revue et complétée par... W. Bode*, pt. 2, Paris.
     B. MORSOLIN, *Tiziano a Vicenza*, Florence.

1894 B. MORSOLIN, *Giangiorgio Trissino: Monografia di un gentiluomo letterato nel secolo XVI*, Florence (2 nd ed.).

1898 O. SCHMIDT - M. FABIANI, *Vicenza*, Vienna.

1900 L. COGO, *La Basilica palladiana nella storia e nell'arte: il suo rilievo architettonico*, Vicenza.

1901 L. COGO, "La nostra Basilica," in *La Provincia di Vicenza*, 3 and 5 August.
     C. MORSELETTO, "La nostra Basilica," in *La Provincia di Vicenza*, 4 August.

1902 F. ANTI, *Relazione sulle condizioni del sottosuolo della Basilica palladiana riguardo alle condizioni statiche del monumento*, Vicenza.
     F. BANNISTER FLETCHER, *Andrea Palladio: His Life and Works*, London.
     C. BASSANI, *Intorno ai guasti delle fabbriche ed in particolare della Basilica palladiana*, Tivoli.
     L. COGO, "L'armamento della Basilica," in *La Provincia di Vicenza*, 16 August and 5 September.
     L. COGO (II), "I ristauri della Basilica palladiana: Considerazioni e proposte," in *La Provincia di Vicenza*, 29 and 30 August.
     L. COGO (III), "Pro Basilica: Al Sig. Flaminio Anti," in *La Provincia di Vicenza*, 18 September and 3 October.
     L. COGO (IV), "La Basilica," in *La Provincia di Vicenza*, 22 November.
     F. SETTI, "La Basilica palladiana," in *Rassegna d'Arte*, September, pp. 136-138.

1903 L. BELTRAMI - A. BRUSCONI, *Relazione sulle attuali condizioni statiche della Basilica palladiana in Vicenza*, Milan.
     A. DE FILIPPI, "I monumenti palladiani a Vicenza," in *Cosmos illustrato*, I, pp. 230-239.

1907 L. FERRO, "Francesco (junior), Gerolamo, Giovanni Battista Albanese," in Thieme-Becker, *Künstlerlexicon*, Leipzig, I.
     A. HAUPT, *Palazzi dell'Italia settentrionale e della Toscana: Verona, Vicenza, Mantova, Padova, Udine*, Berlin (transl. from *Palast-Architektur von Ober-Italien und Toscana: Verona, Vicenza, Mantua, Padua, Udine*, n. p., 1886).

1909 F. BÜRGER, *Die Villen des Andrea Palladio: Ein Beitrag zur Entwicklungsgeschichte der Renaissance-Architektur*, Leipzig.

     G. GEROLA, "Alcune considerazioni intorno al pittore Avanzo," in *Bollettino del Museo Civico di Padova*, XII, pp. 28-33.
     A. MICHEL, *Histoire de l'Art*, Vol. IV, pt. 1, Paris.

1910 "Appunti di Storia Vicentina," in *Bollettino del Museo Civico di Vicenza*, fasc. III and IV (July-December), pp. 45-47.
     D. BORTOLAN, "Di una iscrizione medioevale infissa nell'antica porta Feliciana o del Castello in Vicenza," in *Bollettino del Museo Civico di Vicenza*, fasc. II (April-June), pp. 5-7.

1911 L. SERRA, "Le origini dell'architettura barocca," in *L'Arte*, XIV, pp. 339-358.

1916 G. G. ZORZI, "Il matrimonio di Andrea Palladio," in *Nuovo Archivio Veneto*, n. s., Vol. XXXII (extract).

1919 D. BORTOLAN - S. RUMOR, *Guida di Vicenza*, Vicenza.
     A. E. BRINCKMANN, *Die Baukunst des 17. und 18. Jahrhunderts in den romanischen Ländern*, Berlin.

1921 "Bartolommeo Grazioli," in Thieme-Becker, *Künstlerlexicon*, Leipzig, XIV.
     C. GURLITT, *Andrea Palladio*, Turin.

1922 G. GROMORT, *L'architecture de la Renaissance en Italie*, Paris.
     G. G. ZORZI, "La vera origine e la giovinezza di Andrea Palladio," in *Archivio Veneto Tridentino*, N. 3-4, pp. 120-150 (extract).

1923 G. LOUKOMSKI, "Les palais et les villas d'Andrea Palladio," in *La Revue de l'Art ancien et moderne*, XXVII, pp. 207-216.
     L. SERRA, *Alessandro Vittoria*, Rome.

1924 M. GIRARDI, *La topografia di Vicenza romana*, Venice.
     G. LOUKOMSKI, *Andrea Palladio*, Munich.
     G. G. ZORZI, "Andrea Palladio in Friuli," in *Archivio Veneto Tridentino*, Vol. V, 9-10, pp. 120-145 (extract).

1926 G. G. ZORZI, "Contributo alla Storia dell'Arte Vicentina nei secoli XV e XVI, P. II," in *Miscellanea di Storia veneto-tridentina della R. Deputazione veneta-tridentina di Storia Patria*, s. 4, Vol. II, Venice, pp. 1-330.

1927 G. LOUKOMSKI, *Andrea Palladio: Sa vie et son oeuvre*, Paris.

1928 A. MELANI, *Palladio*, Milan.

1929 L. ONGARO, "Giambattista (e Girolamo) Albanese," in *Enciclopedia Italiana*, Vol. II.

1930 G. C. ARGAN, "Palladio e la critica neoclassica," in *L'Arte*, I, iv, pp. 327-346.
     G. FASOLO, *Note d'Arte*, Vicenza.
     G. FIOCCO, "Bisanzio, Ravenna, Venezia," in *Rivista di Venezia* (February), pp. 1-24.

1931 L. COLETTI, "Altichiero e Avanzo," in *Rivista d'Arte*, XIII, pp. 303-363.

1932 G. FASOLO, "Vicenza retrospettiva," in *Vicenza*, III, x, p. 175.
     G. PERONATO, "Palazzo delle RR. Poste e Torri dei Loschi; La casa e la Torre dei Loschi ed il palazzo delle RR. Poste in Vicenza," in *Vicenza*, III, iii, p. 52; iv, pp. 59-62.
     H. WILLICH, "Andrea Palladio," in Thieme-Becker, *Künstlerlexicon*, Leipzig, XXVI.

1933 A. BARDELLA, "Per il ripristino integrale delle Torri dei Loschi," in *Vicenza*, IV, x, p. 153.
     G. FIOCCO, "Andrea Palladio padovano: Discorso inaugurale dell'Anno Accademico 1932-1933... della R. Università di Padova," in *Annuario della R. Università di Padova per l'Anno Accademico 1932-1933*, Padua (extract).
     B. MUNARETTO, "Il Palazzo della Ragione o Basilica Palladiana," in *Vicenza*, IV, vii, pp. 98-100.

1934 G. FASOLO, *La Chiesa di S. Pietro Apostolo in Vicenza*, Vicenza.
     G. PERONATO, "Casa e Torre dei Loschi," in *Vicenza*, V, iv, p. 62.

1935 G. FIOCCO, "Fortune e sfortune del Palladio," in *Vita di Padova*, fasc. II, pp. 7-16.

G. GIOVANNONI, "Andrea Palladio," in *Enciclopedia Italiana*, Vol. XXVI.

E. GOMBRICH, "Zum Werke Giulio Romanos," pt. 2, in *Jahrbuch der kunsthistorischen Sammlungen in Wien*, N. F., IX, pp. 121-150.

V. MARIANI, *Il significato del portico berniniano di S. Pietro*, Rome.

H. WILLICH, "Michele Sanmicheli," in Thieme-Becker, *Künstlerlexicon*, Leipzig, Vol. XXIX.

1936 L. BECHERUCCI, "L'architettura italiana del Cinquecento," in *Enciclopedia Monografica Nemi*, N. 63, Florence.

R. PALLUCCHINI, "Vincenzo Scamozzi e l'architettura veneta," in *L'Arte*, XXXIX, pp. 3-30.

G. PERONATO, "La Piazza dei Signori: La Sua sistemazione," in *Vicenza*, VII, v, pp. 71-76.

1937 F. FRANCO, "La scuola scamozziana di stile severo in Vicenza," in *Palladio*, I, ii, pp. 59-70.

A. VENTURI, *Storia dell'Arte Italiana: La Scultura del Cinquecento*, Vol. X, pt. 3, Milan.

G. G. ZORZI, "Contributo alla storia dell'Arte Vicentina nei secoli XV e XVI: Il preclassicismo e i prepalladiani," in *Miscellanea di Studi e Memorie della R. Deputazione di Storia Patria per le Venezie*, III.

1938 G. FASOLO, "Notizie di arte e di storia vicentina," in *Archivio Veneto*, XXII, pp. 261-301.

N. GALLIMBERTI, "L'urbanistica della Rinascenza," in *Atti del V Congresso nazionale di Storia dell'Architettura* (October 1936), Florence, pp. 255-269.

E. LANGESKIÖLD, *Michele Sanmicheli*, Upsala.

G. LOUKOMSKI, "I disegni del Palladio a Londra," in *Palladio*, II, i, pp. 15-26.

1939 H. PEE, *Die Palastbauten des Andrea Palladio*, Würzburg.

E. SILVAGNI, "Gli Albanese scultori e architetti," Diss. University of Padua, for the academic year 1938-39.

1940 W. LOTZ, review of H. Pee, *Die Palastbauten des Andrea Palladio*, 1939, in *Zeitschrift für Kunstgeschichte*, X, pp. 216-220.

A. VENTURI, *Storia dell'Arte italiana: Architettura del Cinquecento*, Vol. XI, pt. 3, Milan.

1940-41 G. FIOCCO, "Camillo Mariani," in *Le Arti*, III, ii (December 1940-January 1941), pp. 74-86.

1941 S. BETTINI, "Note sui soggiorni veneti di Bartolomeo Ammannati," in *Le Arti*, III, pp. 20-27.

F. FLORA, *Storia della Letteratura Italiana*, Vol. II, pt. 1, Milan.

1942 G. FIOCCO, "Palladio vivo," in *Primato: Lettere e Arti d'Italia*, III, 20, pp. 384-385.

1943 S. BETTINI, "Quaderno n. 1," in *Quaderni di Archeologia e Storia dell'Arte paleocristiana e bizantina* (1942-43), Padua.

A. M. DALLA POZZA, *Andrea Palladio*, Vicenza.

G. GIOVANNONI, "L'Urbanistica del Rinascimento," in *L'Urbanistica dall'Antichità ad oggi*, Florence, pp. 93-115.

V. MARIANI, "L'Urbanistica nell'età barocca," in *L'Urbanistica dall'Antichità ad oggi*, Florence, pp. 117-136.

N. PEVSNER, *An Outline of European Architecture*, London.

1944 S. BETTINI, *Giusto de' Menabuoi e l'Arte del Trecento*, Padua.

R. MARINI, "Introduzione a Palladio," in *La Porta orientale*, XIV, 7-12, pp. 73-79.

1945 O. CABIATI, "Nota al Palladio," included in the Hoepli facsimile edition of *I Quattro Libri dell'Architettura*, Milan, pp. 5-15.

1947 L. COLETTI, *I Primitivi: I Padani*, Vol. III, Novara.

F. FORLATI, "Il restauro dei Monumenti danneggiati dalla guerra nel Veneto orientale," in *Arte Veneta*, I, i, pp. 50-60.

1948 A. BARDELLA, "Su i tre gradini della Basilica," in *Il Giornale di Vicenza*, 10 November.

R. CEVESE, "Tre interventi sulla questione dei 'tre scalini' della Basilica," in *Il Giornale di Vicenza*, 11 March, 2 October, 13 November.

R. PANE, *Andrea Palladio*, Turin.

1949 S. BETTINI, "La critica dell'Architettura e l'arte del Palladio," in *Arte Veneta*, III, pp. 55-69.

G. FIOCCO, "L'esposizione dei disegni di Andrea Palladio a Vicenza," in *Arte Veneta*, III, p. 196.

F. FORLATI, "Il Restauro dei Monumenti; [Monumenti di] Vicenza," in *Mostra del restauro di Monumenti e Opere d'Arte danneggiate dalla guerra nelle Tre Venezie: Catalogo*, Venice, pp. 9-15, 31-90.

L. MAGAGNATO, "Guida alla Pinacoteca Civica," in *Questa è Vicenza*, Vicenza, pp. 101-104.

L. MAGAGNATO (II), "La questione dei 'tre scalini' di Vicenza," in *Arte Veneta*, III, p. 196.

R. PALLUCCHINI, *Mostra di Giovanni Bellini: Catalogo*, Venice.

G. ROSI, "Mostra del restauro a Vicenza," in *Bollettino tino d'Arte*, XXXIV, iv, pp. 381-382.

R. WITTKOWER, *Architectural Principles in the Age of Humanism*, Studies of the Warburg Institute, 19, London.

G. G. ZORZI, "Ancora della vera origine e della giovinezza di Andrea Palladio secondo nuovi documenti," in *Arte Veneta*, III, pp. 140-152.

G. G. ZORZI (II), "Una restituzione palladiana (Il palazzo Civena di Vicenza)," in *Arte Veneta*, III, pp. 99-103.

1950 F. BARBIERI, "I tre gradini della Basilica palladiana," in *Il Giornale di Vicenza*, 12 March.

A. SCARPA, *Scritti scelti di Giangiorgio Trissino*, Vicenza.

G. G. ZORZI, "Un secolare errore sull'atto di nascita delle logge della Basilica di Vicenza," in *Arte Veneta*, IV, pp. 141-143.

1951 F. FRANCO, "Vicenza: La nuova pavimentazione della piazza dei Signori," in *Palladio*, January-March, p. 48.

P. TOESCA, *Il Trecento*, Turin.

G. G. ZORZI, "Alessandro Vittoria a Vicenza e lo scultore Lorenzo Rubini," in *Arte Veneta*, V, pp. 141-157.

1952 F. BARBIERI, *Vincenzo Scamozzi*, Vicenza.

R. CEVESE, *I Palazzi dei Thiene sede della Banca Popolare di Vicenza*, Vicenza.

G. CHIERICI, *Palladio*, Milan-Florence.

F. FORLATI, "Restauro di edifici danneggiati dalla guerra: Provincia di Vicenza. V. Vicenza," in *Bollettino d'Arte*, s. 4, XXXVII, pp. 266-274.

F. FRANCO, "Andrea Palladio," in *Enciclopedia Cattolica*, Vol. IX.

L. MAGAGNATO, "I 'Taiapiera' in Vicenza," in *Prima Mostra della Pietra di Vicenza: Catalogo*, Venice, pp. 13-27.

L. MAGAGNATO (II), "Le vedute vicentine di Cristoforo Dall'Acqua," preface to *Cristoforo Dall'Acqua: Vedute di Vicenza*, reprinted by the Banca Popolare di Vicenza, Vicenza.

N. POZZA, "Le pietre di Vicenza," in *Prima Mostra della Pietra di Vicenza: Catalogo*, Venice, pp. 29-31.

G. G. ZORZI, "La Basilica palladiana," in *Questa è Vicenza*, pp. 153-157.

1953 F. BARBIERI, "Chiesa e Chiostro di S. Pietro," in *Guida di Vicenza*, Vicenza (1st ed.), pp. 333-341.

F. BARBIERI - R. CEVESE, "La Basilica palladiana," in *Guida di Vicenza*, Vicenza (1st ed.), pp. 86-93.

S. BETTINI, "Nota introduttiva," preface to *Industria artistica tardo-romana* by Alois Riegl, Florence, pp. ix-lxi.

R. CEVESE, "Palazzo Porto Breganze," in *Guida di Vicenza*, Vicenza (1st ed.), pp. 110-111.

R. CEVESE (II), "Casa Zilio," in *Guida di Vicenza*, Vicenza (1st ed.), p. 320.

R. CEVESE (III), "Chiesa di S. Rocco," in *Guida di Vicenza*, Vicenza (1st ed.), pp. 278-285.

Guida di Vicenza, (F. Barbieri, R. Cevese, L. Magagnato), Vicenza (1st ed.).

L. MAGAGNATO, "Chiesa di S. Lorenzo," in *Guida di Vicenza*, Vicenza (1st ed.), pp. 60-71.

R. PANE, *Bernini architetto*, Venice.

G. G. ZORZI, "Una testimonianza inedita del Palladio sulla pietra di Vicenza," in *Questa è Vicenza*, Vicenza, pp. 84-88.

G. G. ZORZI (II), "Nuove rivelazioni sulla ricostruzione delle sale del piano nobile del Palazzo Ducale di

Venezia dopo l'incendio dell' 11 maggio 1574," in *Arte Veneta*, VII, pp. 123-151.

1953-54 R. Brenzoni, "Nuovi dati d'archivio sul Falconetto e su Bartolomeo e Ottaviano Ridolfi," in *Atti dell'Istituto Veneto di Scienze, Lettere e Arti*, CXII, pp. 269-295.

1954 F. Barbieri, "Un altare di Giuseppe e Vincenzo Pittoni," in *Vita Vicentina*, N. 11.
R. Cevese, "Sculture della Basilica Palladiana," in *Questa è Vicenza*, Vicenza, pp. 139-141.
G. Mantese, *Memorie storiche della Chiesa vicentina*, Vol. II, Vicenza.
C. Perogalli, *Monumenti e metodi di valorizzazione*, Milan.
G. G. Zorzi, "Progetti giovanili di Andrea Palladio per palazzi e case in Venezia e in Terraferma," in *Palladio*, IV, iii, pp. 105-121.
G. G. Zorzi (II), "Progetti giovanili di Andrea Palladio per villini e case di campagna," in *Palladio*, IV, i-ii, pp. 59-76.

1955 O. Bison, *S. Vincenzo martire e Vicenza*, Vicenza.
G. B. Giarolli, *Vicenza nella sua toponomastica stradale*, Vicenza.
P. Maltauro, "La ricostruzione del Duomo e del tetto della Basilica palladiana a Vicenza: A proposito della tecnica del restauro monumentale," in *Realtà Nuova*, XX, 3, pp. 271-281.
G. Mantese, *Storia di Schio*, Vicenza.
S. Moschini Marconi, *Gallerie dell'Accademia di Venezia: Opere d'Arte dei secoli XIV e XV*, Rome.
C. Perogalli, *La progettazione del restauro monumentale*, Milan.
P. Portaluppi, *Guida all'architettura*, Milan.
G. G. Zorzi, "Contributo alla datazione di alcune opere palladiane," in *Arte Veneta*, IX, pp. 95-122.

1956 G. C. Argan, "L'importanza del Sanmicheli nella formazione del Palladio," in *Venezia e l'Europa: Atti del XVIII Congresso internazionale di Storia dell'Arte* (Venice, 1955), Venice, pp. 387-389.
E. Arslan, "Le Chiese di Vicenza," in *Cataloghi delle cose d'Arte e di Antichità d'Italia*, publ. by the Ministero della Pubblica Istruzione, Rome.
F. Barbieri, "Chiesa e chiostro di S. Pietro," in *Guida di Vicenza*, Vicenza (2nd ed.), pp. 333-341.
F. Barbieri (II), "Le opere d'Arte [del Duomo di Vicenza]," in *Il Duomo di Vicenza*, Vicenza, pp. 99-183.
F. Barbieri - R. Cevese, "La Basilica palladiana," in *Guida di Vicenza*, Vicenza (2nd ed.), pp. 86-93.
R. Cevese, "Palazzo Porto Breganze," in *Guida di Vicenza*, Vicenza (2nd ed.), pp. 110-111.
R. Cevese (II), "Casa Zilio," in *Guida di Vicenza*, Vicenza (2nd ed.), p. 320.
R. Cevese (III), "Chiesa di S. Rocco," in *Guida di Vicenza*, Vicenza (2nd ed.), pp. 278-285.
R. Cevese (IV), *Ville vicentine*, Milan.
Guida di Vicenza (F. Barbieri, R. Cevese, L. Magagnato), Vicenza (2nd ed.).
L. Magagnato, "Chiesa di S. Lorenzo," in *Guida di Vicenza*, Vicenza (2nd ed.), pp. 60-71.
J. Morresi, "La scuola del Vittoria a Vicenza," Diss. University of Padua, for the academic year 1955-56.
G. G. Zorzi, "Il Teatro Olimpico," in *Questa è Vicenza*, Vicenza, pp. 183-197.

1957 N. Pozza, "La pietra di Vicenza e le sculture all'aperto," in *Vicenza*, Vicenza, pp. 66-67.

1958 G. Billanovich, "'Veterum vestigia vatum' nei carmi dei preumanisti padovani: Lovato Lovati [etc.]," in *Italia medioevale e umanistica*, I, pp. 155-243.
R. Cevese, "Relazione sui problemi di Vicenza," in *Italia Nostra*, 10, pp. 18-29.
A. Chastel, *L'Arte italiana*, pt. 2, Florence.
G. Fiocco, preface to: G. G. Zorzi, *I Disegni delle Antichità di Andrea Palladio*, Venice, pp. ix-xii.
G. Fiocco (II), "Le Arti figurative," in *La Civiltà veneziana del Rinascimento*, Florence, pp. 177-195.
F. Hartt, *Giulio Romano*, New Haven.

C. Jacini, *Il viaggio del Po: Le città. Veneto, Città e ville di Terraferma*, Vol. VII, pt. 4, Milan.
L. Magagnato, *Da Altichiero a Pisanello: Catalogo* (exhibition, Verona, August-October 1958), Venice.
G. Mantese, *Memorie storiche della Chiesa vicentina*, Vol. III, pt. 1, Vicenza.
C. Mutinelli, "La Pietà: Note ed osservazioni di filologia iconografica," in *Mostra di Crocifissi e Pietà medioevali del Friuli: Catalogo*, Udine (extract).
R. Pallucchini, "Giulio Romano e Palladio," in *Arte Veneta*, XII, pp. 234-235.
L. Puppi, "Sanmicheli a Vicenza," in *Vita Veronese*, XI, NN. 11-12, pp. 449-453.
G. G. Zorzi, "L'abside della Cattedrale di Vicenza e il contributo di Andrea Palladio al suo compimento," in *Studi in onore di Federico Maria Mistrorigo*, Vicenza, pp. 271-310.
G. G. Zorzi (II), *I Disegni delle Antichità di Andrea Palladio*, Venezia.
E. Arslan, "Altichiero and Avanzo," in *Encyclopedia of World Art*, Vol. I, cols. 226-229.

1959 F. Barbieri, "L'architettura minore a Vicenza," in *Carnet del Turista*, Winter 1959-60, Vicenza.
G. Fiocco, "Preludio ad Andrea Palladio," in *Bollettino del Centro Internazionale di Studi di Architettura Andrea Palladio*, I, pp. 9-12.
F. Franco, "Piccola e grande urbanistica palladiana," in *Bollettino del Centro Internazionale di Studi di Architettura Andrea Palladio*, I, pp. 17-20.
F. Franco (II), "La Scuola del Palladio," in *Bollettino del Centro Internazionale di Studi di Architettura Andrea Palladio*, I, pp. 20-23.
M. Muraro, review of E. Arslan, "Le Chiese di Vicenza," 1956, in *Bollettino d'Arte*, XIV, pp. 290-291.
R. Pallucchini, "Andrea Palladio e Giulio Romano," in *Bollettino del Centro Internazionale di Studi di Architettura Andrea Palladio*, I, pp. 38-44.
R. Pane, "I Quattro Libri dell'Architettura. La formazione del Palladio e 'il Manierismo'. Lo stile di Palladio. La storiografia palladiana dell'età neoclassica da Bertotti Scamozzi a Magrini," in *Bollettino del Centro Internazionale di Studi di Architettura Andrea Palladio*, I, pp. 45-56.
N. Pevsner, *Storia dell'Architettura europea*, Bari.
"Restauri palladiani," in *Bollettino del Centro Internazionale di Studi di Architettura Andrea Palladio*, I, pp. 94-95.
E. N. Rogers, "Palladio e noi," in *Bollettino del Centro Internazionale di Studi di Architettura Andrea Palladio*, I, pp. 57-60.
R. Wittkower, "Sviluppo stilistico dell'Architettura palladiana," in *Bollettino del Centro Internazionale di Studi di Architettura Andrea Palladio*, I, pp. 61-65.
B. Zevi, "Architecture," in *Encyclopedia of World Art*, Vol. I, cols. 625-710.
B. Zevi, "Problemi di interpretazione critica dell'Architettura veneta," in *Bollettino del Centro Internazionale di Studi di Architettura Andrea Palladio*, I, pp. 70-72.
G. G. Zorzi, "Architetti e scultori dei laghi di Lugano e di Como a Vicenza nel secolo XV," in *Arte e Artisti dei Laghi lombardi*, I, pp. 343-371.

1959-60 L. Puppi, "Intorno allo scultore Angelo di Giovanni," in *Arte Veneta*, XIII-XIV, pp. 30-38.

1960 F. Barbieri, "Una proposta per il regesto di Michele Sanmicheli," in *Bollettino del Centro Internazionale di Studi di Architettura Andrea Palladio*, II, pp. 105-107.
E. Battisti, *Rinascimento e Barocco*, Turin.
S. Bettini, *Le pitture di Giusto de' Menabuoi nel Battistero del Duomo di Padova*, Venice.
R. Bonelli, *Da Bramante a Michelangelo*, Venice.
G. Briganti, "Baroque: Changing Conceptions of the Baroque," *Encyclopedia of World Art*, Vol. II, cols. 257-267.

N. Carboneri, "Bibliografia sanmicheliana," in *Michele Sanmicheli: Studi raccolti dall'Accademia di Agricoltura Scienze e Lettere di Verona*, pp. 200-299.

F. Cessi, *Alessandro Vittoria bronzista*, Trent.

A. Chastel, "Palladio et l'Art des fêtes," in *Bollettino del Centro Internazionale di Studi di Architettura Andrea Palladio*, II, pp. 29-33.

G. De Angelis D'Ossat, "L'arte del Sanmicheli," in *Michele Sanmicheli: Studi raccolti dall'Accademia di Agricoltura Scienze e Lettere di Verona*, Verona, pp. 15-32.

G. Fiocco, "Significato dell'opera di Michele Sanmicheli" in *Michele Sanmicheli: Studi raccolti dall'Accademia di Agricoltura Scienze e Lettere di Verona*, Verona, pp. 1-13 (extract).

D. Formaggio, *Il Barocco in Italia*, Milan.

S. Kozakiewicz, "L'influsso palladiano in Polonia fino alla fine del XVII secolo e dalla fine del XVII secolo fino all'età neoclassica," in *Bollettino del Centro Internazionale di Studi di Architettura Andrea Palladio*, II, pp. 48-53.

G. Mantese, *Vicenza: Panorama storico*, Verona.

Michele Sanmicheli: Catalogo (Exhibition, Verona, May-October 1960), Venice.

V. Martinelli, "Gian Lorenzo Bernini," in *Encyclopedia of World Art*, Vol. II, cols. 459-471.

A. Nava Cellini, "Baroque Art: Sculpture," in *Encyclopedia of World Art*, Vol. II, cols. 313-327.

G. Nicco Fasola, "Giulio Romano e il Manierismo," in *Commentari*, XI, 1, pp. 60-73.

R. Pane, "Dai lavori di villa Cricoli... alle ultime opere vicentine [del Palladio]," in *Bollettino del Centro Internazionale di Studi di Architettura Andrea Palladio*, II, pp. 56-70.

M. C. Pavan Taddei, "Francesco, Giovanni Battista, Girolamo Albanese (Albanesi)," in *Dizionario Biografico degli Italiani*, Vol. I.

W. Timofiewitsch, "Die Palladio-Forschung in den Jahren von 1940 bis 1960," in *Zeitschrift für Kunstgeschichte*, III, pp. 174 ff.

M. Zocca, "Le concezioni urbanistiche di Palladio," in *Palladio*, I-II, pp. 69-83.

G. G. Zorzi, "Alcuni problemi artistici in relazione alla cronologia palladiana," in *Bollettino del Centro Internazionale di Studi di Architettura Andrea Palladio*, II, pp. 88-92.

G. G. Zorzi (II), "Andrea Palladio architetto della Repubblica di Venezia," in *Bollettino del Centro Internazionale di Studi di Architettura Andrea Palladio*, II, pp. 108-113.

G. G. Zorzi (III), "Tre scultori lombardi e le loro opere nel Teatro Olimpico di Vicenza," in *Arte Lombarda*, V, 2, pp. 231-242.

1961   S. Bettini, "Palladio urbanista," in *Bollettino del Centro Internazionale di Studi di Architettura Andrea Palladio*, III, pp. 9-11.

S. Bettini (II), "Palladio urbanista," in *Arte Veneta*, XV, pp. 89-98.

F. Cessi, *Alessandro Vittoria architetto e stuccatore*, Trent.

M. Checchi - L. Gaudenzio - L. Grossato, "I tre itinerari," in *Padova: Guida ai Monumenti e alle Opere d'Arte*, Venice, pp. 3 ff.

L. Crema, "Il rapporto tra i valori dell'Architettura romana e la loro interpretazione da parte del Palladio," in *Bollettino del Centro Internazionale di Studi di Architettura Andrea Palladio*, III, pp. 18-24.

G. Fiocco, "Incunabuli di Andrea Palladio," in *Saggi di Storia dell'Architettura in onore di Vincenzo Fasolo*, ss. 6-8 of the *Quaderni dell'Istituto di Storia dell'Architettura dell'Università di Roma*, Rome, pp. 169-176.

F. Flores D'Arcais, "Il Palazzo della Ragione di Padova," in *Bollettino del Centro Internazionale di Studi di Architettura Andrea Palladio*, III, pp. 108-115.

E. Hubala, "Palladio und die Baukunst in Deutschland in 17. Jahrhundert," in *Bollettino del Centro Internazionale di Studi di Architettura Andrea Palladio*, III, pp. 38-44.

W. Lotz, "L'eredità romana di Jacopo Sansovino architetto veneziano: La Libreria di S. Marco e l'Urbanistica del Rinascimento," in *Bollettino del Centro Internazionale di Studi di Architettura Andrea Palladio*, III pp. 82-88.

Padova: Guida ai Monumenti e alle Opere d'Arte, Venice

R. Pane, *Palladio*, Turin.

R. Pane (II), "Invenzione e restauro nella Basilica palladiana," in *Bollettino del Centro Internazionale di Studi di Architettura Andrea Palladio*, III, pp. 119-120.

M. Praz, "Venezia neoclassica e romantica," in *La Civiltà veneziana nell'età romantica*, Florence, pp. 155-179.

A. Prosdocimi, "Le logge del Palazzo della Ragione," in *Città di Padova*, I, 2, pp. 30-35.

C. Semenzato, "Gian Maria Falconetto," in *Bollettino del Centro Internazionale di Studi di Architettura Andrea Palladio*, III, pp. 70-77.

G. G. Zorzi, "I disegni delle opere palladiane pubblicate ne *I Quattro Libri* e il loro significato rispetto alle opere eseguite," in *Bollettino del Centro Internazionale di Studi di Architettura Andrea Palladio*, III, pp. 12-17.

G. G. Zorzi (II), "Errori deficienze e inesattezze de *I Quattro Libri dell'Architettura* di Andrea Palladio," in *Bollettino del Centro Internazionale di Studi di Architettura Andrea Palladio*, III, pp. 143-148.

G. G. Zorzi (III), "Un architetto vicentino contemporaneo di Andrea Palladio (Pietro di Guglielmo da Nanto)," in *Arte Veneta*, XV, pp. 202-213.

G. G. Zorzi (IV), "Notizie di arte e di artisti nei Diari di Marino Sanudo," in *Atti dell'Istituto Veneto di Scienze Lettere ed Arti*, Academic Year 1960-61, Vol. CXIX, Venice, pp. 472-604.

1962   E. Arslan, "Avanzo," in *Dizionario Biografico degli Italiani*, IV.

F. Barbieri, *Il Museo Civico di Vicenza: Dipinti e Sculture dal XIV al XV secolo*, Venice.

F. Barbieri (II), "Il Palazzo Chiericati sede del Museo Civico di Vicenza," Venice.

E. Bassi, "Appunti per la storia del Palazzo Ducale di Venezia (2)," in *Critica d'Arte*, IX, 52, pp. 41-53.

E. Battisti, *L'Antirinascimento*, Milan.

R. Cevese, review of R. Pane, *Palladio*, 1961, in *Bollettino del Centro Internazionale di Studi di Architettura Andrea Palladio*, IV, pp. 271-291.

E. Forssman, "Palladio e Vitruvio," in *Bollettino del Centro Internazionale di Studi di Architettura Andrea Palladio*, IV, pp. 31-42.

F. Franco, review of R. Pane, *Palladio*, 1961, in *Arte Veneta*, XVI, pp. 202-206.

F. Heinemann, *Giovanni Bellini e i Belliniani*, Vols. I-II, Venice.

E. Lavagnino, *La Chiesa di S. Spirito in Sassia e il mutare del gusto a Roma al tempo del Concilio di Trento*, Turin.

E. Lavagnino (II), "Una novità palladiana," in *Bollettino del Centro Internazionale di Studi di Architettura Andrea Palladio*, IV, pp. 52-60.

L. Puppi, *Bartolomeo Montagna*, Venice.

L. Puppi (II), "Il 'Barco' di Caterina Cornaro ad Altivole," in *Prospettive*, 25, pp. 52-64.

W. Timofiewitsch, "La Chiesetta della Rotonda," in *Bollettino del Centro Internazionale di Studi di Architettura Andrea Palladio*, IV, pp. 262-268.

R. Wittkower, *Architectural Principles in the Age of Humanism*, London, 1962 (3rd rev. ed.).

G. G. Zorzi, "La famiglia di Andrea Palladio secondo nuovi documenti," in *Archivio Veneto*, s. 5, LXX, pp. 15-54.

G. G. Zorzi (II), "Le statue di Agostino Rubini nel Teatro Olimpico di Vicenza," in *Arte Veneta*, XVI, pp. 111-120.

1963   A. Chastel - R. Klein, *L'Umanesimo e l'Europa della Rinascita*, Milan.

A. M. Dalla Pozza, "Palladiana VIII e IX," in *Odeo Olimpico*, IV, pp. 99-131.

G. Fiocco, "La rivincita di Altichiero," in *Il Santo: Rivista antoniana di Storia Dottrina e Arte*, III, 3, pp. 283-289.

G. Lorenzoni, *Lorenzo da Bologna*, Venice.

R. Pane, "Palladio e la Critica," in *Comunità*, XVII, 106, pp. 50-66.

G. Piovene, "Trissino e Palladio nell'Umanesimo vicentino," in *Bollettino del Centro Internazionale di Studi di Architettura Andrea Palladio*, V, pp. 13-23.

L. Puppi, "Giovanni Speranza," in *Rivista dell'Istituto Nazionale d'Archeologia e Storia dell'Arte*, n. s., XI-XII, pp. 370-419.

L. Puppi (II), *Il Teatro Olimpico*, Venice.

A. Sartori, "Nota su Altichiero," in *Il Santo: Rivista antoniana di Storia Dottrina e Arte*, III, 3, pp. 291-326.

C. Semenzato, "L'architettura del Palazzo della Ragione," in *Il Palazzo della Ragione di Padova*, Venice, pp. 21-44.

G. G. Zorzi, "Domenico Groppino di Musso: Un altro architetto lombardo-vicentino imitatore del Palladio," in *Arte Lombarda*, VIII, 2, pp. 114-146.

G. G. Zorzi (II), "Quattro monumenti sepolcrali disegnati da Andrea Palladio," in *Arte Veneta*, XVII, pp. 96-105.

1964   F. Barbieri, review of E. Forssman, *Palladios Lehrgebäude*, 1965, in *Bollettino del Centro Internazionale di Studi di Architettura Andrea Palladio*, VI, pt. 2, pp. 323-333.

F. Barbieri (II), "Palladio e il Manierismo," in *Bollettino del Centro Internazionale di Studi di Architettura Andrea Palladio*, VI, pt. 2, pp. 49-63.

L. Becherucci, "Mannerism," in *Encyclopedia of World Art*, Vol. IX, cols. 443-478.

O. Bison, *La Chiesa di S. Vincenzo martire in Vicenza*, Vicenza.

R. Cevese, "L'Architettura vicentina del primo Rinascimento," in *Bollettino del Centro Internazionale di Studi di Architettura Andrea Palladio*, VI, pt. 2, pp. 199-213.

R. Cevese (II), review of G. G. Zorzi, *Le Opere pubbliche e i Palazzi privati di Andrea Palladio*, 1964, in *Bollettino del Centro Internazionale di Studi di Architettura Andrea Palladio*, VI, pt. 2, pp. 334-359.

C. De Azevedo, "Andrea Palladio e l'influenza italiana nell'architettura portoghese," in *Bollettino del Centro Internazionale di Studi di Architettura Andrea Palladio*, VI, pt. 2, pp. 64-69.

M. Guiotto, "Soprintendenza ai Monumenti del Veneto: Restauri dell'anno 1964," in *Arte Veneta*, XVIII, pp. 251-255.

N. Ivanoff, "Il coronamento statuario della Marciana," in *Ateneo Veneto*, n. s. 2, II, N. 1, pp. 101-112.

G. Mantese, *Memorie storiche della Chiesa vicentina*, Vol. III, pt. 2, Vicenza.

R. Pallucchini, *La Pittura veneziana del Trecento*, Venice-Rome.

R. Pane, "Palladio e la moderna storiografia dell'Architettura," in *Bollettino del Centro Internazionale di Studi di Architettura Andrea Palladio*, VI, pt. 2, pp. 119-130.

G. Piovene, "Il miracolo palladiano," in *Tuttitalia*, N. 162, pp. 469-472.

A. Ventura, *Nobiltà e popolo nella società veneta del '400 e '500*, Bari.

B. Zevi, "Michelangiolo e Palladio," in *Bollettino del Centro Internazionale di Studi di Architettura Andrea Palladio*, VI, pt. 2, pp. 13-28.

G. G. Zorzi, *Le opere pubbliche e i palazzi privati di Andrea Palladio*, Venice.

G. G. Zorzi (II), "Precisazioni su alcune opere attribuite a Michele Sanmicheli," in *Arte Lombarda*, IX, 2, pp. 94-112.

1964-65   L. Puppi, "Giovanni Buonconsiglio detto Marescalco," in *Rivista di Archeologia e Storia dell'Arte*, n. s., XIII-XIV, pp. 297-374.

1965   E. Arslan, "Qualche appunto sul Palazzo Ducale di Venezia," in *Bollettino d'Arte*, I-II, pp. 58-66.

F. Barbieri, "L'Architettura gotica civile a Vicenza," in *Bollettino del Centro Internazionale di Studi di Architettura Andrea Palladio*, VII, pt. 2, pp. 167-184.

F. Barbieri (II), "Nuovi appunti sull'attività dei Montagna a Monte Berico," in *Maestri e Opere d'Arte del Quattrocento a Monte Berico* (Bibliotheca Servorum Veneta), Venice (extract).

R. Cevese, "L'Architettura gotica religiosa a Vicenza e nel Vicentino," in *Bollettino del Centro Internazionale di Studi di Architettura Andrea Palladio*, VII, pt. 2, pp. 207-220.

A. M. Dalla Pozza, "Palladiana X, XI, XII," in *Odeo Olimpico*, V, pp. 203-238.

A. M. Dalla Pozza (II), "Elementi e motivi ricorrenti in Andrea Palladio," in *Bollettino del Centro Internazionale di Studi di Architettura Andrea Palladio*, VII, pt. 2, pp. 43-58.

G. Fiocco, *Alvise Cornaro, il suo tempo e le sue opere*, Venice.

E. Forssman, *Palladios Lehrgebäude*, Stockholm.

G. L. Mellini, *Altichiero e Jacopo Avanzi*, Milan.

S. Pettenati, "Un libro su Altichiero e Jacopo Avanzi," in *Arte Veneta*, XIX, pp. 185-187.

L. Polacco, "La posizione di Andrea Palladio di fronte all'Antichità," in *Bollettino del Centro Internazionale di Studi di Architettura Andrea Palladio*, VII, pt. 2, pp. 59-76.

L. Puppi, "Un'opera di Girolamo Pittoni all'Aquila," in *Bullettino della Deputazione Abruzzese di Storia Patria*, LI-LIII (extract).

P. Toesca, *Il Medioevo*, Vol. II (reprint of 1st ed.), Turin.

G. Toffanin, *Il Cinquecento*, Milan.

S. Wilinski, "La Serliana," in *Bollettino del Centro Internazionale di Studi di Architettura Andrea Palladio*, VII, pt. 2, pp. 115-125.

S. Wilinski (II), "Sebastiano Serlio," in *Bollettino del Centro Internazionale di Studi di Architettura Andrea Palladio*, VII, pt. 2, pp. 103-114.

G. G. Zorzi, "Un nuovo soggiorno di Alessandro Vittoria nel Vicentino. I suoi rapporti con Lorenzo Rubini e i suoi figli Vigilio e Agostino; l'amicizia col pittore Girolamo Forni e con lo scultore Ottaviano Ridolfi (1°)," in *Arte Veneta*, XIX, pp. 83-94.

1966   J. S. Ackerman, *Palladio*, Harmondsworth.

F. Barbieri, review of G. G. Zorzi, *Le Chiese e i Ponti di Andrea Palladio*, 1966, in *Bollettino del Centro Internazionale di Studi di Architettura Andrea Palladio*, VIII, pt. 2, pp. 337-355.

A. M. Brizio, "Raffaello e Palladio," in *Bollettino del Centro Internazionale di Studi di Architettura Andrea Palladio*, VIII, pt. 2, pp. 26-33.

G. De Angelis D'Ossat, "Bramante e Palladio," in *Bollettino del Centro Internazionale di Studi di Architettura Andrea Palladio*, VIII, pt. 2, pp. 34-51.

E. Forssman, "Falconetto e Palladio," in *Bollettino del Centro Internazionale di Studi di Architettura Andrea Palladio*, VIII, pt. 2, pp. 52-67.

E. Forssman (II), "Palladio e Daniele Barbaro," in *Bollettino del Centro Internazionale di Studi di Architettura Andrea Palladio*, VIII, pt. 2, pp. 68-81.

J. J. Gloton, "Vignole et Palladio. La Villa Italienne à la fin de la Renaissance. Conceptions palladiennes. Conceptions vignolesques," in *Bollettino del Centro Internazionale di Architettura Andrea Palladio*, VIII, pt. 2, pp. 82-113.

W. Lotz, "Riflessioni sul tema 'Palladio urbanista'," in *Bollettino del Centro Internazionale di Studi di Architettura Andrea Palladio*, VIII, pt. 2, pp. 123-127.

W. Lotz (II), "La trasformazione sansoviniana di Piazza S. Marco e l'urbanistica del Cinquecento," in *Bollettino del Centro Internazionale di Studi di Architettura Andrea Palladio*, VIII, pt. 2, pp. 114-122.

L. Magagnato, *Palazzo Thiene sede della Banca Popolare di Vicenza*, Venice.

G. Marchini, "Un incontro imprevedibile: il Foligno ad Ascoli Piceno," in *Antichità viva*, V, 1, pp. 3-14.

L. Puppi, *Marcello Fogolino pittore e incisore*, Trent.

L. Puppi (II), *Palladio*, Florence.

M. Rosci, "Studi di ville nel VII libro del Serlio e ville palladiane," in *Bollettino del Centro Internazionale di Studi di Architettura Andrea Palladio*, VIII, pt. 2, pp. 128-133.

C. Semenzato, *La Scultura veneta del Seicento e Settecento*, Venice.

H. Spielmann, *Andrea Palladio und die Antike*, Munich-Berlin.

M. Tafuri, *L'Architettura del Manierismo nel Cinquecento europeo*, Rome.

R. Wittkower, "Palladio e Bernini," in *Bollettino del Centro Internazionale di Studi di Architettura Andrea Palladio*, VIII, pt. 2, pp. 13-25.

B. Zevi, "Palladio," in *Encyclopedia of World Art*, Vol. XI, cols. 59-81.

G. G. Zorzi, *Le Chiese e i Ponti di Andrea Palladio*, Venice.

G. G. Zorzi (II), "Un nuovo soggiorno di Alessandro Vittoria nel Vicentino. I suoi rapporti con Lorenzo Rubini e i suoi figli Vigilio e Agostino: l'amicizia col pittore Girolamo Forni e con lo scultore Ottaviano Ridolfi (2°)," in *Arte Veneta*, XX, pp. 157-176.

1967   J. S. Ackerman, *Palladio's Villas*, Locust Valley (New York).

J. S. Ackerman (II), "Palladio's Vicenza: A Bird's-eye Plan of c. 1571," in *Studies in Renaissance and Baroque Art presented to Anthony Blunt*, London, pp. 53-61.

F. Barbieri, "Il primo Palladio," in *Bollettino del Centro Internazionale di Studi di Architettura Andrea Palladio*, IX, pp. 24-36.

F. Barbieri (II), "L'attività vicentina di Giambattista Barberini," in *Arte in Europa: Scritti in onore di Edoardo Arslan*, Milan, pp. 703-712.

F. Barbieri (III), *Il Palazzo Leoni Montanari a Vicenza, sede della Banca Cattolica del Veneto*, Venice.

E. Battisti, "Storia del concetto di Manierismo in Architettura," in *Bollettino del Centro Internazionale di Studi di Architettura Andrea Palladio*, IX, pp. 204-210.

A. M. Brizio, "Manierismo: Rinascimento," in *Bollettino del Centro Internazionale di Studi di Architettura Andrea Palladio*, IX, pp. 219-226.

R. Cevese, "Proposta per una nuova lettura critica dell'arte palladiana," in *Essays in the History of Architecture presented to Rudolf Wittkower*, London, pp. 122-127.

G. Faggin, "Il mondo culturale veneto del Cinquecento e Andrea Palladio," in *Bollettino del Centro Internazionale di Studi di Architettura Andrea Palladio*, IX, pp. 49-65.

E. Forssman, "Tradizione e innovazione nelle opere e nel pensiero di Palladio," in *Bollettino del Centro Internazionale di Studi di Architettura Andrea Palladio*, IX, pp. 243-256.

W. Hager, "Strutture spaziali del Manierismo nell'Architettura italiana," in *Bollettino del Centro Internazionale di Studi di Architettura Andrea Palladio*, IX, pp. 257-271.

H. Hauser, "L'ambiente spirituale del Manierismo," in *Bollettino del Centro Internazionale di Studi di Architettura Andrea Palladio*, IX, pp. 187-197.

N. Ivanoff, *Palladio*, Milan.

W. Lotz, "Palladio e Sansovino," in *Bollettino del Centro Internazionale di Studi di Architettura Andrea Palladio*, IX, pp. 13-23.

L. Magagnato, "Antonio Maria Dalla Pozza studioso del Palladio," in *Odeo Olimpico*, VI, pp. 27-37.

G. Mantese, "Ancora sul Palazzo Dal Monte a S. Corona," in *Bollettino del Centro Internazionale di Studi di Architettura Andrea Palladio*, IX, pp. 425-428.

G. Mantese (II), "L'ignorato campanile della Chiesa e Monastero di S. Bartolomeo ora Ospedale Civile," in *Bollettino del Centro Internazionale di Studi di Architettura Andrea Palladio*, IX, pp. 429-433.

M. Muraro, "Concretezza e idealità nell'Arte del Palladio," in *Bollettino del Centro Internazionale di Studi di Architettura Andrea Palladio*, IX, pp. 108-120.

R. Pallucchini, "Conclusione del IX Corso Internazionale di Storia dell'Architettura," in *Bollettino del Centro Internazionale di Studi di Architettura Andrea Palladio*, IX, pp. 450-453.

N. Pevsner, "Palladio e il Manierismo," in *Bollettino del Centro Internazionale di Studi di Architettura Andrea Palladio*, IX, pp. 304-309.

L. Puppi, *Francesco Verla pittore*, Trent.

M. Rosci, "Sebastiano Serlio e il Manierismo nel Veneto," in *Bollettino del Centro Internazionale di Studi di Architettura Andrea Palladio*, IX, pp. 330-341.

C. Semenzato, "Gli spazi esterni e il Manierismo di Andrea Palladio," in *Bollettino del Centro Internazionale di Studi di Architettura Andrea Palladio*, IX, pp. 342-353.

G. G. Zorzi, "Urbanistica palladiana," in *Bollettino del Centro Internazionale di Studi di Architettura Andrea Palladio*, IX, pp. 168-184.

1968   F. Barbieri, "Il patrimonio artistico della parrocchia," in *Il patrimonio artistico della Parrocchia di S. Pietro*, Vicenza, pp. 11-70.

R. De Fusco, *Il Codice dell'Architettura: Antologia di Trattatisti*, Naples.

L. Puppi, "Antonio Bianchi: Uno sconosciuto scultore lombardo del '600 attivo nel Vicentino," in *Arte Lombarda*, XIII, 2, pp. 67-76.

1969   C. Semenzato, *The Rotonda of Andrea Palladio*, University Park and London.

INDEX OF PERSONS AND PLACES

Names of persons are indicated by small capital letters; names of places are in italics. Numbers in italics refer to the pages of the illustrations in the text; heavy black numbers indicate pages where the subject named is treated at length.

Key to abbreviations: a. = architect; c. = carpenter; e. = engineer; j. = joiner; m. = mason, bricklayer, or *capomaestro*; p. = painter; s. = sculptor; st. = stonemason.

ILLUSTRATIONS IN THE TEXT

PLATES

SCALE DRAWINGS

PLATES

1 - Vicenza. Palazzo della Ragione with the Palladian loggias and the adjacent piazzas, seen from the northeast. Aerial view

2 - Vicenza. Palazzo della Ragione with the Palladian loggias and the adjacent quarters, seen from the south. Aerial view

3 - Vicenza. Palazzo della Ragione with the Palladian loggias, seen from the north. Aerial view

4 - Palazzo della Ragione: upper part of the outer wall on the south,
above the Palladian loggias and below the roof

5 - Palazzo della Ragione: the roof seen from the top of the Torre di Piazza

6 - Palazzo della Ragione: detail of the northern wall within the upper gallery of the Palladian loggias

7 - Palazzo della Ragione: northern wall within the upper gallery of the Palladian loggias

8

8 - Palazzo della Ragione: northwest corner on the ground-floor level. Above the Late Gothic moulding, an embedded capital from the lower gallery of the Formenton loggias and moulding of a corbel supporting the vaults of the Palladian loggias

9 - Palazzo della Ragione: prison window at the northwest corner of the ground floor, partly blocked at the bottom by the steps of the later Quattrocento stair

10-11 - Palazzo della Ragione: niches at the southern and northwest corners, within the upper gallery of Palladian loggias

9

10

11

12

13

12 - Palazzo della Ragione: detail of the roof from the interior

13 - Palazzo della Ragione: door at the northeast corner of the Hall,
seen from the inside

14 - Palazzo della Ragione: interior of the Hall, seen from the eastern side

14

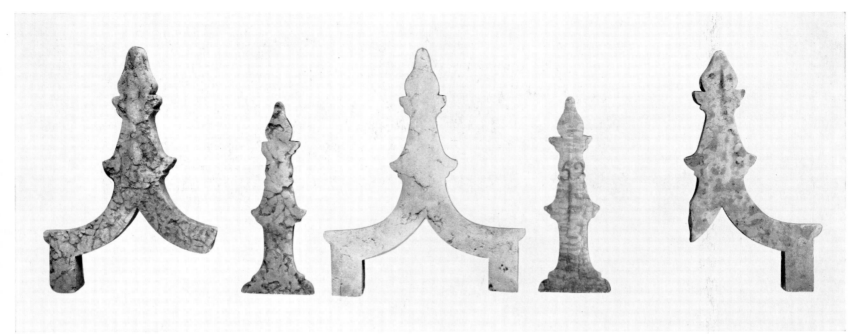

15

16

17

18

15 - Crenelations from the Formenton loggias. Vicenza, Museo Civico

16 and 18 - Late Quattrocento capitals, perhaps remnants of the Formenton loggias. Vicenza, Convent of S. Pietro

17 - Palazzo della Ragione, western side: embedded capital from the lower gallery of the Formenton loggias. Above the capital, moulding of a corbel supporting the vaults of the Palladian loggias

19 - Palazzo della Ragione: column from the lower gallery of the Formenton loggias on the southern side

20 - Palazzo della Ragione: column from the upper gallery of the Formenton loggias on the southern side (incorporated into the Palladian pier)

19

20

21

22

21 - Palazzo della Ragione: detail of the masonry under the oculi during restoration (1947-49)
22 - Palazzo della Ragione: shops on the northern side

23 - Palazzo della Ragione: shops under the northern stair

24 - Palazzo della Ragione: northern stair

25 - Palazzo della Ragione: northern stair and interior of the lower gallery of Palladian loggias

26 - Palladian loggias: overall v

the northern and western sides

27 - Palladian loggias: northern side

28 - Palladian loggias: northern side and western corner

29 - Palladian loggias: northwest corner of the upper gallery

30 - Palladian loggias: western side

31 - Stairway between Piazzetta Palladio and Piazza delle Erbe at the southwest corner of the Palladian loggias

32 - Palladian loggias: detail from Contrà Muschieria

33 - Palladian loggias: southern side, detail

34 - Palladian loggias: southern side

35 - Palladian loggias: interior of the lower gallery on the western side

36 - Palladian loggias: interior of the upper gallery on the northern side

37 - Palladian loggias: piers in the upper northeast corner, seen from inside

38 - Palladian loggias: pier and arch in the upper northeast corner, seen from inside

39 - Palladian loggias: vaults of the upper northern gallery

40 - Palladian loggias: interior of the upper gallery on the northern side,
view of the piers from the northeast corner

41 - Palladian loggias: interior of the upper gallery on the southern side

42 - Palladian loggias: interior of the upper gallery on the southern side, view of the piers

43

43 - Palladian loggias: northern stairwell
44 - Palladian loggias: a Doric pier

45 - Palladian loggias: an Ionic pier

46 - Palladian loggias: an Ionic arch

47 - Palladian loggias: detail of the base of an Ionic pier

48 - Palladian loggias: detail of the base of a Doric pier

49

50

49 - Palladian loggias: Doric frieze, ox-skull

50 - Palladian loggias: Doric frieze, pa-tera

Palladian loggias: *mascheroni* on the key-stones of the lower gallery

51 - GIROLAMO PITTONI, *mascherone* on the first arch from the left on the west

52 - MARCANTONIO PALLADIO (nephew), *mascherone* on the sixth arch from the left on the north

53-54 - MARCANTONIO PALLADIO (son), *mascheroni* on the fifth and third arches from the left on the north

51

52

53

54

55

56

57

58

Palladian loggias: *mascheroni* on the keystones of the lower gallery

55-56 - Marcantonio Palladio (son), *mascheroni* on the second arch from the left on the north and the third arch from the left on the west

57 - *Mascherone* on the fourth arch from the left on the west

58 - Francesco Albanese the Elder, *mascherone* on the fifth arch from the left on the west

Palladian loggias: *mascheroni* on the keystones of the lower gallery

59 - FRANCESCO ALBANESE THE ELDER (?), *mascherone* on the fifth arch from the left on the south

60 - GIAMBATTISTA ALBANESE (?), *mascherone* on the eighth arch from the left on the south

Palladian loggias: *mascheroni* on the keystones of the upper gallery

61-62 - FRANCESCO ALBANESE THE ELDER and workshop, *mascheroni* on the fourth arch from the left on the north and the fourth arch from the left on the west

63

64

63 - GIROLAMO ALBANESE (?), group of statues on the southwest corner of the balustrade

64 - GIAMBATTISTA ALBANESE(?), group of statues on the northeast corner of the balustrade

65 - GIAMBATTISTA ALBANESE (?), group of statues on the northwest corner of the balustrade

66

67

68

66-67-68 - GIAMBATTISTA ALBANESE (?), statues on the northern balustrade: seventh, sixth, eighth piers from the left

69 - GIAMBATTISTA ALBANESE (?), statue on the second pier from the left on the western side

70 - CAMILLO MARIANI (?), statue on the fifth pier from the left on the western side

71 - CAMILLO MARIANI (?), statue on the fourth pier from the left on the western side

72-73-74 - CAMILLO MARIANI (?), statues on the northern balustrade: fourth, third, second piers from the left

75 - FRANCESCO ALBANESE THE YOUNGER; BARTOLOMEO MUGGINI (?), statue on the seventh pier from the left on the southern side

76 - Camillo Mariani (?), statue on the third pier from the left on the western side

77 - GIAMBATTISTA ALBANESE (?). Palazzo della Ragione: memorial to a praetor over the northern door of the Hall,
overall view

78 - GIAMBATTISTA ALBANESE (?). Palazzo della Ragione: memorial to a praetor, detail of the figure of Hercules

79 - GIAMBATTISTA ALBANESE (?). Palazzo della Ragione: memorial to a praetor,
detail of a female figure

80 - ALBANESE WORKSHOP. Palazzo della Ragione: two figures of Fame and the coat-of-arms of Vicenza, over
the gate of the southern stair

81 - Palazzo della Ragione: tablet of 1261 in the southern wall, within the upper gallery of loggias

82 - Palazzo della Ragione: niche for a coat-of-arms in the northern wall, within the upper gallery of loggias

83 - Palazzo della Ragione: shops on the southern side

84 - GIANNANTONIO GRAZIOLI. Palazzo della Ragione: framing for a tablet of the Emperor Gordian, in the northern wall within the upper gallery of loggias

SURVEY REPORT

THE SURVEY WAS CONDUCTED BY DR. ARCH. GILDA D'AGARO
IN COLLABORATION WITH DR. ARCH. MARIA TARLÀ AND MARIO TOMASUTTI

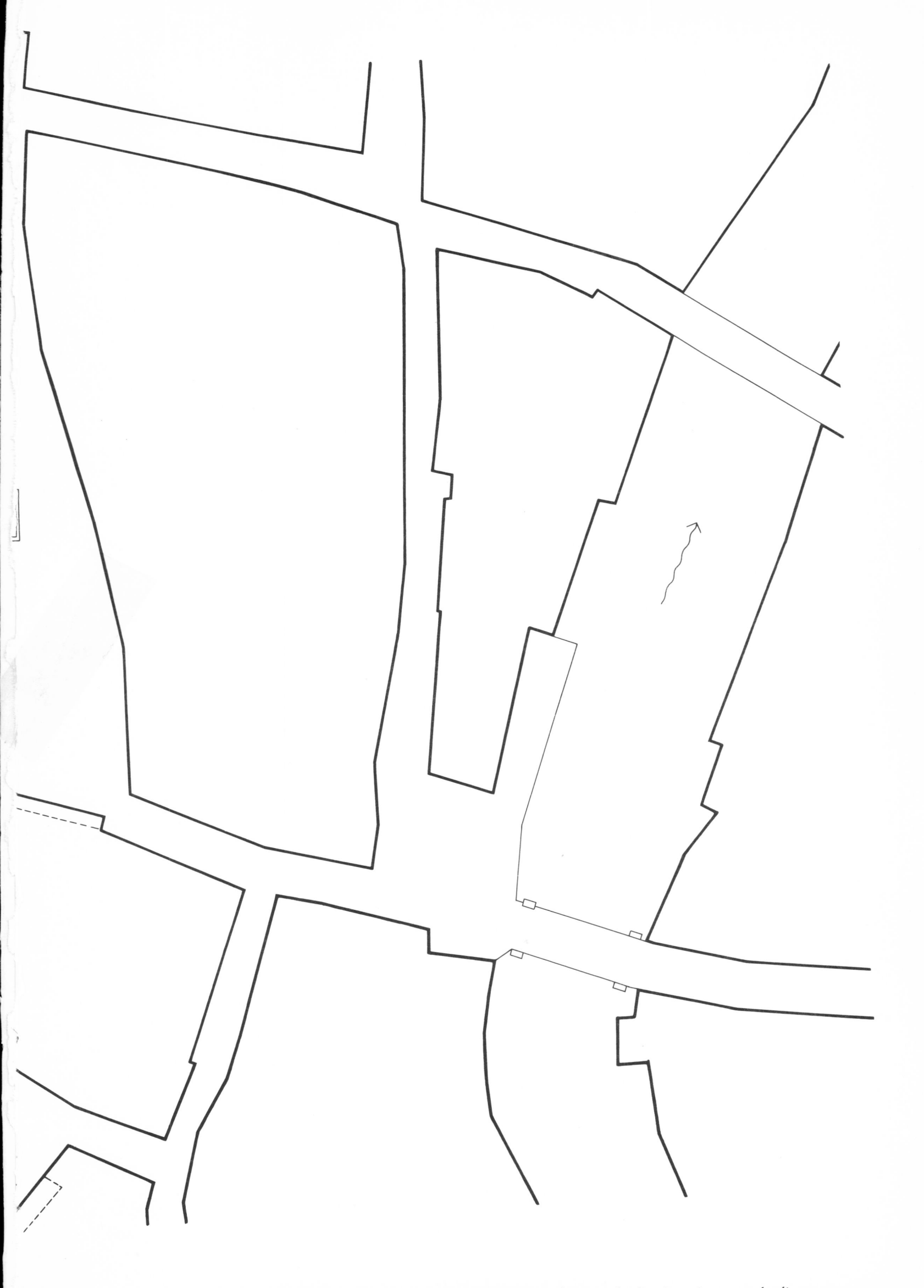

a - General topographical plan of the Palazzo della Ragione showing the loggias, piazzas, and adjacent quarters

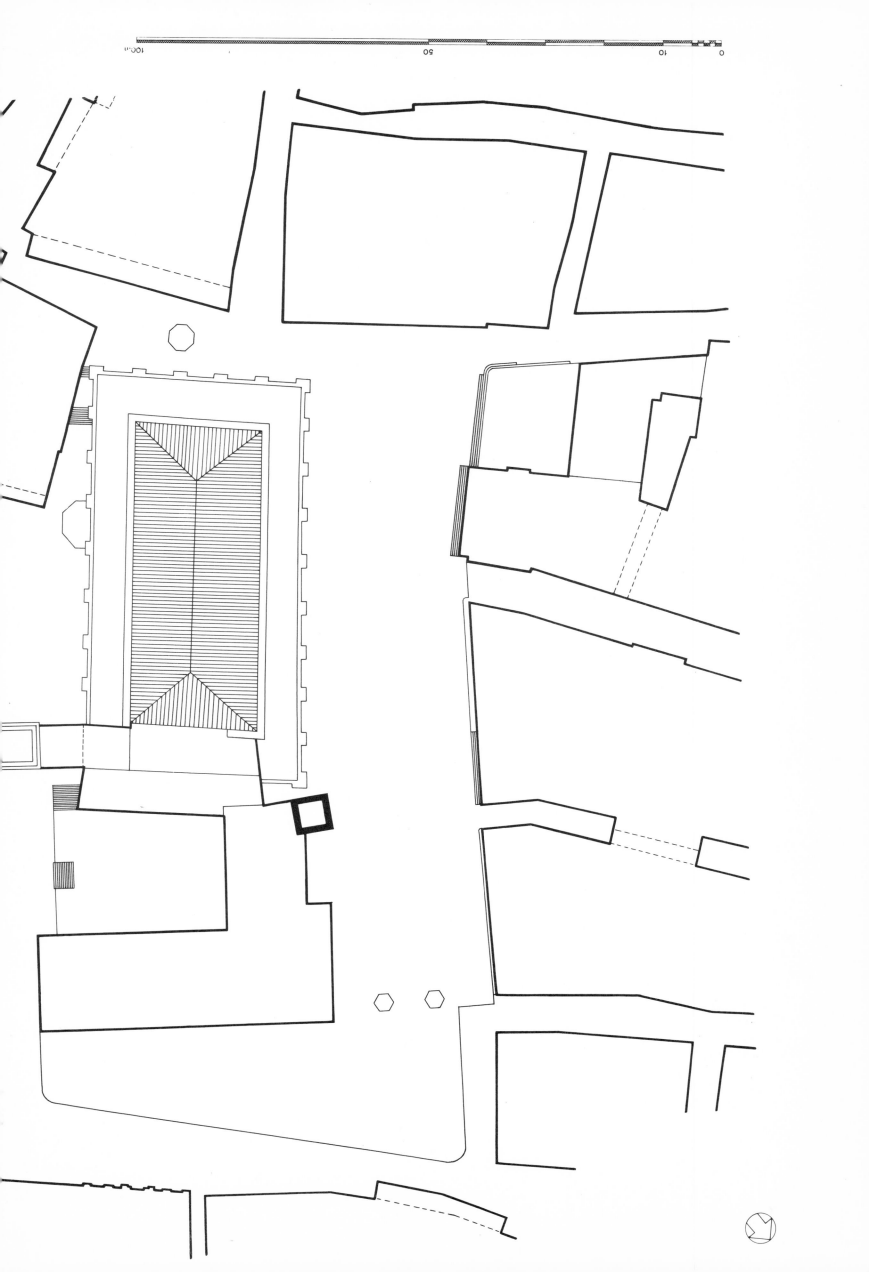

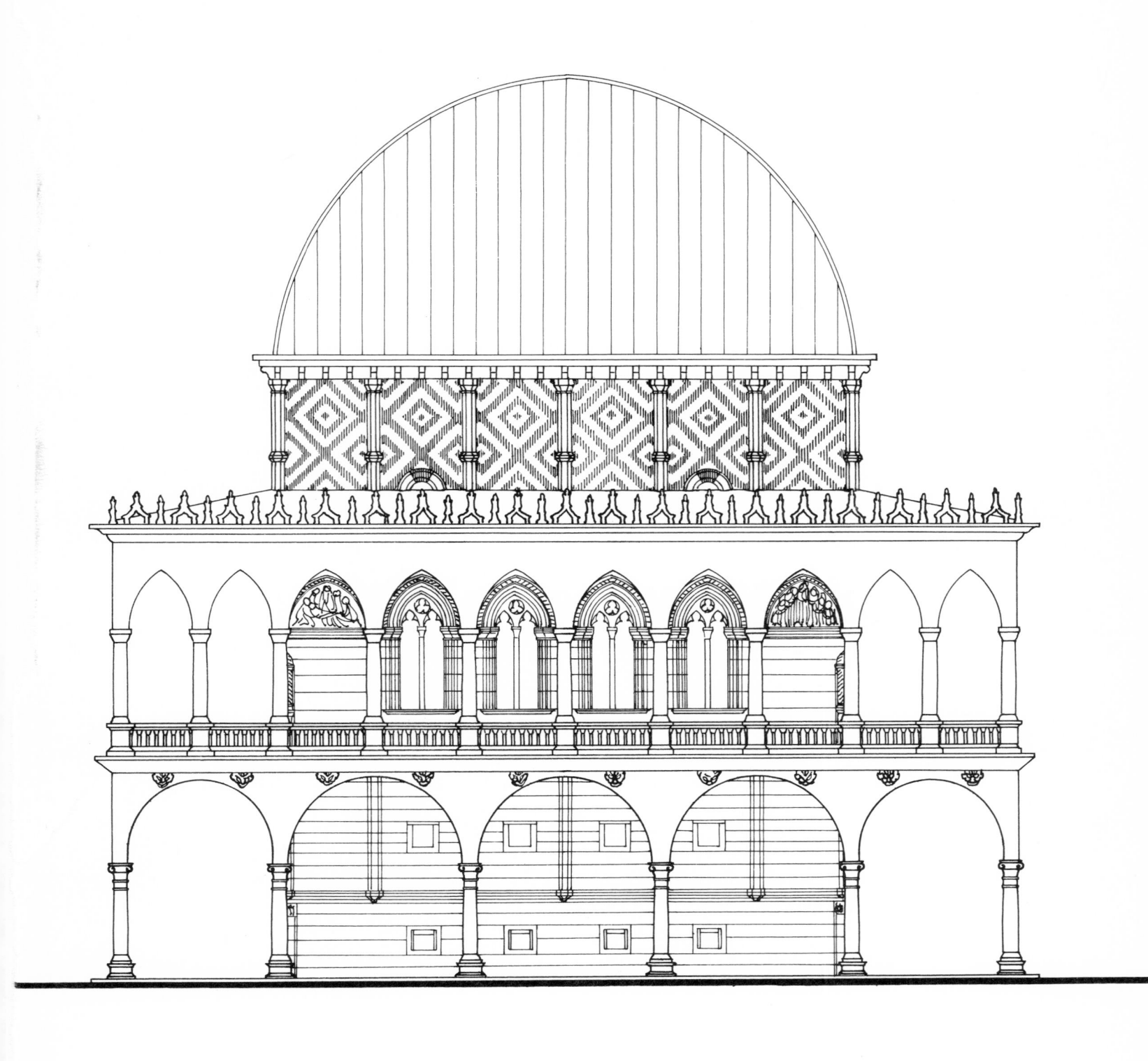

c - Palazzo della Ragione with the Formenton loggias, western side (reconstruction)

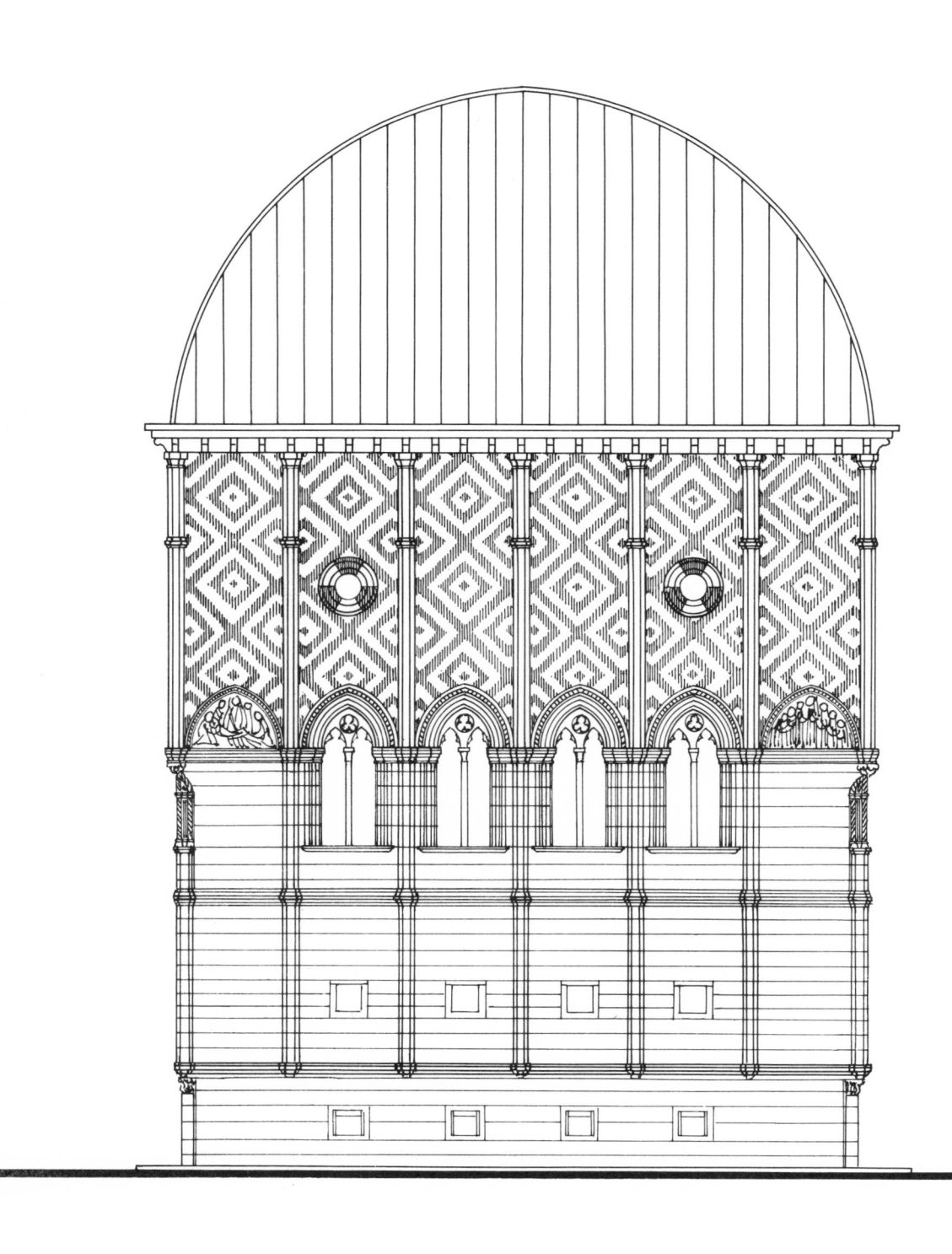

b - Domenico da Venezia's Palazzo della Ragione, western side (reconstruction)

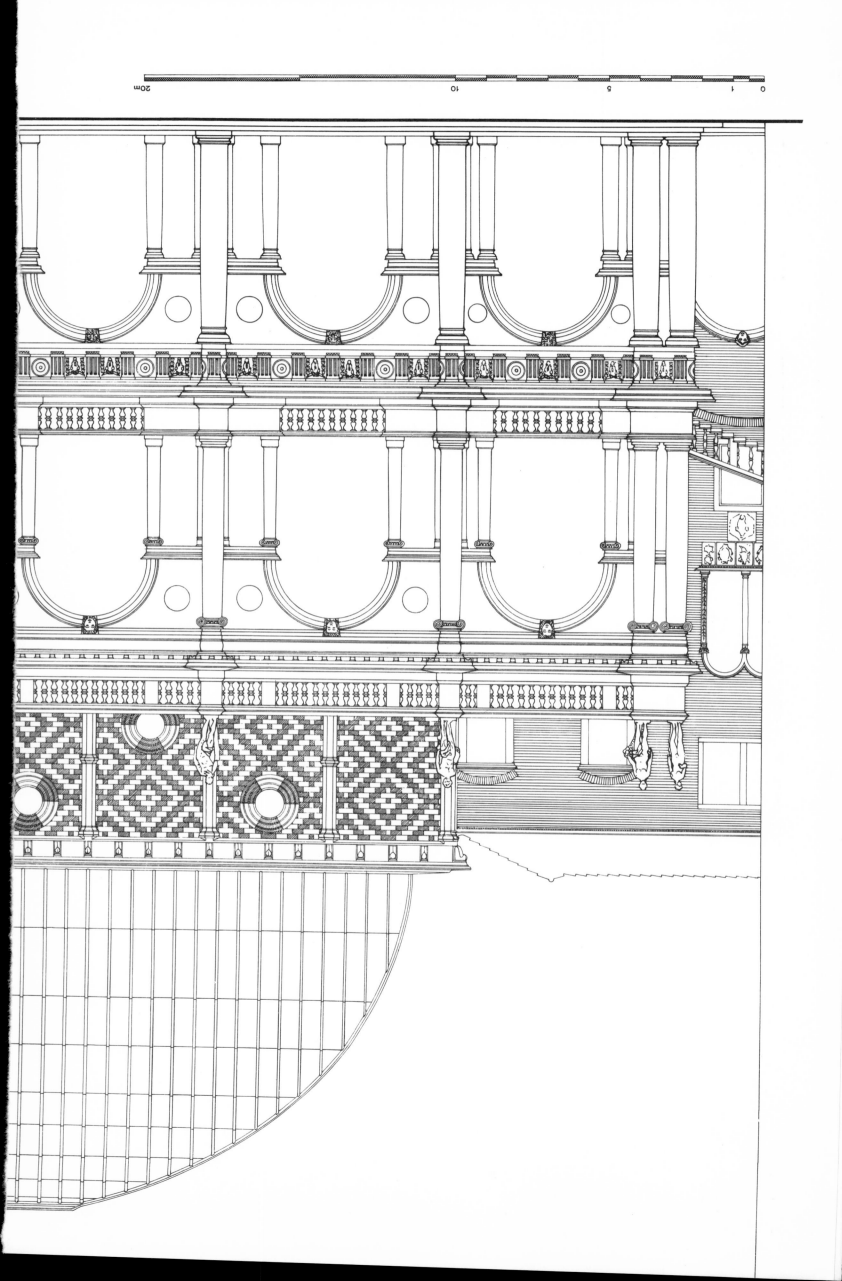

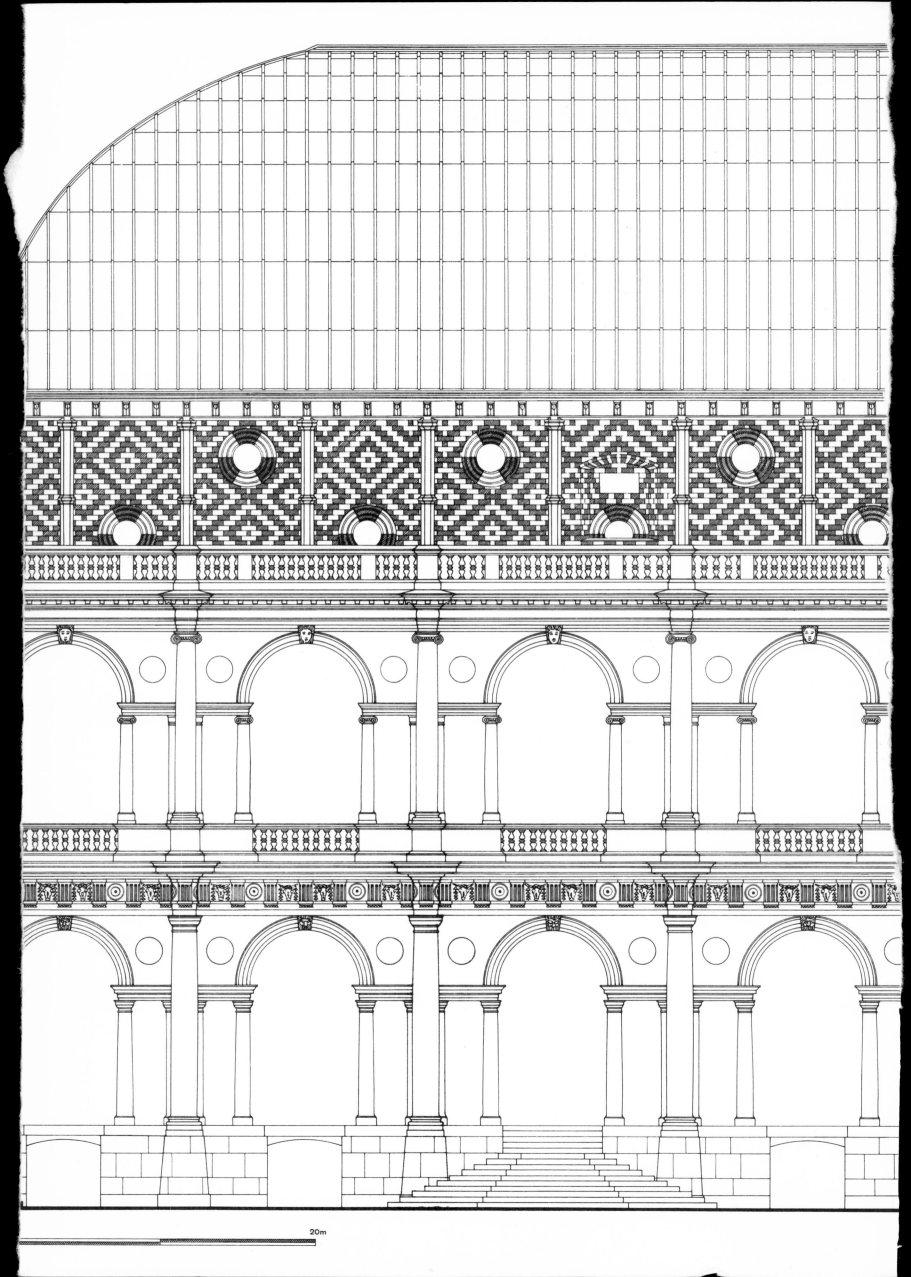

20m

e - Palazzo della Ragione with the Palladian loggias, southern side: elevation

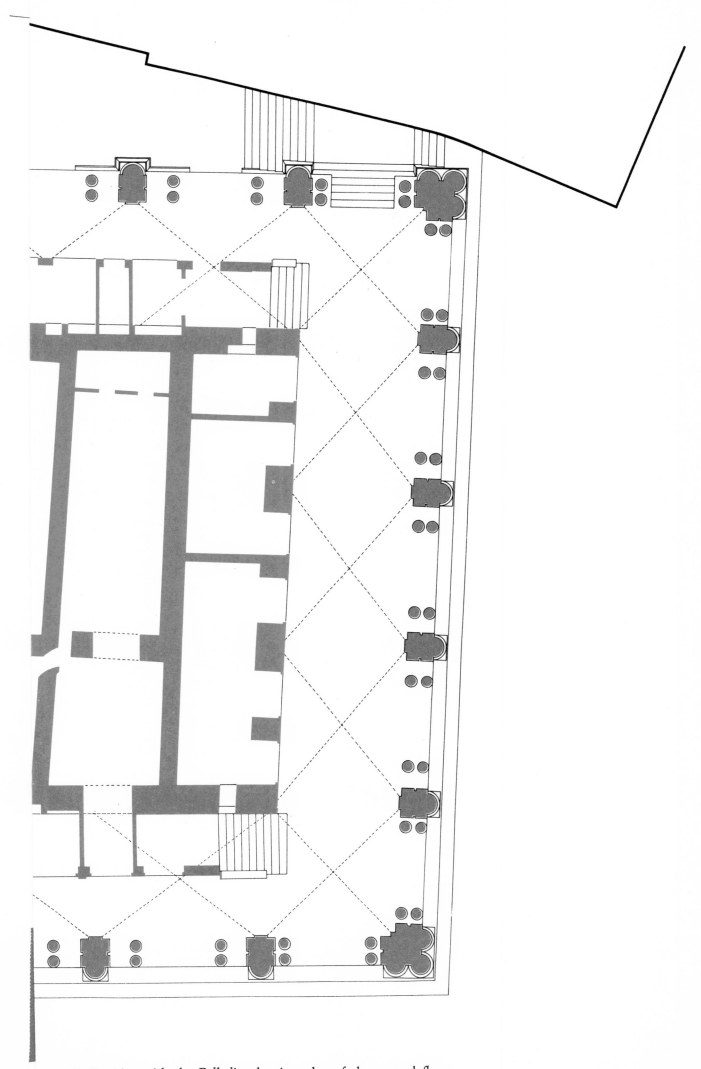

...zzo della Ragione with the Palladian loggias, plan of the ground floor